Challenges of HEALTHCARE IN INDIA

Economics and Administration

Challenges of HEALTHCARE IN INDIA

Economics and Administration

DR. R. KUMAR
MBBS, MS Ex PGI
Eye Specialist, Health Columnist and
Medical Tourism Advisor,
Chandigarh

Foreword by

DR. DEVI SHETTY
Chairman, Narayan Hrudalaya,
Health City, Bangalore

DEEP & DEEP PUBLICATIONS PVT. LTD.
F-159, Rajouri Garden, New Delhi-110027

Challenges of

HEALTHCARE IN INDIA

ECONOMICS AND ADMINISTRATION

ISBN 978-81-8450-084-4

Typeset by S.S. COMPOSERS,
3190, Mohindra Park, Shakur Basti, Delhi-110034.

Printed in India at MAYUR ENTERPRISES,
WZ Plot No. 3, Gujjar Market, Tihar Village, New Delhi-110018.

Published by DEEP & DEEP PUBLICATIONS PVT. LTD.
F-159, Rajouri Garden, New Delhi-110027.
Phones: 25435369, 25440916
E-mail: ddpbooks@yahoo.co.in • ddpubs@gmail.com
Showroom:
2/13, Ansari Road, Daryaganj, New Delhi-110002 • Telefax: 23245122

Contents

Foreword

The responsibility of the healthcare sector is two fold, i.e. preventing ailments and thus reducing child mortality, improving maternal health and combating HIV/AIDS, malaria and other diseases, and providing world class medical/surgical services in the hospitals for the Indian people. While providing health for our own people, it is also necessary to cater to the needs of global village. Development of skilled manpower for the areas mentioned above is important. Clearly, investing in human resources for health is imperative for development. Similarly greater allocations in healthcare can enhance human resource development. Furthermore, as a nation's economic productivity is linked to the health of its citizens, the economic impact of poor health systems may become significant. In the past brain drain of the highly qualified doctors has been a great problem, but now healthcare being a sunrise industry in India many natives are coming back. At issue is not only the availability of healthcare workers but also the long-term viability of healthcare systems. This entails changing the conditions for native healthcare workers, including increasing wages and opportunities for training and improving working conditions.

The development of most highly skilled persons is a gray area. India needs the development of skill in healthcare sector the most. While a lot of emphasis is being laid on the infrastructure of buildings and equipment, where are the highly skilled people and the trainers to run the hospitals and impart training in medical institutions? Thus a lot of hardware is being built and there is an acute shortage of software, i.e. skilled manpower and the trainers for such manpower.

The majority of growth in the health sector over the last

two decades has been in urban areas, with 75% of health infrastructure now being located in that area. Between 1991 and 2000, 7,044 new hospitals opened up in the country, most of them in the private sector. Unfortunately private healthcare is expensive and unaffordable for a large majority of people and only a small percentage of well to do people can avail it without tilting their budget.

No doubt world class hospitals like Narayan Hrudalaya are required not only to offer the best of services to our people but also to promote medical value travel to earn foreign exchange for the country's development.

But the poor rural people and the workers in the unorganized sector, who constitute majority of our population, have also a right over such centers of excellence, to avail life saving treatment. We are providing such a care at our centre at Rs. 10 per month to 30 lakh farmers of Karnataka, Now the state Government want this coverage to be extended to 1.2 crores schedule cast and schedule tribe of our state. We can extend the insurance to the entire population of Union territory of Chandigarh.

The patients are coming from countries like Bangladesh where treatment may not be available. There are over 30 million NRIs/PIOs spread across 110 countries and they definitely are our brand ambassadors besides being our potential customers. A large number of NRIs come to our hospitals for treatment. The Arabs, post 9/11, are now coming to India in increasing numbers. We also get patients from Nepal, Afghanistan and the CIS countries, which have poor health infrastructure. We are also getting patients from western countries as well due to better affordability and no waiting period.

Dr. R. Kumar from Chandigarh has taken a great initiative in writing this book to improve healthcare in India and to promote medical tourism. I hope and wish that he succeeds in his endeavors.

DR. DEVI SHETTY
Chairman, Narayan Hrudalaya,
Health City, Bangalore

Introduction

The responsibility of the healthcare sector is two-fold, i.e. (i) providing world class medical/surgical services in the hospitals for the Indian people, (ii) realization of the Millennium Development Goals of reducing child mortality, improving maternal health and combating HIV/AIDS, malaria and other diseases. Development of skilled manpower for both the areas mentioned above is important. Numbers is only half the story—the quality of skill in each of them is all important. Clearly, investing in human resources for health is imperative. This also explains the recent launch of the Public Health Foundation of India (PHFI) by the Prime Minister; a public-private initiative, which aims to train more than 1,000 public health professionals annually. These non-medical, but public health professionals will take care of the preventive aspects.

Highly skilled manpower

The creation of most highly skilled surgeons and trainers is all important. One of the pivotal factors to sustain the projected growth of the healthcare industry in India would be the availability of a trained workforce, besides cheaper technology, better infrastructure, etc. Worldwide shortage of doctors, nurses and paramedical staff has led to an exodus of such manpower from India. A major challenge for our nation and the healthcare industry would be not only to retain the healthcare workforce but also to develop an environment, which would attract those abroad to return. Even if the number of doctors were to increase from 0.6 to 0.8 per 1000 population and number of nurses were to increase from 1.5 to 2 per 1000 population to catch up with middle rung countries, India needs 0.2 million doctors and 0.5 million nurses right away, besides need for other paramedical and healthcare management personnel. One of the encouraging trends has been the growing interest of physicians of Indian origin whose number is more than 60,000, working in other nations and willing to return home. The world class infrastructure of corporate hospitals along with salary levels to facilitate the living index at par with the west are just two reasons that are encouraging top notch doctors to come back. Dr. Pratap Reddy and Dr. Naresh Trehan both from Apollo group, are just two examples. Growing restrictions on licensing and practice within the European Economic Community is also translating into a large number of Indian doctors looking to relocate back from the UK which accounts for over 15,000 doctors of Indian origin.

There is a great need to focus on the software, i.e human resource (knowledge and skills) for healthcare, their numbers matter but more importantly do their skills. The development of most highly skilled persons is a gray area. India needs the development of skill in healthcare sector the most. While a lot of emphasis is being laid on the infrastructure of buildings and equipment, where are the highly skilled people and the trainers to run the hospitals and impart training in medical institutions? Thus a lot of hardware is being built and there is an acute shortage of software, i.e. skilled manpower and the *trainers* for such manpower. The premier medical colleges of Punjab; viz. Patiala, Amritsar, Faridkot are in shambles—with most of the wards and operation theatres closed or nearly so. This all is not due to lack of financial allocations alone. There is no dearth of patients either. Private Doctors in these and other cities are earning a lot of money. With moderate user charges these public hospitals could have become self-financing. In fact it is the staff and faculty of these institutions who have lost initiative to work and learn the latest technological skills. This trend has to be reversed to revive these premier institutions. Development of the highly skilled manpower in the healthcare sector is the most important input and the lack of it is the most important matter of concern. Solution to provide adequately trained medical teachers (and well versed in modern surgical techniques) has to be found at the highest level.

More healthcare workers and more institutions

Undoubtedly, more workers and better skilled workers is the need of the hour to improve public health. The government has to take care of this aspect. Several foreign institutions will also be working in the area of public health all over India. The Bill and Melinda Gates Foundation is providing a $15-million grant to support the initiative. McKinsey and Company, along with other private sector players, is working in a *pro bono* capacity to support the cause. Another recent initiative has been the setting up of a task force on planning for human resources for health services. "Most of the investments in health have been as targeted interventions in health programs. Demographically, India is a young nation that can capitalize on the opportunity to have trained personnel to meet the healthcare needs of the ageing countries. Contrarily, the proportion of the elderly in India is estimated to increase from 6.9% to 11.8% by 2025. This too calls for an added health workforce. The World Health Day theme this year is dedicated to the significance of health workers. There are 59 million health workers worldwide. A workforce of seven million is available for the entire South East Asian region. There is an urgent need for 4.35 million more workers! "Almost 90,000 extra health professionals are required in India at the moment. PHFI aims to bridge the gap between supply and demand of healthcare professionals in the private as well as public domain," says Harpal Singh, Chairman, Fortishealthcare. Health work force is required not only to battle diseases but also emergency crises like earthquakes and tsunami. Chronic non-communicable diseases account for 51% of deaths and 44% of the disease burden in the South East Asian region.

Reversal of brain drain

There has been a constant brain drain from India to developed countries from early sixties onwards. Emigration of healthcare workers has weakened the already failing health systems in the country. At the same time, the graying of the industrialized world has placed pressures on industrialized countries to find a solution for scarce or poorly distributed healthcare labour to support their ageing populations. It is still unclear what the new rules of engagement will be to retain and train healthcare workers, where they are most needed and to mitigate the grave imbalance between the rich and the poor with regard to healthcare. How can healthcare workers with needed skills maintain their freedom of movement and the opportunity to respond to more favourable employment offers outside their country or region of origin without damaging the fundamental right of their own population to a basic standard of healthcare?

Nurses, in particular, are leaving their home countries in greater numbers. The number of nurses in the UK from non-EU countries grew from approximately 2,000 in 1994-95 to more than 15,000 in 2001-02. In the US, the percentage of nurses trained abroad increased from six percent in 1998 to 14 percent in 2002. Even the Philippines, a traditional sending country, sent more than three times the number of nurses abroad in 2001 than in 1996, primarily to the UK, Ireland, and Saudi Arabia. Such trends persist despite severe or emerging shortages in home countries. In fact, long-time source countries like India and the Philippines face health worker shortages themselves in rural and underserved areas.

To some extent, the Philippines, India, and Cuba have invested in the training of health workers for export. In return, migrants contribute to their home countries with remittances and enhanced skills when they return. However, in a study by the Joint Learning Initiative at Harvard University notes that "while the absolute numbers may not be large, the outflows can be 'fatal' for disadvantaged people in source countries." Although the home country may gain from remittances, such transfers do not necessarily go to the health system or to public coffers. Furthermore, as a nation's economic productivity is linked to the health of its citizens, the economic impact of poor health systems may become significant. At issue is not only the availability of healthcare workers but also the long-term viability of healthcare systems.

The recommendations focus on changing the *conditions* for *native* healthcare workers, including increasing wages and opportunities for training and improving working conditions. In addition, they suggest that developed countries should work to minimize their reliance on foreign health professionals by placing native health professionals in underserved areas (e.g., through programs focused on loan repayment and recruitment from rural areas). Host countries as well as representatives from organizations such as Physicians for Human Rights and the International Council of Nurses have called for regulated recruitment from developing countries facing a critical shortage of healthcare workers. China has initiated agreements to send medical professionals to England for training purposes. Such arrangements have also been initiated by countries with health worker shortages. South Africa has proposed bilateral agreements which aim to stop active recruitment of its health workers with several countries. Similar to mandates and codes of practice, bilateral agreements face challenges of private sector enforcement. Other recommendations under consideration include changing the visa policies of wealthy countries to promote skills development through short-term visas. The hope is that such training could improve healthcare treatment and retention in the healthcare profession within origin countries. Many of the tens of thousands of health professionals living outside of their country of origin are willing to contribute their skills to their home countries. There are a range of tools available to countries to promote such transfers, including allowing dual citizenship to foster more circular migration. There is a tremendous need for more research on healthcare migration. The scale and nature of skills shortages in the healthcare sectors, especially in rich countries, is poorly understood, as is the relationship between recruitment and retention. Sorting out challenges of geographical distribution *versus* those posed by scarce supply will continue to be important.

India is now creating an environment for the NRI brain bank to flow back towards the home country, so that the fruit of advancement in science and technology could be tasted by the natives.

Return of the natives to corporate healthcare

NRI doctors are coming back to be a part of the sunrise sector-healthcare. The great brain drain is just getting reversed. Dr. Ramcharan Thiagrajan, a liver transplant surgeon, who practiced for 15 years in the US, joined Manipal Health Systems, Bangalore as Consultant, Surgical Gastroenterology, Multi-organ Transplant. He is not alone.

Fifteen percent of doctors at the Kerala Institute of Medical Sciences, Thiruvanthapuram are former Non-Resident Indians (NRIs). Twenty-eight specialists at Wockhardt Hospitals Group have recently returned from abroad. Fifteen former NRI specialists are working with Image Hospitals, Hyderabad. Around 80 percent of the doctors at the Madras Medical Mission are former NRIs.

There are more than 20 NRI doctors working with Yashoda Hospitals, Hyderabad. Six NRI, doctors have joined yet-to-open Artemis Health Sciences (AHS), New Delhi. Global group of hospitals at Hyderabad has been established by an NRI doctor.

Apollo Hospitals Group has been receiving applications from NRI doctors ever since the first hospital was inaugurated in Chennai, nearly 25 years ago. Dr. K. Hari Prasad, CEO, Apollo Hospital, Hyderabad, says, "Over 70 percent of doctors working in our Hospital have had an international stint. Aditya Birla Memorial Hospital (ABMH), Pune, is another case in point. For Dr. Sanjeev Singh, Senior Medical Administrator in AIMS, Kochi, what is encouraging is the changing trend of trained and experienced hands in the West, looking to settle in India."

According to Dr. Parvez Ahmed, Executive Director, Max Healthcare, there are three categories of NRI doctors returning to India. The majority are those who have done their post-graduation abroad. The second category is one with 5-10 years experience abroad. "Typically, it's the 40-plus category that wants to return," says Daljit Singh, President, Fortis Healthcare. The third group, the least among the others, includes those with more than 15 years of experience.

The Pull Factor

The pull factor is that high-value private players are entering healthcare and rapidly creeping in the corporate culture. "Corporate hospitals are taking keen interest in these doctors and from the doctors' perspective they see a lot of opportunities to work in a professional environment. The unfavourable change in the immigration laws in UK, abolishing the permit free training for overseas doctors and mainly Indians are key reasons for the turn of the tide. Agrees Dr. Girish

Dewnany, who works as a Consultant Orthopaedic Surgeon at PD Hinduja Hospital and Asian Heart Hospital, Mumbai and worked in the UK for 10 years, "The reason bulk of doctors return, especially from the UK, is the lack of progress in their career or being stuck in middle grade."

Dr. P. Sharat Kumar, Consultant Orthopaedic Surgeon and Sports Medicine Consultant, Apollo Hospitals, Hyderabad who has stayed in the UK for nearly 11 years agrees. "I believe this change won't have much effect on well established Indian doctors in the UK."

Dr. Amit Trehan, a Gastroenterologist working with Fortis Hospital, says the reason for joining Fortis is more for its esteem. "A reputed hospital with good infrastructure is a preference for NRI doctors. This is because of the environment they are used to and so can prove their skills," he explains.

Dr. Sujeet Jha, an Endocrinologist with Max Healthcare, New Delhi who, after being in the UK for 11 years, came back feels that established brands help establish oneself. Based on several visits to different corporate hospitals, he selected Max Group, on the basis of infrastructure, opportunity to grow and its preference towards promoting ethical practices.

According to Dr. Dewnany, choosing a brand that replicated the working conditions in the West was easier said than done. "Once you have been in the West for more than five years, you will find it difficult to return to India as your package Dr.ops Dr.amatically," echoes Dr. Jha. When it comes to remuneration, NRI doctors command around 30 percent more than their Indian counterparts.

Dr. Jha feels that, "Many of the hospitals in India still do not practice internal medical audit system which critically reviews the internal systems with the established standards."

NRI doctors bring in an edge with them. Maybe that's the reason why hospitals and high-tech medical centres catering to medical tourism prefer to recruit them because of the quality and prestige of their international credentials. R. Basil, MD and CEO, Manipal Health Systems, says, "These doctors have an edge in terms of International Board Certifications that attracts international patients who come to India."

Recruiting NRI physicians is an opportunity for a hospital to develop areas that fall under specialized fields. As

Dr. Ahmed puts it, "India, that has such high rates of infectious diseases, has chosen not to develop this as a sub-speciality, and we don't find specialists who have been trained especially in infectious diseases." AIMS is keen on taking trained hands from West in the areas of joint replacement, spine, cardiac transplantation, single lung transplantation, non-invasive neuro-radiology, nanotechnology, stem cell research, etc.

Multi-organ transplant surgeon Dr. Ramcharan is a case in point. Doctors from fields like organ transplant, neonatology and sports physicians are also in demand. "Since it's easier to conduct research here than in the US, most doctors prefer to return to India when they want to carry out clinical research since the laws are easier here," adds Trehan.

In India, it has been largely specialty-driven where NRI doctors look for an institution to teach undergraduates and post-graduates, and carry out clinical trials and research. "I recently hired a physician with an experience in bone marrow transplantation that can also help us further develop this unit," says Dr. Parthasarathy.

Public health is trailing

The forefathers of Indian Constitution envisaged a nation with equitable access and assistance to the sick and underserved. We have crossed several milestones but still there is a long way to go. We have been successful in eradicating small pox and guinea worm and in reducing the incidence of malaria, leprosy and polio to remarkable levels. The $17 billion Indian healthcare industry, contributing about 4% to the GDP, is expected to grow at a rate of 13% annually in the next five years. However, several challenges remain. India records the largest number of oral cancer patients and diabetics in the world. With 5.1 million HIV/AIDS cases, it is the second largest in the world after South Africa. With 16.5% of the global population, India contributes to a fifth of world share of diseases. There are only 59 doctors per 1,00,000 population compared to nearly 200 in most developed countries. The Report of the National Commission on Macroeconomics and Health (NCMH), Equitable Development Healthy Future, states that "the probability of the poor falling sick is 2.3 times more than the rich and there is an 18-year difference in the life expectancy at birth between 72 years in Kerala and 58 in Madhya Pradesh." India's performance is worse than Bangladesh and Sri Lanka. Against India's infant mortality rate of 68 per 1,000 live births, Sri Lanka has only 8. Also, Bangladesh's under-5 mortality rate at 69 per 1,000 live births is far below India's 87, states the report. Estimates suggest that by 2015 the number of HIV/AIDS cases would increase three-fold and cardiovascular and diabetes incidence will double. However, there is a degree of obsession with AIDS allocations and the attention given is out of proportion as compared to other public health problems.

McKinsey estimates that the healthcare spending in India will increase from Rs. 86,000 crore in 2000-01 to over Rs. 200,000 crore by 2012. World Health Organization (WHO) attributes 60% of all deaths to chronic diseases. McKinsey report also highlights the poor health infrastructure in India. It has only 1.5 beds per thousand people as against middle-income countries like China and Korea with an average of 4.3 beds. Although the per capita health expenditure has increased from Re 1 in 1950-51 to about Rs. 215 in 2003-04, more needs to be done especially on the human infrastructure front. "There are many improvements that can be made in the status of health professionals without necessarily undertaking reforms *per se*, such as developing systems for quality education and training of various health personnel categories; supporting and protecting them; enhancing their effectiveness; and tackling health imbalances and inequities. The improvement strategies include relevant skills preparation and maintenance for such skills, using the right mix of professionals, dealing with influences that affect their performance, and assisting countries in formulating effective national strategies," says Dr. S.J. Habayeb, WHO representative to India.

Growth of Private Healthcare

Goldman Sachs has said the country's healthcare market will grow more than seven times to $286 billion in size by 2020 from $40 billion in 2005, implying a CAGR of 14%. Healthcare spending by four developed countries has risen 27 fold over 25 years to $2.75 trillion in 2005. Phase III pipelines are static despite $238 billion in R&D spend over 2001-06 and global brand sales worth $189 billion will be vulnerable to generics between 2007 and 2011, the Goldman Sachs report said.

The majority of growth in the health sector over the last two decades has been in urban areas, with 75% of health infrastructure now being located in that area. Between 1991 and 2000, 7,044 new hospitals opened up in the country, most of them in the private sector. 20,000 new doctors are trained each year and the pharmaceutical industry has grown enormously in the country—all in the private sector (Deogaonkar). The sorry state of healthcare is revealed in the Para below.

- 80% of general practitioners that practice allopathic care are not properly trained.
- 73% use cost as their first point of reference when prescribing medicine.
- 75% were aware of the PHCs in their area but did not have information on who the health workers there were.
- 29% know how to make Oral Re-hydration solution to treat diarrhoea, but almost all of them handle that condition regularly.

Udaipur health survey supported this data by finding that only 37.7% of private doctors had an MBBS (qualifications to practice modern medicine) or higher specialty degree. 13.9% of "private doctors" in this survey had no formal qualifications and 36% did not have a college degree in any subject. Even more alarming was that this survey showed that a large majority of non-medical staff also saw patients. "the dominance of the private sector not only denies access to poorer sections of society, but also skews the balance towards urban-biased, tertiary level health services" (Deogaonkar). While legitimate growth of the private sector occurs in urban areas, rural areas are seeing a private sector dominated by quacks or poorly trained "doctors". This has resulted in over 20 million Indians being pushed below the poverty line every year because of health-care costs.

While the World Health Organization has said the largest healthcare burdens in the developing world will shift from infectious diseases now to the so called 'disease of civilisation' by 2020, this is further illustrated by studies by Goldman Sachs in diabetes, oncology and cardiovascular disease that suggest there would be a larger number of patients with purchasing power in the BRICs countries by 2025 than in Japan, EU or the US. An overall assessment of the Indian healthcare system points to large-scale lacunae.

World Health Organization (WHO) estimates that tuberculosis continues to be the biggest killer of young adults in India, taking a toll of 1,000 persons every day. The proportion of births by skilled health professionals is just 42.5 as per World Health Report 2005. "We need to enhance the numbers and quality of public health professionals by bringing honour and dignity to this profession. We need to recognise that a developed India means not only a literate and educated India but also a healthy India," says R.A. Mashelkar, Director, Council for Scientific and Industrial Research (CSIR). National Commission on Macroeconomics and Health reports that India has an adverse nurse population or nurse doctor ratio. Only an estimated 40% of registered nurses are active because of low recruitment, migration, attrition and drop-outs due to poor working conditions. The quality of nurses' training is also poor due to non-adherence to teacher-student norms, inadequate infrastructure, insufficient budget and insufficient hands-on training for students. Also, India's doctor-population ratio of 59.7 per lakh population is worse than most developed countries. Hospitals and clinics are understaffed by 15-20%.

Corporate hospitals: Viability questioned

The unmet demand for good healthcare in India coupled with the growing opportunities to raise resources through the capital market set off a few corporate hospitals projects in the last decade. A few years and many disappointments late, there are questions if a hospital run on purely business lines will survive at all.

The cost factor

Sophisticated diagnostic equipment have had a big positive impact on the practice of medicine, though the cost of installing them is fairly high. And given the rapid progress in technology, the likelihood of obsolescence is high. The cost of constantly upgrading diagnostic equipment is heavy—a factor that appears to have played a role in pushing corporate hospitals floated in the last decade into heavy debt. Heavy debt, in turn, leads to a vicious cycle of hospitals charging heftily for diagnostics to cover the interest cost. But this may affect the frequency with which these diagnostics are used. The outcome is that the income generated may simply not be enough to cover the cost of loans. For instance, a couple of years ago, Tamilnad Hospital—located near Chennai—had to pay an interest charge of Rs. 14 crore when the total income was Rs. 11 crore.

High debt and other disappointments

Corporate hospitals that were not backed by careful planning and had high debts, have failed. Hospitals are long-gestation projects. Therefore, the right mix of debt and owned funds is critical to their success. An industry observer feels that if more than one-third of the hospital project cost were to be funded by borrowings, as against owned funds, the viability would be in doubt. A look at Apollo's funding pattern is interesting. In the early 1990s, it borrowed Rs. 2 for every rupee of owned funds. At the time, the company's interest payment was about 13 percent of its income, far higher than the top-rung companies across other sectors. Later on Apollo reduced its borrowed capital to 50 paise for every rupee of its owned funds. Simultaneously, the interest cost had fallen to about 6 percent of its income. If Apollo had not controlled its borrowing, the company might have gone the way of other disastrous hospital projects. There are a few striking similarities between corporate hospitals and other businesses promoted at the same time by raising public money. The most obvious ones are poorly conceived projects based on unrealistic assumptions and a lack of accountability. The story was repeated in other sectors, notably steel. Many dotcom ventures went down the same path too.

Health insurance is essential

Access to quality healthcare in the private sector is limited by the high cost. However, this is changing dramatically with the advent of health insurance as a preferred tool to finance most healthcare expenditures. Health insurance is destined to grow exponentially in the coming years with large and diverse players having entered the fray and enticing consumers with an ever growing array of schemes. Less than 10% of India's population today has some sort of health insurance cover: either voluntary or as part of the Employees State Insurance, Central Government Health Scheme or Community Insurance. Private players in the voluntary health insurance sector saw spectacular growth in their collections last year. Healthcare insurance premium collected in 2005-06 registered a growth of 35% over year 2004-05. The private players registered a growth of 77% over year 2004-05 and public players a growth of 25% over 2004-05. The entry of pure Health Insurance companies into the marketplace in 2007 promises a plethora of innovative products. They estimate a potential of US$ 7,700 million in health insurance premium by 2015. Foreign Direct Investment (FDI) limit in health insurance may be raised from 26% to 49%, which would result in surge of international players and even more customized offerings targeting all sections of society. In the event of the minimum capital requirement of US$ 22 million being reduced to US$ 11 million, a number of standalone players would enter the fray as is the trend across the world for health insurance.

Famous Dr. Devi Shetty is in the process of offering health insurance coverage to the farmers of Karnataka. In the Phase-I they are going to cover 10 percent of the State's population, that is roughly about 50 lakh farmers. Each farmer-member is expected to contribute Rs. 5 to Rs. 10 a month and he/she will be insured for all types of operations starting from appendices to heart surgery. These procedures will be totally free and other than this free service they will also get medical treatment at a concessional rate.

His Excellency, the Governor of Punjab and Administrator of Chandigarh, U.T. observed that every citizen of Chandigarh must have an insurance cover to meet the medical/surgical needs.

The private sector has an estimated premium potential of over Rs. 4,500 crore. But the private sector will target only those who can afford its premiums. Private insurance companies are unlikely to provide coverage to the poorest of the poor in the rural areas, who need it the most. The state in collaboration with NGOs should provide insurance to all its citizens; especially those who cannot afford the treatment/premium of medical insurance. However, the overcharging from the insurance companies by the hospitals concerned is a serious malady. This if not checked can lead to the ruinous path of 'American system', letting the system go haywire.

The other side of the story is that for most general insurance companies, health is a loss-making portfolio and companies are currently facing claim ratios of over 100%. A huge base still remains to be covered by different kinds of innovative products." The potential that health insurance holds can be seen from the fact that LIC of India has recently said that it wants to start a company exclusively offering health cover, though with a lower capital requirement. However, Insurance Regulatory and Development Authority (IRDA) chairman C.S. Rao's proposal of a higher minimum capital requirement of Rs. 100 crore as against expected Rs. 50 crore for standalone health companies could prove to be a hurdle in developing the health insurance sector. Till date, only one standalone health insurance company, Star Health and Allied Insurance Company Ltd. has come up. Promoted by a number of individuals, in association with Oman Insurance Company and few overseas partners, Star Health will have a capital base of Rs. 105 crore and will be headed by V. Jagannathan, former CMD of United India Insurance (UII). At present, most of the activity in health insurance is concentrated on the mediclaim policy, marketed by the public sector insurance companies. According to Gopal Verma, Director, E-Meditech Solutions, a third-party administrator, "Between undercutting and stagnant pricing of policies, most of the market growth is lost. While actual cost of medical procedures and related issues like medicines, medical tests, room rates have gone up by 150%, the pricing structure has been revised upwards only by 5-6%. A regular re-pricing at least once in three years is absolutely necessary." A recent Parliamentary committee report pointed out that an additional burden had been thrust upon the insured by increasing the premium costs by 6% to meet the cost of service rendered by TPAs. Further, many a time, there is a nexus between doctors, hospitals and the policy-holders to cheat insurers by inflating the bills, doctoring the medical reports and other methods. In order to arrest the rampant abuse of health insurance facilities by medical-providers, standardization of services with appropriate acquisition cost should be done with immediate effect at all levels, say experts. Again, there is cross-subsidization in the health insurance segment—rural and semi-urban policy-holders subsidize urban policy-holders as the premium rates are uniform throughout the country. And between the individuals and the corporates, individual policy-holders subsidize the latter. Agrees Verma, "The pressure to accept a lower premium rate is much more in the case of a corporate client as nobody wants to lose bulk business." However, the rural health insurance remains largely ignored. "Lack of awareness about various schemes has been one of the major challenges in spreading rural health insurance. The other challenges are selecting an appropriate distribution channel to meet the needs of the widely dispersed population and tying up financial support for premium funding in the economically weaker sections," says Jacob.

Poor governance

Why has the state failed in delivering the necessary healthcare to its people? A few broad factors explain it all—poor governance, dysfunctional role of the state and the lack of a strategic vision. "The entire system needs overhauling which can come only through bureaucratic and political will. Disparities abound, be it gender equality, intra-state equality, inequalities across economic and social groups or the rural-urban bridge. It must be addressed. Also, successful models need to be replicated," says Kalaivani, Additional Director, National Institute for Health and Family Welfare. The need of the hour is to act because benefits far outweigh costs. NCMH estimates that a 50% reduction in mortality rates due to CVD can raise India's GDP by 2-5%.

Dr. Ajay Mahal, Assistant Professor, Harvard School of Public Health, USA, in Choosing Investments in Health contends, "India needs to prioritize interventions and targets. A range of low cost solutions like peer education, access to condoms, use of anti-retroviral drugs would help in tackling HIV/AIDS". Other strategies include yoga for tackling lifestyle diseases and better hygienic practices to reduce the incidence of diarrhoea. Dr. Harpal Singh Kalsi of Fortis opines that "a physical health infrastructure is already in place but the delivery and availability of services is not good. A large part of the government expenditure should be towards covering the minimum needs of the people. It should make a fundamental shift from being a provider of services to a payer of services". He adds, "This will also improve the reach of services in the rural areas because once the private sector knows that the costs involved are secure it will definitely venture forward. While primary healthcare should be taken care of by the government, the citizens should be encouraged to pay for the higher and tertiary services." Sri Ramachandran University hospital is following this model, purely in private sector.

Medical Value Travel

Five-star facilities lure foreign tourists to a Rs. 15-billion-plus market growing at over 30% per year. An estimated 150,000 foreigners visiting India every year for medical procedures, and the number is mounting. Corporate hospitals going all out to woo patients from abroad. That's the scenario in medical tourism—one of the hottest sectors in India today. A recent study by the McKinsey consulting firm estimated that India's medical tourist industry could yield as much as $2.2 billion in annual revenue by 2012. Says Daljeet Singh, CEO, Fortis Healthcare, "Medical Value Travel is on a take-off stage in India. India has all the advantages to become the healthcare hub of Asia." Fortis Healthcare, in the last couple of years, has set-up state-of-the-art hospitals in Punjab and NCR Delhi, besides taking over the Escorts Heart Institute and Research Centre (EHIRC). This corporate hospital group, while catering to well-heeled citizens in the country, is also keeping an eye on the air loads of patients looking for world-class medical treatment in India. Well, this has been happening across the board. The largest of the estimated half-dozen medical corporations in India serving medical tourists in Apollo Hospital Enterprises. The first patients were Indian expatriates who returned home for treatment; major investment houses followed with money and then patients from Europe, the Middle East and Canada began to arrive. The company has a partnership with hospitals in Kuwait, Sri Lanka and Nigeria.

According to Ashok Anantram, president, International Business, Apollo Hospitals, roughly 10-15% of the total patient mix is foreign. "Of the 60 countries we cater to, the largest share would be from the SAARC countries, Oman, Bahrain, UAE, and some African countries. Over the last couple of years a good increase in the number of patients from UK, US and Canada has also been witnessed." The reasons why patients travel for treatment vary. Many medical tourists from US are seeking treatment at a quarter or sometimes even a 10th of the cost at home. In UK, tired patients, who have had to wait for years for treatment by the National Health Service, and cannot afford private hospitals, see India as a viable option? For others, it is a chance to combine a vacation with elective or plastic surgery. Currently the NHS does not fund British patients to go to India. It has told Indian hospitals that it cannot refer UK patients because flying time to India exceeds the three hours limit set for transferring patients. "Most Western patients we get are covered by insurance or pay out of their own pocket," says George Eapen, Chief Executive Officer of the Apollo Hospital. But hospitals hope the situation will change in the coming years through arrangements with insurance companies and governments. "Canadian patients now get 75% of their expenses reimbursed after treatment here," says Mr. Eapen.

Dr. Aninda Chatterjee observed the following in an editorial written in November 2007 issue of Journal of Indian Medical Association.

Medical tourism is the latest bug

What makes India the favoured destination for medical tourism? The reason is a blend of several unique features that include: (1) Over 60,000 cardiac surgeries are done every year. (2) Multiorgan transplants are successfully performed at 1/10th the cost in comparison to the west. (3) Patients from over 55 countries are treated in Indian hospitals. (4) India's education system provides an estimated 30,000 doctors and 100,000 nurses each year to meet the growing demands. (5) The Indian government spending on the healthcare sector is expected to be around 8% of its GDP by 2010. (6) Care of patients by internationally qualified specialists. (7) Latest equipment and infrastructure. (8) Adherence to international accreditation standards like JCI and CAP. (9) Strict blood safety and infection control processes. (10) International consultation possible for second opinion from top centres in US and Europe through telemedicine network. (11) English as a language widely understood and spoken by Indian medical fraternity. (12) Good hotels in the vicinity of the hospitals have ensured comfortable stay for the patient's family and relatives. (13) Niggling worries like a shuttle service to and fro from the airport, the acceptance of international credit cards and the availability of international cuisine are taken care of. (14) Small or no waiting time for any kind of treatment. (15) India is a country that views a human being in totality. Here treatment is based on the physical, psychological, social, nutritional, ecological, environmental and spiritual needs of each individual:

Our holistic therapy integrated traditional medical systems like ayurveda and homeopathy with complimentary therapies like yoga and acupuncture to speed up the healing process.

Source of medical treatment can be due to: (1) The US Medicare Trust Fund is going to be bankrupt by 2019. (2) The French healthcare system ranked as best in the world is losing Euros 23,000 per minute and will he bankrupt by 2020. (3) The National Health Service (NHS) of UK has a long waiting period for elective treatment. (4) Americans in large numbers (approximately 416 millions) cannot afford healthcare insurance premium. (5) Post 9/11 WTC bombing for which the whole patient bulk from Middle East Asia has difficulty in procurement of VISA for undergoing treatment in US and Europe. (6) In 2006 alone, about 500,000 Americans have ventured out of the country for medical treatment which is likely to grow further.

The price offered by Indian Hospitals seem to be quite lucrative compared to price band in US, UK and even in Thailand eg, heart surgery: $40000 (US)/$23000 (UK)/$7500 (Thailand)/$6000 (India); knee replacement : $20000 (US)/ $12000 (UK)/$8000 (Thailand)/$6000 (India); cosmetic surgery: $20000 (US)/$10000 (UK), $3500 (Thailand), $2000 (India).

How much is hype?

A recent Newsweek article on "Medical Mecca's" failed to list even a single Indian corporate hospital. Instead, the All India Institute of Medical Sciences was cited as an oasis for India's poorest. However, the Institute evidently does not focus on the high paying foreign patients. Despite the evident advantage of low cost, world class hospital infrastructure, superior treatment outcomes and some of the best trained medical staff, the flow of foreign patients is still a trickle. Significant improvement would have to be made in public health infrastructure, connectivity and reduction of visa formalities.

India's neighbours and PIOs need healthcare support, too

The patients are coming from poorer countries like Bangladesh where treatment may not be available. "There are 25 million NRIs/PIOs spread across 110 countries and they definitely are our brand ambassadors besides being our potential customers. A large number of NRIs come to our hospitals for treatment. The Arabs, post 9/11, are now coming to India in increasing numbers. We get patients primarily from Bangladesh, Nepal, Afghanistan and the CIS countries, which have poor health infrastructure," says Singh of Fortis. "If it started with a tourist accidentally falling ill while visiting the country, today, people across the world seek out Indian hospitals not only because of the cost factor, but the standard of treatment, which is comparable to the best in the world," says Dr. Sanjay Sharma, business development head, EHIRC. "About 30-40% of our total patient base is foreign patients. This is just the beginning for us. It is less than 18 months that our flagship hospital at Max Devki Devi Heart and Vascular Institute, Delhi, a super specialty hospital in cardiology, came into function and the response is extremely encouraging," says Sanjay Rai, Director, Sales and Marketing, Max Healthcare. While NRIs and people from SAARC countries were always interested in seeking treatment in India, CIS nations, West Asia and Africa, also see a lot of patients flying to India, adds Dr. Sharma. "The cost of a heart surgery in India is one-fifth of that in UK and one-tenth of that in US. This itself is a major incentive." Adds Dr. Rashmi Taneja, consultant plastic surgeon,

Sir Ganga Ram Hospital, Delhi. "For example, botox in US is anywhere from $10 to 12 per unit. In India the cost is approximately $7. For a surgery like eye bags it would cost almost $8,000 or more. In India the same surgery costs Rs. 35,000 or $800 to a maximum of $ 1,000." Foreign patients also appreciate the greater accessibility to the doctor. "This is unlike the Western medical community where you would have to call the office or the answering service and even then deal with the nurses or ancillary staff. In India they have direct access to the doctor." Of late, cosmetic surgery and dental care have emerged as two new areas attracting a number of foreign patients. "Persons seeking cosmetic surgery commonly ask for liposuction, botox, and the whole gamut of surgical procedures that are common including eye bags, tummy tuck, breast reduction or augmentation, facelift, thread lift, etc." adds Dr. Taneja. And the hospitals are laughing all the way to the bank. The National Health Policy says that treatment of foreign patients is legally an "export" and has been deemed "eligible for all fiscal incentives extended to export earnings." Eager to cash in on the trend, private hospitals offer services tailored for foreign patients, such as airport pickups, Internet-equipped private rooms and package deals. Says Dr. Sharma, "We facilitate visa and forex matters, accommodation, ambulance service and provide for an intrepeter." "Cardiac, orthopaedics, neurosciences, IVF, cosmetic surgery, dental care and ophthalmology have great potential for India. Alternative systems of medicine are also drawing a major section of health travelers to India. Kerala has been drawing the biggest chunk of this market," says Singh. And the private health sector is working hard on attracting more international patients. Delhi alone has a Rs. 60-crore healthcare tourism market, says Rai.

The accreditations

Joint commission international is a respected body to give accreditation to the best hospitals of the world. The Indian Healthcare Federation in coordination with the CII committee on healthcare has prepared quality parameters, which are to be adhered to by 55 hospitals across 15 cities in the country. "This will not only standardize the level of healthcare facilities but also help develop brand equity. This domestic accreditation system along with a code of ethics, besides ensuring a uniform price band is expected to go a long way in ensuring a set standard of services." "There is a considerable potential for developing medical tourism but for this to happen it has to be marketed as an integral part of the Indian Tourism product offer just as we market Indian cultural tourism, wild life tourism, beach tourism, etc."

City beautiful to Medi-city

The Union territory's consumers are not just the richest (on per capita income), but also the biggest spenders (per capita expenditure) among the top 50 cities in India. At Rs. 86,629, the annual per capita income here is over three times the national per capita income, which stands at Rs. 25,716. Chandigarh is ahead of Delhi, whose per capita income is Rs. 61,676. Among the neighbouring states, Punjab has registered a per capita of Rs. 33,848, Haryana has Rs. 38,832 and Himachal Pradesh has Rs. 33,805 as its per capita annual income. "While incomes in the public sector are stagnant, the private sector is witnessing a boom here. However, with the VIth Pay Commission's Report round the cover, the salaries in public sector will see a big rise. And it's not just IT sector alone which can boast of high income but sectors like medicine have become lucrative. The city has several thousand private clinics in various systems of medicine and surgery. Many super specialty clinics and hospitals have come up in the private sector. It is believed that nearly one lakh patients visit the outdoor clinics of the public hospitals plus private clinics for various treatments (all specialties and all systems put together). Chandigarh caters to the healthcare needs of 600 lacs of population of northern India (population equal to Thailand). As elsewhere, 80% OPD patients visit private clinics and bear the expenditure from their own pockets. Despite the present facilities being better than adjoining states, the city needs to expand its healthcare services, quantity as well as quality-wise.

Recently the city has conceived a medi-city to make the healthcare services world-class. This will take care of the growing needs of the people of the region as well as attract foreign medical tourists from all over the globe. As per recommendations made it will be a cluster of hospitals, one each being in the field of cardiology, oncology, obesity, geriatrics, orthopedics and neuro-surgery, cosmetic and reconstructive surgery, gynecology, ophthalmology, dental, etc. In addition, it will have a world class convention centre, training programme for medical teachers, CME for nurses and paramedics and a wing for poorer segments of society. The medi city would generate revenue so that new public hospitals as big as PGI could be set-up.

Sources

Morbidity, Healthcare and the Condition of the Aged; Report No. 507 National Sample Survey Report, 60th Round.

Morbidity and Treatment of Ailment Report No. 441, National Sample Survey Report, 52nd Round; November 1998.

The Metrics of Physician Brain Drain; Mullan F., MD; *The New England Journal of Medicine*; Vol. 353:1810-1818; October 27, 2005.

SEZ Act 2005.

Health Insurance—A Horizontal Study; Ministry of Finance; Eleventh Report, Committee on Public Undertakings (2005-06); Fourteenth Lok Sabha.

Report on Population Projection for India; National Commission on Population.

http://www.bumrungrad.com/

Redefining Hospitals; Cover Story, Business World; 18 December 2006, p. 38.

The Unorganized Sector Workers; Social Security Bill, 2005.

First Health Summit, Nov. 7, New Delhi, Technopak.

The Tribune, Chandigarh, 14th Nov. 2007.

Aninda Chatterjee, The Art, Science and Commerce of Medical Tourism, *JIMA*, Vol. 105, No. 11, Nov. 2007.

CHAPTER

1

Lack of Quality in Public Health

Era of Transition

It is well known fact that public healthcare system is inadequate in quality as well as quantitry. India's economic growth is bringing with it an expected "health transition", in terms of shifting demographics, socio-economic transformations and changes in disease patterns—with increasing degenerative and lifestyle diseases and altered healthcare behaviour. The growing demand for the quality healthcare and the absence of matching delivery mechanisms pose a challenge and certainly a great opportunity. We stand at the threshold of an exciting opportunity to design and engineer healthcare delivery systems, develop numerous commercially viable and customizable delivery formats for the growing, demanding and health conscious Indian populace—the collective size and economic clout of which is indeed hard to fathom. And as if this colossal market isn't big enough, the Indian price and human resources advantages have already made Indian shores the new haven for medical value travel. In short, we are witnessing a classic case of demand far in excess of supply, both qualitatively and quantitatively.

Healthcare spending

In India, public health services are provided by the government through publicly financed and managed health services from the primary to the tertiary level. These services, accounting for about 18 percent of the overall health spending and 0.9 percent of the GDP, are provided more or less free of cost to the patients. Private and voluntary sectors have emerged as important arms of the health sector. It accounts for about 82 percent of the overall health expenditure and 4.2 percent of the GDP. Nationwide healthcare utilization rates show that private health services are directed mainly at providing OPD services and are financed from meager out of pocket resources. This places a disproportionate burden on the poor.

State and local governments incur about three-quarters and the central government about one-quarter of public spending on health. Health is primarily a state responsibility, and the central government is responsible for health services in union territories. It is also responsible for developing and monitoring national standards and regulations, linking the states with funding agencies, and sponsoring numerous schemes for implementation by state governments. Goals and strategies for the public sector in healthcare are established through a consultative process involving all levels of government through the Central Council for Health and Family Welfare (CCHFW).

Concurrently, the country is a victim of double whammy, i.e. suffering the burden of both communicable and non-communicable diseases at the same time. Some infectious diseases thought to have been conquered have returned with a vengeance or have developed stubborn resistance to drugs. These include viral hepatitis, tuberculosis, malaria, and pneumonia. Furthermore, new and previously unknown diseases such as HIV/AIDS, the ebola virus, and food- and water-borne diseases continue to emerge. In addition lifestyle ailments like obesity, diabetes, hypertension, heart disease and caners have made their presence felt in a big way. Unfortunately, the advances in healthcare are accessible to only a small percentage of well to do Indians. The healthcare inequality is bound to widen, if huge investment in healthcare is not made and the deficit of 10 lakhs of beds (as per WHO assessment) is not taken care of. Corporate hospitals are known for "poaching" doctors from government institutions, and also to deny even emergency medical care to the poor, without advance deposits. How can a country allow its hospitals built on a land provided at a subsidized price and its doctors, who were educated at the people's expense, to cater to only affluent patients, when more than 1300 poor people die every single day from a completely curable disease such as tuberculosis? India is probably the world's leading exporter of trained medical professionals (doctors, nurses, paramedical workers). Some of the world's poorest people living in rural India actually subsidize the medical care provided to the richest people from developed countries, either in the form of health tourism or "export" of medical skills. Quality healthcare delivery requires that trained professionals are made available where they are needed. The National Rural Health Mission launched by the prime minister is a sincere effort, yet looks too ambitious. It is reassuring to note the government intends to raise the annual spending on public healthcare to more than 2% of gross domestic product, which had fallen to 0.9% in the past few years.

The fundamental deficiency in the public health system lies in the gross understanding of the system rather than in the infrastructure per se, which, in reality, is far more robust than what is available in several other countries. The public health sector in India is unique in that it must take responsibility not only for producing a steady supply of professionals but also for stimulating demand for them. Optimising costs is largely dependent on the production, acquisition and management of labour resources, and then on the productive delivery of services. (Sangita Reddy)

Quality healthcare is a right

A seminar held under the aegis of the Jan Swasthya Abhiyan, at the Asian Social Forum, Hyderabad (arranged by CEHAT—Centre for Enquiry into Health and Allied Themes in partnership with the Global Health Council, U.S.A.) emphasized that access to quality healthcare is a right of every citizen. While the 'Right to Health' would be the ultimate aim, the Right to Healthcare could be a first step. India is known to have poor health indicators in the global context, even in comparison with other developing countries. The per capita public health expenditure in India at Rs. 21 per person is among the lowest in the world. The 'Right to Life' (Article 21) enshrined in the constitution, as well as the directive principles regarding Nutrition, Standard of living and Health (Article 47), and various Supreme Court Judgments in favour of healthcare, point to the underlying need to accord a right to healthcare to the people of India. The 93rd amendment in the constitution accepting Education as a fundamental right has strengthened the case of right to healthcare to be accepted as people's right. The International Covenant on Economic, Social and Cultural Rights, in its Article 12 clearly recognized the right of everyone to the enjoyment of the highest attainable standard of physical and mental health and creation of conditions which would assure to medical attention in the event of sickness. The Alma Ata declaration of 'Health for all by 2000' signed in 1978 was yet another declaration which the government endorsed. It was agreed that adequate financial allocation, political will, awareness of this right among people and strong political mobilization will be required to realize this right. Earlier Bhore Committee had recommended universal healthcare for Indian citizens. Strengthening public health system could be an effective strategy towards gaining the 'Right to Healthcare'. There should be a health worker in every village. Giving the health worker a meaning and context will help build a major mobilization of people for this right to healthcare. Systematic efforts should be made to include the issue in the election manifestos and generate political will.

Medico Friend Circle (MFC) an active member of the Jan Swasthya Abhiyan, feels that the existing system of healthcare is not geared towards the needs of the majority of the people: the poor. It requires fundamental changes. Some of MFCs recommendations include:

- Healthcare should be made available to everyone irrespective of her/his ability to pay.

- Healthcare should be guided by the needs of our people and not by commercial interests.
- The pattern healthcare should be geared to the rural health concerns of India.
- The medical curriculum should be tailored to the needs of the people of India.
- Medical science should be popularized and demystified.
- An appropriate healthcare systems should be established in which different categories of health professionals are regarded as equal members of a democratically functioning team.
- The primary role of preventive measures to solve health problems should be established.
- Due importance should be given to curative technology in saving a person's life, alleviating suffering or preventing disability.
- The public health system should be sensitive and comprehensive.
- There should be active participation by the community.
- Healthcare services should be based upon human values, needs and equality.
- Research on alternative medicine should be encouraged.

Health spending is declining

Andhra Pradesh was one of the first states to initiate reforms in 1995-96, followed by Karnataka, Punjab, West Bengal, Maharashtra, Orissa and Uttar Pradesh. Capital expenditure on medical and public health (such as upgrading hospitals) has increased, largely thanks to World Bank loans. However, on closer examination, if the contribution of user fees is accounted for, the decline in health spending in the reforming states is larger. There is actually no difference between reforming and non-reforming states. This implies that health sector reforms, far from enhancing the public health budget, have not helped even to maintain the current levels of health spending.

- Health sector reforms have diverted finances and personnel away from other programs. For instance, central and state governments are supposed to share the drug costs for tuberculosis (TB) on an equal basis. But since 1999, there has been no state allocation for anti-TB drugs.
- Commitments under the reform program to create administrative changes, such as a state Policy and Strategic Planning Unit, has led to diverting personnel away from disease control programs, like malaria control.
- 'Levering in' external assistance (through the World Bank) has led to 'levering out' of overall planning. Effectively, disease control programs have been left out from overall state level planning as they come under various national programs.
- Healthcare reforms do not integrate disease control programs within the development of the public healthcare system in the state.

Health indicators

- More than one-third of married Indian women have chronic energy deficiency; more than half of them are anemic.
- Forty-five percent of children under three are severely and chronically malnourished.
- Only 42 percent of children between the age of 12 and 24 months have completed their immunization schedule; a massive 14.4 percent have not received a single vaccine.
- Only 31 percent of the rural population has access to potable water supply and only 0.5 percent enjoys basic sanitation.
- In 2001, people continue to die for the same reasons they did when India became independent in 1947: infectious diseases.
- Babies continue to die every day of treatable respiratory infections, diarrhoea and other

illnesses either preventable through clean water, nutritious food and cheap vaccines, or treatable with basic drugs. See Appendix 1 for details on 'Invest in children'.

- AIDS is one more infectious disease in the landscape today.
- As the entire Indian population ages, many more people are being struck down by non-infectious ailments. Some people believe that cancers, diabetes and heart disease will soon overtake infectious diseases as the killers.
- There are wide variations, from the populous northern state of Uttar Pradesh (with an IMR of 88/1,000) to the southern state of Kerala (16/1,000), whose health indicators rank among those of developed countries.

Infectious and parasitic diseases

The killer diseases include tuberculosis and other infections including sexually transmitted diseases, AIDS, tropical diseases, respiratory infections and maternal conditions. Epidemics of deadly cerebral malaria have been reported in many parts of the country. Every year, scores of children in the rural areas die of measles, exacerbated by malnutrition. One in two Indians is infected with the TB bacillus, and 1.5 percent of the population has radiologically active TB. Between one and two million new cases occur every year, with a case load of over 11 million patients. India has more TB cases than any other country in the world.

a. TB affects the poorest sections of society. An estimated 26 percent of all deaths in the economically most productive section is due to TB.
b. The TB pandemic is further complicated by the spread of HIV/AIDS. It is estimated that there are 250,000 HIV-related TB cases annually by 2000.
c. It is estimated that the economic cost of TB to India is more than US $2 billion (Rs. 8,000 crore) each year.

d. Almost 100,000 people died from respiratory infections in 1998.
e. Some 1,25,000 women died from complications of pregnancy in 1998.
f. 100,000 deaths in 1998 could be attributed to nutritional deficiencies, more than half of which were simple protein-calorie malnutrition.
g. HIV affected 3.5 million Indians in 1998, according to UNAIDS estimates, though the overall prevalence of HIV in India is still low. Official surveillance data suggest that the epidemic is progressing rapidly.
h. One in two new HIV infections takes place in people below the age of 25; one in four HIV infections in India are amongst women, most of whom have no risk factor other than being married.
i. However, doubts have been expressed on the quality of epidemiological data. It has also been argued that the HIV epidemic should be seen in the context of other conditions such as diarrhoea, respiratory infections and tuberculosis, which have a higher morbidity and mortality.
j. Malaria affects 2.6 million people each year, and killed at least 20,000 people in 1999.
k. India has the largest burden of leprosy patients in the world, with a caseload of over 4 million patients.

Chronic diseases take a greater toll.

- Cancers killed 653,000 people in 1998, the single largest type being mouth and oropharynx cancer. An estimated 1.5 million new cases occur each year.
- Cardiovascular diseases, which includes those with an infectious origin, such as rheumatic heart disease, killed 2,820,000 people in 1998.
- Diabetes: there were more than 33 million diabetics in 2005, according to World Health

Organisation estimates. One in four diabetics will be Indian. Diabetes was responsible for 102,000 deaths in 1998. Up to 75 percent don't even know they're diabetic. Diabetic retinopathy, the most common cause of blindness in urban, middle-class Indians, is on the rise, though most of it is preventable. Diabetes is also the most significant cause of end-stage kidney disease and of amputations in India. The costs of drugs for diabetes, already high for the average Indian, are expected to go up in the near future.

Disabilities are common

A benchmark survey was carried out by the National Sample Survey Organization in 1991. It was estimated that 1.9 percent of Indians were disabled. Later estimates suggested that between 6 and 10 percent of the population in any developing country is affected by disability, which means 60-100 million Indians are affected by disability. The incidence of disabilities remain high even in the latest studies.

Ten percent of the child population—or 30 million children up to the age of 14—have special educational needs of various kinds. Unfortunately, in the absence of comprehensive support services, not more than 3-4 percent of children with disability have access to education.

Most Indian women suffer ill health

a. In a study in rural Maharashtra, researchers found that one in two women interviewed reported an illness in the previous month. They spoke of chronic, non-infectious, long-standing problems, related to their reproductive health, to various aches and pains, or to mental health. Illnesses were often linked to their working and living environment, childbearing and contraception. Almost half tolerated their illnesses without treatment—either they couldn't afford the treatment, or they felt it couldn't be treated, or health facilities were inaccessible.

b. A considerable proportion of women suffer silently from a range of gynaecological problems—reproductive tract infections (RTIs), menstrual problems, cervical erosion, infertility, uterine prolapse, and so on. The most frequent complaint is of vaginal discharge. RTIs are acquired through sexual transmission, medical procedures such as IUDs, tubectomies, abortion and childbirth, or from overgrowth of the body's own bacteria. Numerous studies have demonstrated that gynaecological morbidity is a serious problem in India.

c. 100,000 Indian women die of pregnancy-related causes each year. The maternal mortality ratio (number of deaths for every 100,000 live births) is 50 times higher than developed countries and six times higher than neighbouring Sri Lanka. The six major causes—haemorrhage, anaemia, eclampsia (pregnancy-related hypertension), infection, abortion and obstructed labour—account for 85 percent of pregnancy-related deaths. There are also a number of background factors: nutrition and health status, age, number of children, marital status, gender disparities, lack of information, socio-economic conditions and poor access to health services all influence maternal mortality and morbidity.

d. Abortion, which has been legal in India since 1971, accounts for at least 12 percent of maternal deaths. Only ten percent of the estimated 5 million abortions ('medical termination of pregnancy' or MTP) that take place in India annually, are performed in approved health services.
   - Authorized MTP centers are concentrated in the urban areas, and in a few states. Many approved centers may not be providing services, many are inadequately equipped, with poorly-trained or insufficient staff. The private sector provides a large proportion of services.
   - A rural community-based study in the state of

Maharashtra found that one out of six women who underwent an abortion did so to abort a female fetus. Two out of three suffer health consequences serious enough to affect their daily lives. Less than one-third of women are counseled about the procedure's risks, but more than half are given contraceptive advice, and many are forced to accept contraception in order to get an abortion.

e. However, women's health problems extend beyond their reproductive health. While maternal mortality and morbidity have been the focus of women's health efforts, public health specialists have argued that mortality data from the government's model registration scheme indicate that communicable diseases are the most significant cause of death for women.

More than one-third of all deaths take place in children under the age of five.

According to the World Health Report, 2005, one in every three of the world's malnourished children lives in India and about 50 percent of all childhood deaths in India are attributable to malnutrition. About 10 percent of the 27 million infants born each year do not survive for five years. And infectious diseases continue to be the biggest killer, a scenario unchanged since independence, according to estimates available. Coupled with the lack of public funding for basic healthcare in the rural areas, the crux of the problem has been poor disbursal and ineffective management. In 1999, 98 of every 1,000 children died from an infectious disease before their fifth birthday, placing India 49th out of 187 countries in the under-five mortality rate. As many as 429,000 children died of diphtheria, pertussis (whooping cough), tetanus, measles or polio, in 1998. One in two polio deaths in the world occurs in India. All of these are preventable. 733,000 children under the age of five died of diarrhoeal diseases in 1990 (250 million cases annually). 777,000 children under the age of five died of respiratory infections in 1990 (nearly 500 million cases annually). 333,000 children died of complications following low birth weight in 1990. These deaths are preventable through adequate nutrition to mother and child, clean water supply and sanitation, effective immunization and an accessible health service to provide prompt treatment.

Commission on macroeconomics and health (CMH)

The CMH was established in January 2000 by the then WHO Director-General, Dr. Gro Harlem Brundtland, to assess the place of health in global economic development. The most important point that the CMH highlighted was the importance of investing in health to promote economic development and reduce poverty. Most important, the India health report (IHR) points out that the biggest problems with the Indian health system are the lack of government spending in the health sector (0.9 percent of GDP against an average of 2.2 percent by lower-middle-income countries) and the inefficiencies and misuse of the available meagre resources. Since 84 percent of healthcare is out-of-pocket expense, the system is set-up to favour those who can pay. The ambitious goal of providing universal healthcare for all (in 1978, India was a signatory to the Alma Ata declaration, undertaking to provide "Health for All" by 2000) was far from being achieved. As the report suggests, the current system needs to be overhauled, both in terms of financial and human resource. Policy-makers need to define realistic goals and allocate much higher levels of resources for the health sector. These resources should not be allowed to fritter away or siphoned out. This will require strict monitoring, so as to ensure that funds are being utilized for the purpose they were meant for.

Healthcare is passing in private hands. This has resulted in spiraling medical care costs and rural indebtedness. An assessment of utilization patterns of public and private healthcare providers shows that despite the provision of free or low-cost services at government health facilities, demand for public sector outpatient services are low even amongst that part of the population which falls below the poverty line. The poor are increasingly turning to private providers, even for treatment of infectious disease such as

HIV, TB and Malaria, which are designated as primary responsibilities of the public health system. This is because of the reason that most of the staff in public healthcare institutions is either absent from duty or unhelpful.

Primary healthcare is scarce

Primary healthcare in India is provided through government-operated Primary Health Centres (PHCs), at village and town levels. A medical officer (a qualified MBBS doctor) is appointed at each of these PHCs and is supposed to diagnose and manage all medical and surgical illnesses at the primary level, and refer selected patients for higher investigations and treatment or expert opinion to centers based at the district level—the CHCs, where at least one post-graduate surgeon, one physician and one obstetrician-gynaecologist are posted. PHCs should play two equally important roles: (i) First, diagnosis of diseases based on symptoms and simple laboratory tests, and their treatment either at the centers or through referral. (ii) Second, health education leading to family planning, better hygiene and sanitation, and prevention of communicable diseases, especially sexually transmitted diseases.

At present, the major problems at the primary level in healthcare can chiefly be attributed to: (i) absenteeism of the staff; (ii) shortage of qualified doctors to be posted at PHCs; (iii) non-availability of proper infrastructure, including equipment and consumables at the PHCs; (iv) poor motivation of the public to seek timely help from the PHCs owing to misbeliefs, superstitions and lack of health education. With the result of non-functioning PHCs the ailing rural population has to travel to urban areas thus increasing the load on hospitals in the urban areas and ending up with serious complications.

Health infrastructure in India

1. Public health services

India has a vast healthcare sector, estimated at Rs. 126.27 billion in 1998. This healthcare sector is broadly divided into the public and private sectors. Public health services consist of the following 'step-up referral' network of sub-centres, primary health centres, community health centres and district hospitals:

- 140,000 sub-centres manned by two multipurpose health workers; 23,000 primary health centres (PHCs) with a medical officer, 14 staff and 4-6 patient beds, with each PHC acting as a referral unit for six sub-centres; 3,000 community health centres (CHCs) with four medical specialists, 21 staff, 30 beds and basic surgical and lab facilities, with each CHC a referral unit for four PHCs; 550 district hospitals and 1,012 at the sub-divisional level.
- In the urban areas, the network consists of urban family welfare centres for contraceptives, urban health posts and hospitals. (Figures as of June 1999, according to the health ministry).

2. Doctors, nurses, hospitals and dispensaries

In 1998, about 523,000 allopaths and 115,500 practitioners of other systems of medicine provided health services to the Indian population. Institutional services were provided by 17,000 hospitals and 28,000 dispensaries (mostly privately owned and in the urban areas), with 95,000 beds, and supported by 566,000 nurses. Health providers are trained at 165 medical colleges, which turned out 12,000 graduates and 3,140 post-graduates in 1991. However, more than 80 percent of out-patient services and a smaller proportion of hospital services were provided in the private sector.

3. Private sector provides most of the out-patient services

It provides at least 80 percent of health services in the country. The role played by non-governmental organizations working in health is also significant.

4. Indigenous medicine

India has perhaps the world's largest community-based tradition of indigenous systems of medicine—

a. Every rural community has its own local health tradition, using thousands of plants for medicinal purposes. As many as 700,000 traditional dais (midwives) conduct the majority of rural deliveries, 60,000 bone-setters treat orthopedic problems, 80,000 herbal healers provide primary healthcare for various conditions. Millions of people use home-based remedies.

b. The classical systems include Ayurveda, Siddha, Tibetan medicine, Unani-Tibb and Homoeopathy. Some of these date back thousands of years, and depend on a codified system of knowledge, some documentation, and institutions of teaching, research and manufacture. Medical practice is largely not institutionalised.

c. Yet only four percent of the national health budget is devoted to these systems. There have been very limited efforts to evaluate these systems. Most Ayurvedic colleges do not have the required infrastructure and faculty. The Central Council of Research in Ayurveda and Siddha has 80 research centres, but there is a general lack of perspective on the proper research design to validate the claims of ayurveda based on its own theoretical formulations rather than isolating active principles for allopathic medicine. Overall, there has been no effort to strengthen these systems.

Lack of Quality in Healthcare

The Indian health system is ill-equipped to cope with the rising number of elderly and the changing disease patterns, with an average of just 0.7 hospital beds and 0.6 physicians per thousand populations. India faces the continuing challenge of fighting infectious diseases like malaria, tuberculosis and leprosy alongside increases in lifestyle-related problems faced by the developed world, such as cancer, cardiovascular disease and diabetes.

The top is laden with treatment facilities comparable with the best in the world and at the bottom rung is a situation where there are only an estimated .7 beds per 1,000 people, comparing poorly even with countries like China, Brazil and Thailand that have an average of 4.3 beds per 1,000. The quality of healthcare available in India is extremely variable—from corporate hospitals with the latest equipment, highly-qualified doctors and patient-friendly services, to small outfits with unqualified staff, lacking even basic equipment or a continuous supply of water and electricity. An estimated 1.36 lakh maternal and one million newborn deaths take place each year, according to the recently released 'World Health Report 2005—Make Every Mother and Child Count'. India has the third highest maternal mortality rate at 407, below Timor-Leste (800) and Nepal (415) in the South-East Asia region. At 68, it has the second highest infant mortality rate in the region. The report places India in the list of 51 countries showing slow progress in maternal and child health.

General practitioners in slums charge for injections of limited efficacy and possible harm. Traditional health practitioners—many providing allopathic medicines—serve a large proportion of the population, many of them practicing allopathic medicine for which they are not trained. Unethical practices such as unnecessary investigations and surgeries and kickbacks for referrals are rampant. Many private hospitals over-charge and deny the patient information about diagnosis and treatment. Though medical services were recently brought under the Consumer Protection Act, there are no enforceable standards for private hospitals. Regulatory bodies such as the medical councils are unwilling to fulfil their responsibilities, the legal system is ill-equipped to handle the burden of medical litigation, and aggrieved patients and their relatives cannot afford the costs.

Indian pharmaceutical is a silver lining

India is the third-largest active pharmaceutical ingredients (API) manufacturing country, with sales of $2 billion during 2005. By 2010, the active API market in India is expected to touch $4.8 billion to reach to the second slot with a growth rate of 20%.

A number of US companies source pharmaceutical raw materials from India. In comparison with China, the wide use of English in commerce is mooted as an advantage to US companies, along with India's tradition as an exporting nation. India should prove to be a useful regional production base. Partnering an Indian company may also provide a good route to commercialization in targeted markets such as Brazil or Russia, where Indian companies have an established presence. In addition, India has a large and varied patient base along with the necessary chemical and analytical skills at a comparatively low cost to make it an attractive base for clinical trials. R&D alliances are already being forged between multinationals and domestic companies. India accounts for less than two percent of the world market for pharmaceuticals, with an estimated market value of US$10.4 billion in 2007 at consumer prices, or around US$9 per capita. The vast majority of pharmaceuticals available in India are already off patent and generics are likely to dominate the market for the foreseeable future.

Abbreviated New Drug Application (ANDA) has to be submitted with USFDA for marketing approval for off-patented drugs. India is the leading country which has filed the maximum number of ANDAs with the USFDA. During 2005, Indian firms have filed 144 ANDAs with the USFDA, accounting for 25% of all ANDA filings submitted to the FDA API magic. Indian pharma industry ranks fourth in the world in terms of volume, Accounts for 8% of global production, Ranks twelfth in terms of value, Accounts for 2% by value, Has the second-largest number of USFDA approved plants after the US, Exports worth over Rs. 21,000 crore in 2005-06 and has $2-billion biotech industry.

Models of healthcare

(i) Physician-patient relationship model

From the Hippocratic perspective, the focus of medical action gravitates around the physician-patient encounter. This means that the physician's duty toward the individual patient overrides all other considerations except insofar as these affect the physician's ability to fulfil her or his patient-related duties. Cost-benefit and cost-effectiveness considerations must be completely abandoned because they violate the fiduciary obligation that this physician has toward this patient here and now.

(ii) The social perspective model

It construes medicine as one among several social enterprises of which the overall purpose is to advance the well-being of members of society. The sole distinguishing feature of medicine when viewed from this perspective is that, unlike other social undertakings, its focus is the health status of members of society. It entails profession's mandate to advance the welfare of members of society in general. That is why, in order to be able to exercise this socially derived office, society accords physicians certain privileges. For instance, it is the physicians alone who may prescribe drugs, perform surgeries, or engage in the other health-oriented interventions that society prohibits to all other individuals—all on the assumption that unless physicians have this socially mandated service-provider monopoly, the welfare of society will be worse-off. It also means the greatest good for the greatest number.

(iii) The business approach

A third approach to medicine, and one that also affects the nature of resource allocation, may be called the business model. Here it becomes one among many other types of profit-making enterprises that are allowed by society in economic terms. Here the professional medical ethics becomes a species of business ethics. Here the economics of the marketplace become the primary determinants, and allocation decisions become a purely financial matter. Not to put too fine a point on it: A patient's right to healthcare resources becomes defined in terms of the patient's financial capacity.

Each of these approaches has its own unique problems. The first model captures the fact that the physician's efforts should primarily be directed toward the best interests of the patient; the social service model captures the fact that medical practice occurs in a social setting and that therefore societal considerations are more relevant; and the business model captures the fact that physicians are professionals and therefore entitled to give some weight to entrepreneurial concerns.

The hospital sector has become the largest component of the healthcare industry with its varied size,—services offered, age and modernity of the physical plant and its equipment, overall mission (service, education, research), ownership and influence of unionization. The problem of cost inflation in the healthcare industry is extremely complex. There are a number of separate factors that can potentially contribute to healthcare costs. It involves the nature of health service technology, the nature and incidence of illness, the response of health providers and the response of the healthcare consumers to the changes. An ideal market system for healthcare should ensure an optimum amount of resources devoted to healthcare, an optimum combination of resources, an optimum distribution of healthcare and an optimum investment of resources between current provision of healthcare and future needs through research and education.

For the privileged consumer class the organized sector, the medical or health insurance with its tax incentive (income tax deduction) has in part become responsible for over-insurance on the one hand and excessive utilization of health services on the other. But, of course, while this section forms a significant proportion of the prime health consumers, their proportion will increase with the entry of more private and foreign insurance companies, making this a key factor to be considered.

Despite the above scenario, emerging medical or health economics is tragically still not given importance in education that most physicians, who invariably decide the cost of healthcare, have limited knowledge of the cost associated with hospital treatment. It is well recognized that cost containment is crucial to the growth and development of the health sector. The prime strategy that has increasingly come to be adopted is a market-oriented and dependent strategy which is a combination of a number of factors viz. increasing consumer choices through consumer education and development of alternative health delivery systems, increasing consumer cost sharing, changing the tax treatment of insurance and medical care and controlling the terms of employment-based insurance. The logic is that competition is the greatest leveller that very soon the market dynamics will force the healthcare industry to offer different packages of services according to the economic status and choice of the customer. Here, it assumes that there will be a large number of competitors in the market and not a monopolistic tendency. Sceptics believe that such an ideal market condition is a myth.

National Health Information Highway

Five researchers (Ashwin Srinivasan, Sumit Negi, Chandan D. Nath, Ponani S. Gopalakrishnan and Vishal Batra) are currently working with IBM's Business Consulting Services on a pilot program with a large healthcare group. The team has faced a couple of challenges: building healthcare standards that are specific to India and convincing healthcare entities across the nation to integrate those standards into their business processes. The partnership formed with a large hospital chain in India will facilitate the formation of a working committee, consisting of hospitals and the IT and Health ministries, to create health data standards for the country. IBM has already deployed Clinical Document Architecture (CDA) over the data grid to demonstrate standards-driven claim data exchange. And, as the first pilot program is progressing, other programs will be rolled out to two hospitals and two insurance third-party administrators.

National Health Information Highway system offers information technology to help reduce medical errors, improve efficiency, assist planning (locations of specialty hospitals or medical schools, crisis management, drug and equipment supply and budgeting, and more), and accelerate research and training (using diagnosis data to train medical students or using medical problems captured on the network to build test cases). In 2002, India's healthcare industry contributed five percent to the Gross Domestic Product (GDP) and employed approximately four million people. By 2012, it is projected to contribute 8.5 percent of the GDP. Healthcare spending in the country will double over the next 10 years with private healthcare contributing a large portion of this spending, rising from US $14.8 billion to US $33.6 billion. Because the traditional system of medicine is faced with escalating healthcare costs, the state health systems desperately need to improve efficiency in how they allocate and use health resources to combat the many problems the rapidly developing country has. These problems include infant and maternal mortality rates that are still high; basic reproductive and child health services, supplies and infrastructure needs that are unmet; and universal immunization of children against all vaccine-preventable diseases has not yet been achieved. In addition, the government is striving to achieve zero-level growth of HIV/AIDS, reduce mortality from vector- and water-borne diseases by 50 percent, and increase the use of public health facilities—all by 2015.

Other healthcare highway capabilities include:

- facilitating electronic data exchange (which will automate the current manual process and reduce the time it takes to settle claims from the current four to six weeks),
- providing data standardization (which will allow for interoperative and collaborative networks),
- middleware-based (to allow flexible collaboration among multiple third-party administrators and hospitals nationwide),
- supporting information integration and extraction (to answer queries from the doctors and administrators),
- supporting hybrid client platforms and programming languages (to allow different TPAs and hospitals to be part of the network),
- using industry standard interfaces (so that cross-training and re-training won't be necessary),
- offering security through an authorized data channel (so that only authorized personnel can access this highly confidential information), and
- provide auditing, which is required by the IRDA, the insurance regulatory body in India.

High-tech, five-star hospitals have pushed costs sky-high. A simple headache will warrant a CT scan to rule out a brain tumour. Doctors have used the CPA to further justify expensive and sometimes unnecessary investigations and therapies. On the other hand, sophisticated equipment is available in government hospitals, but it is often not in working condition. According to the VHAI report, the government's annual public health expenditure is about Rs. 10,000 crore—a pittance compared to an estimated expenditure in the private sector of between Rs. 40,000 and Rs. 60,000 crore. Private services are supported by politicians and bureaucrats, who often get free treatment—which is actually intended for the poor, and is a condition for the various concessions and tax benefits that these hospitals get. The entry of the corporate hospital signals an open focus on profit rather than people's needs. Private medical colleges and high-tech private hospitals proliferate nationwide. For the people behind these ventures, medical education and healthcare are like any other industry which must make a profit.

Sources

Reddy, Sangita (2007): Issue in Public Health, *Economic Times of India*, Nov. 13, 2007.

Sen, Amartya: Public action to remedy hunger, Arturo Tanco Memorial Lecture, August 2, 1990.

Bethune, Norman: The scalpel, the sword, Ed. Gordon Sydney and Ted Allan, Monthly Review Press, 1973.

Jain, Kalpana: Public healthcare in disarray fills the coffers of private hospitals, *The Times of India*, February 5, 1999.

Editorial, Be Indian, be happy, *The Times of India*, January 1999.

CHAPTER

2

Indian Economy and Health

Healthcare Systems in India

The Indian economy is witnessing phenomenal growth. It is currently at 8.5% of Gross Domestic Product (GDP); a fiery pace that most analysts predict is sustainable and likely to accelerate further, making it one of the fastest growing economies in the world. The last decade has seen the healthcare sector transition from a static and seemingly inconspicuous industry to an increasingly dynamic and significant industry today. A decade ago in India, healthcare sector was not considered as a key driver of national economic performance. However, over the years, there has been a fundamental change to this paradigm, with incontrovertible evidence from the world over firmly establishing that improved health leads to better economic performance. The direct as well as unquantifiable benefits from healthcare have become too large to be ignored. Small wonder that healthcare planning and investment have become the buzzwords for corporate planners the world over.

Health is influenced by general economic prosperity and social cohesion, and economic and social inequalities, said Nobel Laureate Amartya Sen. Drawing parallels between India and China to highlight his point on the role of economic prosperity in facilitating good health, the Nobel Laureate said China had managed to achieve astounding progress in general health and longevity along with economic growth. Those parts of India that had high life expectancy by 1979, partly because of following the Chinese model of social commitment,—particularly Kerala and now Himachal Pradesh—have continued to have high rates of longevity and mortality reduction. Ensuring health coverage for all as a part of the human right need not await the distant possibility of the disappearance of inequalities in income and wealth.

We have certain worrying features in our system. We have 21 percent of global burden of disease. Twenty-five percent of all maternal deaths take place in our country and same may be true for neonatal mortality. Are people protected against the high cost of medical care? So any health system should see to it that the financial protection is extended against the catastrophic illnesses and the poor people who are really worst affected with the high cost, are not constrained to seek care. Several studies have indicated that poor don't seek care on account of poor purchasing power.

Expenditure on health

Last decade has been witness to phenomenal growth in numbers hospitals, the medical colleges, nursing colleges and other similar training institutions. However, the quality of training and learning left a lot to be desired. It will be useful to see as how we are doing in terms of spending? Overall, Government spending is 0.9% of GDP, which is very low. WHO has pointed that we are really in the bottom quintile in the world in terms of public sector spending in the healthcare? The policy documents are explicit for increasing public spending to 2% and then 5% within next 10 years. In terms of expenditures 80 percent of all spending is on health from the private side, it's kind of out-of-pocket expenditures because the health insurance is yet to catch imagination of masses. Out-of-pocket expenditure includes risk of falling in debts after hospitalization.

Strategic opportunities for foreign investment and collaboration mark the sector, as leading Indian players draw out global expansion plans.

- The Healthcare Delivery market is estimated at US$ 18.7 billion. Nearly 65 percent of the healthcare services market has been captured by the private sector.
- The industry is growing at about 13 percent annually and is expected to grow at 15 percent over the next four to five years.
- A recent CII-McKinsey and Co. study forecasts growth from US$ 18.7 billion to around US$ 45 billion—equivalent to 8.5 percent of GDP by 2012. Private healthcare is expected to account for 75 percent of this spending.

The Confederation of Indian Industry's (CII) and Indian Healthcare Federation (IHF) estimate fresh investments of US$ 25 billion over the next 8-10 years to establish that facilities will put the sector on the global healthcare map. With US$ 12-15 billion expected in domestic investments, the Indian healthcare sector represents a US$ 10 billion opportunity for foreign investors. Over the past two decades, a number of Indian private sector companies have set-up hospital facilities and clinics. Prominent examples include Apollo, Max, Fortis, Escorts and Wockhardt; out of an estimated total of 150 that represent a rapidly growing number of high-end facilities that offer top-of-the-line medical treatment.

- Private hospitals account for over 32 percent of hospital beds in India. Besides providing basic health and medical care services, these corporate hospitals often undertake complex surgeries like liver transplant, bone-marrow transplants, open-heart surgeries and kidney transplants.
- Another area witnessing increasing corporate presence is diagnostic services. Premier Indian players in this segment include SRL-Ranbaxy, Metropolis Health Services and Dr. Lal's Pathlabs. The emergence of corporate hospitals on a larger scale is an important development. It has added the much needed infrastructural capacity, and,

more importantly, been a catalyst in the professionalisation of hospital management. In turn, it has also facilitated impressive growth in the hospital management education industry.

Use of Information Technology

An important and positive development in the Indian healthcare sector is the use of information technology for upgrading the delivery of healthcare services and improving efficiency levels. Some examples include—

- Computerization of medical records,
- Networking of various departments in a hospital, and
- Providing tele-medicine services.

Online reporting of laboratory and radio-diagnostic results over a Local Area Network (LAN) introduced by some medical colleges has significantly reduced reporting lag and patient movement. It has made the following partnerships possible: Wockhardt and Harvard Medical International Inc., USA, Fortis Healthcare and Partners Healthcare System, USA. Birla Heart and Research Centre And Cleveland Clinic Foundation, USA.

Public private and voluntary sector health systems

We have commented on Primary Health Cente (PHC) as the heart of public health services in the country. Some description of PHC is given in this chapter. In the private sector we have dedicated medical practitioners, who provide service against fee. Some of them are not earnest about the service component, while several others are not qualified. Most of the recent investment in healthcare is in the private sector with the result many corporate hospitals have been set up, which provide world class care at a high end of fees. Some of such hospitals are mentioned below. Similarly, there are serving clinics and hospitals in the voluntary sector (NGOs), which provide service either free or on payment of a nominal amount. Let us study some of the corporate hospitals first.

Top corporate hospitals

Apollo Group of Hospitals

Apollo Hospitals has emerged as the single largest private hospital group in south Asia. It operates hospitals, dispensaries, clinics and laboratories. Specialty services provided by the group include open-heart surgery, angioplasty surgery and renal transplants. The company has several firsts to its credit. It was the first hospital to obtain ISO 9002 and ISO 14001 quality certification in India. It was the first to set-up a health insurance administration company. It was the first to introduce preventive healthcare in India. It was the first Indian hospital to introduce new techniques in coronary angioplasty, sterio-tactic radiotherapy and radio-surgery. Apollo Hospitals got accredited with the Joint Commission International (JCI), an arm of the US-based Joint Commission on Accreditation of Healthcare Organisations (JCAHO).

Escorts Heart Institute (EHIRC)

The Escorts Group has a presence in specialized cardiac treatment and multi-specialty care hospitals providing a whole gamut of specialized medical services. Escorts operates ten hospitals across India. The group is also reputed for tertiary care services such as neurology, neurosurgery, plastic surgery and urology. Escorts Heart Institute and Research Centre (EHIRC) has introduced innovative techniques of minimally invasive and robotic surgery. EHIRC is a 325 bed tertiary care institute, with 9 operation theatres, 5 cath labs, 2 heart command centres and world class facilities. It has carried out over 80,000 angiographies, 17,000 angioplasties and 43,000 cardiac surgeries over the past fifteen years—which is a world record. It is an ISO 9001 approved facility, which was recently adjudged the best cardiac care hospital in the country. It has been purchased by Fortis group recently.

Fortis Healthcare

It a company founded by the promoters of the Indian pharmaceutical major, Ranbaxy Laboratories, started operations in 2001. Fortis Healthcare has ambitious growth plans in the hospitals segment. The company aims to have a number of multi-specialty Fortis Healthcare centres over the next three to five years through an investment of close to US$ 217 million. The company is focusing on increasing its capacity to 4,000 beds in 10 hospitals, up from the existing 600 beds in 4 hospitals. As part of this initiative, Fortis will be setting up a medi-city at Gurgaon in Haryana based on the John Hopkins Medical Centre in the US. To be known as Fortis International Institute of Medical and Biosciences (FIIMBS), it will house a medical college, an attached hospital, an allied sciences institute and a referral centre, among other facilities.

Max Healthcare

Max Healthcare, a fully owned subsidiary of the highly diversified Max Group, is focusing on becoming the largest healthcare player in northern India with a chain of clinics and hospitals with a bed capacity of 1200. On an average, Max Healthcare treats 30,000 patients every month, with 200 new patients visiting the facilities every day. Max has a presence in all three verticals of the healthcare delivery segment (Primary, Secondary and Tertiary care). The institute has developed a three-tier business model for delivering healthcare services. This is a hub and spokes model, where the hub is the super specialty hospital and the spokes are its own clinical and diagnostic centres. The model comprises Dr. Max Clinics at the primary level, Max Med-centers at the secondary level and Max Devki Devi Hospital at the higher end.

Wockhardt

It is among India's leading pharmaceutical and healthcare companies. Since inception in 1989, the Wockhardt Hospital and Heart Institute has become a renowned tertiary level heart centre providing cardiac care to patients of all age groups including newborns. It has earned the recognition of a "Centre of Excellence" in cardiac care and has become a treatment destination for cardiac patients from neighbouring countries. It has an international alliance with Harvard Medical International, and has tie-ups with many global health insurance giants, including the BlueCross and BlueShield. It's sister hospital 'Multispeciality Hospital' at Bangalore is a world class service.

Aravind Eye Hospital

This hospital in south India is the single largest provider of eye surgery in the world. In 1998, its hospitals saw 1.2 million outpatients and performed 183,000 cataract surgeries. It costs about US$ 10 to conduct a cataract operation. It costs hospitals in the United States about US$ 1,650 to perform the same operation. Since it's opening in 1976, Aravind has given sight to millions. Aravind's surgeons are so productive that the hospital has a gross margin of 40 percent. This is despite the fact that 70 percent of the patients pay nothing or close to nothing, and the hospital does not depend on donations. The Aravind Eye Hospital business model is taught as a case study at the Harvard Business School.

The Jaipur Foot

It is named after its birthplace, the capital of the Indian state of Rajasthan, is an extraordinary prosthesis, or artificial limb, and has revolutionized life for millions of land-mine amputees. According to the Time magazine, which profiled its founders as one of fifteen 'Heroes of Medicine', "The beauty of the Jaipur foot is its lightness and mobility—those who wear it can run, climb trees and pedal bicycles, and its low price. While a prosthesis for a similar level of amputation can cost several thousand dollars in the US, the Jaipur Foot costs only US$ 28 in India.

Other developments in private healthcare

The US-based Atlas Medical Software, which specializes n developing software solutions for the healthcare industry, has set-up its operations in India. Bayer Diagnostics, one of the largest diagnostic businesses in the world, with a presence in more than 100 countries is represented in India through Bayer Diagnostics India Limited (BDIL) in which Bayer AG of Germany owns 32.67 percent of the stake. In India, it is mainly into the manufacture of chemical and immuno chemical test systems, medical diagnostic equipment (blood analyser and serum analyser) and electrolyte serum analyzer.

German medical instruments major Drager Medical AG, a joint venture between Dragerwerk AG and Siemens AG, is keen to enter India through a wholly owned subsidiary. Drager Medical manufactures a range of medical products like anesthesia equipment, monitoring equipment, ventilation equipment, pediatrics and medical emergency equipment, oxygen and aerosol therapy equipment. GE-BEL, a joint venture between GE and Bharat Electronics Limited is the only manufacturer of X-ray and CT tubes in South Asia. Global Technology Operations—India (GTO) is an ISO 9001 certified Software Development Centre that designs and develops products and solutions for GE Medical Systems using the latest computer platforms. GE Medical Systems Information Technology is a joint venture between GE and Citadel Health Ltd. of Hyderabad, for HIRePSTMa state-of-the-art Hospital Information System. UK-based iSOFT Group (iSOFT), one of the world's leading suppliers of application systems for hospitals and healthcare organisations, will be investing U$ 100 million over the next three years in its Offshore Development Centre (ODC) in Chennai in southern India, which was set-up in 2001.

Philips has set a target of emerging as a distinct number two in the Indian medical systems market in another four to five years. The company today sells about US$ 43-49 million worth of medical systems in India. The aim is to take it to US$ 100 million. Philips is also looking at tele-medicine, with its DisHA (Distance Healthcare Advancement) initiative to be piloted in two states. Philips will work with state governments, hospitals and other partners to provide affordable, accessible healthcare through mobile vans equipped with medical equipment under DisHA.

The US-based healthcare products major, Proton Healthcare is making an entry into India with its range of digital health monitoring devices such as digital blood pressure monitors, ultrasonic nebulisers, body fat scales and thermometers. Proton has entered into a strategic tie-up with the Delhi-based SM Logistics for distributing its products in the Indian market. Siemens is a leading manufacturer of medical equipment with a market share of more than 30 percent in India. The range of products includes X-ray systems, intensive care systems, hearing instruments, ultrasound instruments and equipment for nuclear medicine, among others.

Wipro GE Medical Systems, a joint venture between GE Medical Systems and Wipro Corporation, is India's largest medical systems sales and service provider. Wipro GE, which manufactures and exports products to global markets, pioneered the manufacture of Ultrasound and CT Scanner systems in India for global markets.

India is becoming a competitive outsourcing destination for high-end laboratory and diagnostic testing. For hospitals in the United Kingdom, United States and West Asia, it is cheaper to outsource laboratory and diagnostic tests to India.

Healthcare BPO could potentially be a US$ 4.5 billion opportunity for India by 2008, offering employment to about 200,000 people. It includes offshoring of processes such as medical billing, disease coding, forms processing and claims adjudication. Already, over a dozen companies are either consolidating operations or have kicked off pilots in this space. These include Indian companies such as Apollo Health Street (AHS), iHealthcare, Paramount Healthcare, Hinduja TMT, Ajuba, Affiliated Computer Services, Cognizant Technology Solutions and Vision Healthsource. As healthcare BPO players mature, other businesses like claims repricing, medical diagnosis and actuarial work are expected to gain momentum. The opportunity is being driven by the US$ 1.4 trillion US healthcare industry, trying to rationalise costs. The American Healthcare Association estimates that the profitability of US hospitals fell from 6.1 percent, six years ago to 2.8 percent in 2002. Almost 40 percent of the US hospitals make losses. State-owned insurer Medicare has US$ 20 million in liabilities. Hospitals need to offshore the US$ 350 billion administrative functions and US$ 50 billion billing and coding tasks to be able to bring down their costs.

Public Health System

While the network exists to serve rural and poor areas,

these centers are grossly under funded and understaffed. Then there is a real problem of absenteeism of the health staff.

Rural Healthcare System in India

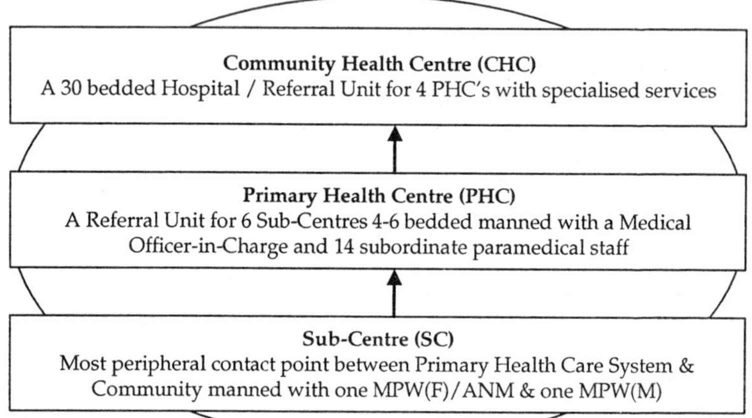

Source: Bulletin on Rural Health Statistics in India, 2006.

The center of the public health system is primary health center (PHC). Each PHC has five to six sub-centers located closer to rural villages that are managed by an Auxiliary Nurse. Each sub-center is meant to serve three to four villages. Overall, one PHC can serve anywhere from 25,000 to 48,000 people. The National Health Policy report of 2002 found that the current infrastructure of public health needs to increase by 16% in order to adequately serve the population (Ministry of Health and Family Welfare).

Rural areas already have much fewer staff and beds than urban areas. Doctor to patient ratios are six times lower in rural areas, and doctor to bed ratios are fifteen times lower (Deogaonkar). A 2004 health survey in rural Udaipur found that each PHC served over 45,000 people and had on average of 5.8 medical personnel and 1.5 doctors appointed (Banerjee). Having such few staff serve such large populations no doubt contributes to their inefficiencies.

Modern *v/s* CAM

Unfortunately, 80% of general practitioners practice modern medicine without proper training (Patil). The same is true of the private healthcare. A survey found that the average distance to a public health facility was 2.09 km and to a PHC was 6.7 km (Banerjee). For many rural people, who don't have transportation, traveling 6.7 km to closest doctor when ill is a great distance and could be a factor in their choosing unqualified private practitioners who are closer. The rural Udaipur survey showed that the people chose to go to private doctors almost twice as much as public facilities. In fact Patil tells us that 70% of rural families spend 60% of their annual income on health. The rural health survey supported this data by finding that only 37.7% of private doctors had an MBBS (qualifications to practice modern medicine) or higher specialty degree. 13.9% of "private doctors" in this survey had no formal qualifications and 36% did not have a college degree in any subject. Many quacks and practitioners of CAM (complementary and alternative medicine) use modern medicine with impunity.

Urban *v/s* Rural

Agriculture is still the primary economic driver in rural India, and still holds 60% of the workforce of the whole country. However despite having the greater percentage of the workforce, it only comprises about 20% of the GDP. It is service-based jobs and industrial jobs that comprise the majority of India's GDP (51.4% and 28.1% respectively). This has created an imbalance of economy and of opportunity.

	Rural	*Urban*	*Reference Year*
Population (%)	72.2	27.8	2001
Birth Rate	26.4	19.8	2003
Death Rate	8.7	6.0	2003
Infant Mortality Rate	66	38	2003

Source: *SRS Bulletin*, April 2005, Sample Registration System, Registrar General, India.

Urban India, despite having a smaller percentage of the overall workforce, is driving the economy and therefore controls where new opportunities in technology, lifestyle, and health are placed. In fact, 75% of the health infrastructure and medical personnel in India are concentrated in urban areas (Patil). This has translated into different health scenarios for rural *vs.* urban India. When measuring health, the three factors that are considered most informative about standards of living are mortality, morbidity and life expectancy. These measures allow us to examine rate of life, death and disease in an area and draw conclusions about the population health in those areas.

Surprisingly, birth rates nearly triple death rates in both rural and urban India. This tells us that the population is growing very quickly all across the country. The population in rural India continues growing larger, and they are also dying at a greater rate than urban India. The death rate there is almost 50% greater in rural India, and Infant Mortality is nearly twice as much. Maternal mortality rates (MMR) are also significantly high at 407 deaths/100,000 live births. In fact, MMR has actually risen over the last decade (Deogaonkar). There are many reasons for this, some of which are outlined below (Patil):

- 51% of deliveries are conducted at home by an untrained attendant.
- 75% of women have their first pregnancy before they turn 18.
- Only 67% of women complete their antenatal checkup.
- Only 30% of women get postnatal check-ups.

The good news out of all of this is that most rural deaths are preventable. They arise from infections and communicable, parasitic and respiratory diseases (Patil). The bad news is that mortality and morbidity rates in rural India have not shown significant improvement over time. Healthcare delivery in India comes in three major forms.

Indicators of health status of the Indian population

Annual incidence of cataract, the cause of 80 percent of blindness, is 3.8 millions of cases. The total potential for surgical cataract removal is 1.75 million cases per year.

The total number of cancer cases in India was estimated at 924,790 in 2001. This is projected to increase to 1,229,968 by 2011 and to 1,557,800 by 2021. The mortality rate due to cardiac arrest and related causes was estimated at 2.4 million in 1990. With increasing urbanization the problem is on the rise. Malaria is Projected to increase from 2.03 million cases in 2001 to 2.62 million cases in 2021.

Hypertension, diabetes and renal diseases: These stress and lifestyle related disorders are on the rise. The diabetic population in India is projected to increase from 40 million of 2001 to 47 million people in 2010. Hypertension is lower in rural areas but on an increase in urban cities. Prevalence rate in Delhi alone is 17.34 percent. Both hypertension and diabetes further cause renal disorders.

The current prevalence rate for neurological disorders is 15 to 20 people per thousand. The most common ailments are epilepsy, migraine, cerebrovascular disorders, Parkinson's disease and peripheral neuropathies. It is estimated that 1 percent of the population is suffering from serious psychiatric illnesses, 10-15 percent have neuro-disorders, and 2.5 percent are mentally retarded. (*Source*: ICRA report on Indian Healthcare.)

As part of rural Primary healthcare network alone, a total of 1.6 lakh sub-centers, (with 1.27 lakh. ANMa in position) and 22975 PHCs and 2935 CHCs (with over 24000 doctors and over 3500 specialists to serve in them) have been set-up. To promote Indian systems of medicine and homeopathy there are over 22000 dispensaries, 2800 hospitals. Besides 6 lakh angawadis serve nutrition needs of nearly 20 million children and 4 million mothers. The total effort has cost the bulk of the health development outlay, which stood at over Rs. 62.500 crores or 3-64% of total plan spending during the last fifty years. On any count these are extraordinary infrastructural capacities created with resources committed against odds to strengthen grass roots. There have been facility gaps, supply gaps and staffing gaps, which can be filled up only by allocating more funds and determined will to ensure good administration and synergy from greater congruence of services. It has got more firmly established at the periphery/sub-center level and dedicated to RCH services only. At PHC and CHC levels this has further been compounded by a weak referral system. PHCs and CHCs are funded by States, several of whom are unable to match Central assistance offered and hence these centers remain inadequate and operate on minimum efficiency.

How can healthcare be made affordable?

Participating in a debate organised by *Economic Times* V. Raja, CEO, GE Healthcare observed: What we need is a paradigm shift. Today's primary care physician should be armed with the sophisticated technology of today's specialists: portable ultrasound units to detect early heart disease, advanced bone mineral density scanners to catch osteoporosis and electronic medical records (EMRs) to improve the quality and safety of care.

This shift can help clinicians detect disease earlier, access more information and monitor and intervene earlier with targeted treatments, enabling patients to live their lives to the fullest and reduce costs.

The key challenges that India must address to make healthcare affordable and accessible are: liberalising health insurance, digitisation of healthcare, create awareness about early health as a concept amongst the masses, and increasing the level of integration between government, hospitals and equipment manufacturers to improve the healthcare system. With insurance covering just 3% of the total population, India remains one of the most under-insured countries in the world. A strong effort must be made to communicate who is covered, how to access benefits, and what screening and other preventive care is available under government and private-pay policies.

We need to develop healthcare infrastructure to cater to the projected demand for healthcare services. Private providers have already made substantial inroads and have set up facilities both in India and overseas. The government can help this through targeted incentives that can reduce the cost of creation of facilities by up to 30%.

Another area India can do well is tele-radiology and tele-cardiology. Given the shortage of skilled healthcare professionals, experts can provide diagnoses and second opinions remotely. We can overcome the shortage of manpower and reach more people in the rural areas, potentially saving millions of dollars and inconvenience in the process. (V. Raja, GE)

On the other hand Shubnum from healthcare institute stated that "The key to sustainability of India's rapid economic growth lies in the health of its people.

Containing rising healthcare costs challenges all nations irrespective of their GDP or quantum of healthcare spends. However, it is not necessary that a higher spend results in better health-care outcomes.

In India, unlike many other low and lower middle income countries, an individual incurs the largest out-of-pocket expenses on health.

As healthcare costs have increased it. is, therefore, not surprising that medical expenditure, which on a yearly basis can amount up to 60% of an individual's annual income, is one of the leading causes of indebtedness. If we were to analyse the drivers for rising healthcare costs they would fall into three main categories—consumer, provider and supplier driven.

Physicians, in are influenced by myriad circumstances, from emergence of new epidemics, evidence based quality practice of medicine to legal and institutional challenges in providing the best possible care. All these help fuel a perception of what is perceived as "unnecessary hospitalisation and over investigation."

India, according to Ficci, would require an investment of $78 billion in the next decade to fund the addition of approximately 1,000,000 beds which are needed. It is anticipated that government, given its lacklustre performance in its healthcare spend of 1% of the GDP, will contribute $8.2 billion and the private sector $69.7 billion."

Global Burden of Disease (GBD) study

The disease burden affects the wage earning capacity as well as productivity. It also entails expenditure on medical treatment, travel, attendants and the unfortunate premature death. The study shows that sixty percent of morbidity is due to infectious diseases and common tropical diseases, a quarter due to life-style disorders and 13% due to potentially preventable per-natal conditions. We were able to control small pox and guinea worm diseases. It has now been proposed to eliminate or control the following diseases.

- Polio Yaws and leprosy which seems distinctly feasible though the removal of social stigma and reconstructive surgery and other rehabilitation arrangements in a decade.
- Kalaazar by 2010 and Filalriasis by 2010 which also seems feasible due to its localized prevalence and the possibility of greater community based work.
- Blindness prevalence to 0.5% by 2010 sees less feasible due to a graying population.
- AIDS reaching zero growth by 2007 appears to be problematic as there are disputes even about base data on infected population.

Eleven out of thirteen diseases recommended by the Bhore Committee were infectious diseases and at least three of them may well continue to be with us for the next two decades, i.e. TB, Malaria and AIDS to which diarrhoea in children and complicated and high risk maternity should be added in view of their pervasive incidence and avoidable mortality among the poorer and under served sectors.

Tuberculosis

It is estimated that about 14 million persons are infected, from radiologically active tuberculosis. More than 300,000 deaths occur every year. The prevalence among working age adults (15-59) is even higher. TB is a wide-spread disease of poverty among women living and working in ill ventilated places and other undernourished persons in urban slums. No universal screening is possible. Drugs are prescribed on the basis of fever and shadows as a result incomplete cure becomes common and delayed tests only prove the wrong diagnosis. Treatment costs in case of drug resistance can soar close to ten times the normal level of Rs. 3000 to 4000 per person treated. There is reason to hope that DOTS programs would prove a greater success over time with increased community awareness. With commitment and full use of infrastructure it will be possible to arrest further growth in absolute numbers of TB cases keeping it at below 1.5 million till 2010 even though the population will be growing. Once that is done TB can be brought down to less than a million, i.e. within internationally accepted limits and disappears as a major communicable disease in India by 2020.

Malaria

At present India has a large manpower fully aware of all aspects of malaria but often low in motivation. There is evidence of reemergence with focal attacks of malaria with the virulent falciparum variety especially in tribal areas. About 2 million cases of malaria are recorded all over India every year with seasonal high incidence local failures of control. Drug resistance in humans and insecticide resistant strains of mosquitoes present a significant problem. There is growing interest and community awareness of biological methods of control of mosquito growth. As regards a vaccine, there seems to be no sufficient incentive for international R&D to focus on a relatively lower priority or research. The search for a vaccine continues but has little likelihood of immediate success. It is necessary that routine tasks like timely spraying and taking blood slides testing and their analysis and organic methods of reducing mosquito spread are carried out diligently. Malaria can certainly be reduced by a third even upto a half in ten years, and there is a prospect of near freedom from malaria for most of the country by 2020.

AIDS

The Draft NHP 2001 seeks to stop further infection by educating and counseling and condom supplies. Further such awareness efforts must be followed by multi-pronged and culturally compatible techniques of public education that go beyond segments easier to be convinced or behaviour changed. In about a decade vaccine development may possibly be successful and drugs may by more effective but they may not always be affordable nor can be given free. A recent analysis reveals that the three drug regimen recommended will cost $10000 per person per year from Western companies and the treatment will be life long. Three Indian companies are offering to Central Government anti-retro; viral drugs at $600 (Rs. 30,000) per person per year and to an international charity at an even lower price $ 350 (Rs. 13,000) per year. It has been public policy in Brazil that the drug is supplied free to all AIDS patients.

Child Health and Nutrition

There is a issue of infant and child mortality, (70 out of 1000 dying in the first year and 98 before five years) and low birth weight (22% UW at birth and 47% EJW at below 3 years). Most mortality occurs from diarrhoea and the stagnation in IMR in the last few years is bound to have a negative effect on population stabilization goals. At the same time, more streamlined RCH services are getting established as part of public systems and through private partnerships. Therefore there is every reason to hope that the NPP 2000 target of 30 per thousand live births by 2010 will be met barring a few pockets of inaccessible and resource lean areas with stubborn persistence of poverty and dominantly composed of weaker sections.

As regards childhood diarrhoea, deaths are totally preventable with simple community action and public education by targeting children of low birth weights and detecting early those children at risk from malnutrition through proper low cost screening procedure. The success can be built upon till 2025 for reaching levels comparable to China.

Mild and moderate malnutrition still prevalent in over half of our young population can be halved if food as the supplemental pathway to better nutrition becomes a priority both for self-reliance and lower costs. There has been a tendency for micro-nutrient supplementation to overwhelm food derived nourishment. This trend is assisted by foreign aid but over a long-run may prove unsustainable. By engaging the adolescents into proper nutrition education and reproductive health awareness we can seamlessly weave into the nutritional security system of our country a corps of informed interconnected and imaginative ideas can be tried out.

Voluntary and Non-Government Organisations (NGOs) Sector

Traditionally, providing relief of pain, distress and ill health has been considered as an act of 'Dharam' by Indians. Our scriptures bear testimony to this fact. Government of India also recognises free medical/surgical treatment as an act of charity and encourages it. While several charitable clinics are set-up only to muster publicity or to extract money from the state or foreign agencies, many others do provide selfless medical care of high quality. While the acts of tokenism need to be curbed, genuine voluntary healthcare is the need of the hour, where 42 crore people in the unorganised sector do not have any health cover at all. One good example of NGO sector is illustrated below.

Voluntary Health Services (VHS), Chennai

The Voluntary Health Services (VHS), a registered non-profit society, was founded in July 1958, in Chennai (Madras), India, by the late Dr. K.S. Sanjivi, a renowned physician, a respected teacher and a visionary. Its basic concepts are the prevention and cure of serious illnesses, and the fostering of the family as a unit for medical care, with a family insurance scheme that is income-based. The family membership scheme covers the head of the family and his dependants. A membership card is issued on payment of the subscription, valid for one year from the date of enrolment. It has to be renewed every year. The subscription is based on the income. Those who do not opt for family membership can be treated as individual members. Members with a monthly income below Rs. 750 are given free treatment, while, for higher income groups, charges are levied in a graded manner. Over 70% patients get free treatment in this hospital. In addition to curative care, each member is entitled to a free medical check-up on enrolment and once a year thereafter, on the subscription being maintained.

A special feature of the scheme is that it is the service provider, namely, the VHS hospital itself, who is implementing it, and there is no third party involved. Further, as VHS has almost all the specialities, with a wide range of investigative facilities and a 24-hour Blood Bank, Intensive Care Unit, etc., the members get all their benefits under a single roof.

Today, the VHS Medical Centre is a tertiary teaching 405-bed hospital with almost all the specialities—ranging from general surgery and medicine to neurology and nephrology. About 70 percent of the patients (those with a monthly income below a certain limit) are treated free of cost, which includes free diet and medicines. The VHS offers a unique Medical Aid Plan that was evolved as an insurance scheme to be utilized by the middle and lower income groups. The family is taken into account as the unit of healthcare and the head of the family is enrolled as a member, on payment of an annual membership fee which is income-based, and his family members are included as his dependants and the medical services are availed by them.

Sri Ramachandra Medical Centre, Chenni attached to the University (same name) is another hospital that provides free medical treatment to all its patients, who come to the block meant for non-paying patients. Most of the services are absolutely free, even when such patients require services that are not listed in the non-paying category, the charges made from these patients would be nominal. Their official brochure says that 2500 OPD patients and 750 in patients receive free care daily, including surgical and obstetric care. Since the institute is non-profit making but self-sufficient hospital, the revenue generated from paying patients and fee received from graduate/post-graduate medical students from home and abroad is ploughed back for the care of poor patients. this model can work for improving healthcare in our country.

As mentioned elsewhere, Dr. Devi Shetty of Narayan Hrudalaya fame is rendering yeoman's healthcare service for poor farmers of Karnataka through medical insurance at a nominal price. This model can also work, if well-to-do people earning from paying patients (other industry) can divert their spare resources for the healthcare of health-nots. However, the quality should not be compromised in the name of free service.

Sources

Banerjee, Abhijit, Angus Deaton and Esther Duflo. "Healthcare Delivery in Rural Rajasthan", *Economic and Political Weekly*, February 28, 2004, Vol. 39, Issue 9. pp. 944–49.

Express Healthcare Management. Rural Healthcare, 16th August 2005. http://www.expresshealthcaremgmt.com/20050831/ruralhealthcare01.shtml.

Patil, Ashok V., K.V. Somasundaram, and R.C. Goyal, "Current Health Scenario in Rural India", *Australian Journal of Rural Health*, January 2002. pp. 129–53.

Deogaonkar, Milind. "Socio-economic inequality and its effect on healthcare delivery in India: Inequality and healthcare", *Electronic Journal of Sociology*, 2004. http://www.sociology.org/content/vol18.1/deogaonkar.html.

CIA. CIA World Fact Book 2002, 2002. CIA, 1 January 2002, http://www.faqs.org/docs/factbook/geos/in.html.

Bardhan, Pranab. "Globalization and Rural Poverty", World Development, December 2005.

Government of India. Ministry of Health and Family Welfare, National Rural Health Mission Document, 2005.

Government of India, Ministry of Health and Family Welfare, Bulletin on Rural Health Statistics in India 2006. 2006, http://mohfw.nic.in/dofw%20website/Bulletin%20on%20RHS%20—%2006%20—%20PDF%20Files/bulletin_on_rural_health_statistics.htm

Government of India, Ministry of Health and Family Welfare, National Health Policy-2002, 2002, http://mohfw.nic.in/np2002.htm.

CHAPTER

3

Reforms in Healthcare

Long Way to Go

India's healthcare system needs a lot of improvement, is a well accepted fact. Government has the constraint of funds, whereas private sector is out to make only profits. Voluntary sector is more of a tokenism. There is an urgent requirement of wide ranging and deep reforms in this sector to provide a responsible universal healthcare delivery.

A committee on policy framework for private investment in health education, and rural development, comprising of Mukesh Ambani (convenor) and Kumarmangalam Birla (member) appointed by prime minister's council on trade and industry suggested the following reforms in the field of healthcare, in April 2000. Some portions, relevent to healthcare are reproduced here. The recommendations if implemented can bring changes for the better. It is learnt that Mukesh Ambani himself has taken initiative to set up model primary healthcare centres all over the country. While his brother Anil has launched himself in setting up world class hospitals.

'There are many infirmities in the existing health infrastructure. These infirmities do not assure India either of a healthy society or of a healthcare industry that can be a force for economic growth. Reforms in health are vital to secure India's future. The Indian health system has to make available affordable, quality healthcare to a population that is growing from one billion now to one and a quarter billion in fifteen years time. It has to care for life threatening diseases that affect a large number of underprivileged, while simultaneously addressing lifestyle diseases that impact a large number of relatively well-off people. If India has to provide health for all, public expenditure has to be significantly stepped up and focused on the poor and indigent groups. At the same time, there has to be greater play for private participation in the health sector. Several innovative financing mechanisms have to be institutionalized. India has the potential to be at the forefront of modern healthcare, given its strong base in quality healthcare professionals and cost effective research. India has the opportunity to harness these strengths to deliver quality healthcare not only for its people but to larger geographical regions as well. India has to see health not as a social cost but as an investment in human capital for economic growth.

At present adequate healthcare is unaffordable for the vast majority of India's population. Current funding is being used sub-optimally and is not directed to maximizing health gains. Significant disparities exist between urban and rural areas, between different states and between poorer and wealthier segments of the population. The current structure of the healthcare delivery system, especially public healthcare, does not provide enough incentives for improvement in efficiency. There are stark deficiencies in healthcare quality and regulation is weak. An improvement in health systems and infrastructure is vital to assure India's future. The vision for India in the area of health should be 'to foster a healthy society through provision of quality healthcare services to all citizens'. To realize this vision, India has to focus on health development with the mission of 'creating an affordable and efficient healthcare system, balancing preventive and curative measures and establishing an enduring public-private partnership'.

The agenda for reforms

It aims to focus on free government funded healthcare to the most needy. It induces those who can pay for healthcare to do so, but through new financing mechanisms designed to ease the burden of obtaining healthcare when it is most needed. The current system of individual spending should migrate to collective spending on healthcare. The government should facilitate this migration though introducing multiple healthcare financing schemes targeted at different socio-economic segments of the population. This should be through a mix of private and public sources. In addition, there could be other measures such as reallocation of funding and increased revenues for the government.

Steps, to ensure that these measures do not unduly increase healthcare costs across the society, have to be taken, primarily through increased insurance coverage. The organised sector should be mandatorily covered though social insurance. The existing schemes (such as CGHS & ESIS) should be consolidated at the state level.

A safety net, fully sponsored by the government, should be available for the poor and the vulnerable sections of the society. The rural population should be covered through community insurance operated at the panchayat samiti levels. Voluntary social insurance should be encouraged for people employed in the unorganised sector. In addition, private insurance for people who can afford and want better facilities should be available. There should be provision for selective user charges in government funded schemes to prevent misuse.

In the area of preventive health, it is imperative that such factors as nutrition, hygiene, water supply and sanitation, food adulteration, quality of drugs, environmental protection, quality of household fuels and health programmes in schools and occupational areas are addressed. An inter-sectoral approach in collaboration with other agencies dealing with these areas is essential. A decentralised approach right up to the village level is advocated.

India's population is expected to be around 1.24 billion by the year 2015. To meet its obligation for a healthier society, large investments in the health sector are required. The total expenditure on health in 2015 is estimated at Rs. 1,81,120 crores, at current prices. Of this, Rs. 1,17,423 crores (65%) should be in the public sector and Rs. 63,697 crores (35%) in the private sector. This pattern of spending between public and private will be a reversal of the current situation where government spending is about 22% of the total health expenditure. The government will have to spend about five times its current spending on health, but focusing on primary and preventive health. Appropriate utilization of .available resources is a must, lest the scarce funds are plundered.

As for human resources, the number of doctors will have to increase three times from the existing level of 3.6 lakhs to 12.4 lakhs by 2015. Similarly, there is need for substantially increasing the number of paramedical professionals for meeting the increased healthcare needs. The costs are huge, but there are enormous payoffs in long-term investment in healthcare. Such investments can not only raise quality of life for all citizens but also make the healthcare industry in India a great force for economic growth.

The recommendations of the committee are given below:

A. Healthcare Delivery

1. Strengthen the Referral System

For treatment at the secondary level, a referral from the primary level has to be made. In case there is no referral from the primary health centre at either the secondary or the tertiary centre, the patient be charged a higher fee.

2. Decentralized Health Delivery System

Form a health association accountable and responsible to the panchayat samiti. The key responsibilities of the association would include monitoring health status at village level, effective inter-sectoral co-ordination and mobilising community involvement. Form a healthcare federation of the health associations at the district level and accountable to the zilla parishad. The key responsibilities of this federation would include monitoring the overall health status of the district, effective management of the referral network between community health centres and district hospitals, inter-sectoral planning with the departments of education, sanitation, sewage and water (all key factors affecting health) for focused and coordinated action plans.

3. Enhanced Private Sector Participation for Increased Coverage

This would enhance the reach of the health delivery system and also reduce the need for extensive infrastructure to be established by the government.

4. Quality of Healthcare

Institute a mechanism to monitor the quality of services offered at both public and private facilities.

5. Competition

Encourage the participation of private sector in the secondary and tertiary sectors through infrastructure creation. This could be in the form of tax breaks and incentives.

6. Use of Technology

Devise a detailed plan for use of information technology in healthcare delivery, referral, training and administration.

B. Healthcare Financing

1. User Pays Principle

Ensure that the different segments of the population contribute to the cost of healthcare, according to their ability to pay. The free healthcare and government expenditure should be used for the indigent group and services such as communicable disease control, immunization and family welfare.

2. Private Sources of Finance to Augment Government Spending

Encourage private sector and NGO initiatives in healthcare through appropriate tax breaks and incentives.

3. Multiple Financing Options to Provide for Healthcare

Migrate from the current system of individual spending to collective spending on healthcare. This should be through a mix of private and public sources.

4. Insurance

Provide insurance cover to the rural population through community insurance operated at the panchayat samiti levels. Encourage voluntary social insurance for people employed in the unorganized sector. Prevent misuse of government funded schemes by a provision for selective user charges.

5. Safety Net

Provide a safety net, fully sponsored by the government, for the poor and the vulnerable sections of the society.

6. Tax on Tobacco and Liquor

Levy additional tax on areas which will increase the healthcare costs such as use of tobacco and liquor.

C. Government's Role

1. Develop Inter-Sectoral Linkages, Especially in Promotive and Preventive Services

Address the areas which impact health in a co-ordinated manner with all the agencies at all levels, as against the current practice of inter-sectoral linkages in an *ad-hoc* manner.

2. Effective Regulatory Mechanism

Regulate critical service related regulations such as accreditation and mandatory quality assurance systems. The current regulatory mechanism is extremely weak. Decentralise the regulatory mechanism to the state level made immediately. However, the centre should set the regulations, which will be applicable all over the country.

3. Corporatisation of Government Hospitals

Allow select government hospitals autonomy and self-determination through the route of corporatisation.

4. Separate Purchase and Delivery Functions

Separate the government roles of financier, purchaser and provider.

5. Role of Government

Redefine the role of the Ministry of Health to include—purchasing the agreed range of health services at optimal prices from a range of providers. The quality should not be compromised on any count.

6. Refocus Government Expenditure

Shift from the current emphasis on curative, advance and urban services to increase funding for preventive services and better services in the rural areas. The government expenditure should cover both healthcare for the poor and health promotion and disease prevention for all.

7. Government Focus on Preventive and Primary Healthcare

Focus more on preventive and primary healthcare and reduce the government's direct intervention in the secondary and tertiary levels. Ensure provision of free medical attention to the indigent and needy.

Recent studies indicate that the cost of healthcare delivery in India in comparison to the developed countries is extremely economical. This is a huge opportunity, and can be utilized to increase the financing for the healthcare needs of India.

Managed Care: An Economic Commodity

Managed care will be introduced in India. It's simply a matter of time that it will be 'exported' to India as it has been to Latin America. "Healthcare is being converted from a social service to an economic commodity, sold in the marketplace and distributed on the basis of who can afford to pay for it." The key difference, is that with regular indemnity insurance (such as MediClaim), it is the doctor who decides the medical treatment and the insurance company simply pays money. Thus, the financial risk of falling ill is underwritten by the insurance company, leaving the doctor the sole authority, with no one to cross-question his medical decisions. However, managed care organizations (called HMOs, or health maintenance organizations), play an active role in managing how money is spent. They set guidelines for medical care, choice of medications, and can limit access to specialists in order to improve cost-effectiveness. Treatment decisions by physicians often require the "authorizations", of HMOs, who can refuse to pay for care if they do not think it is appropriate—and this can hurt both patient and doctor.

Let's start with the problems patients face. The biggest one is of access, and it's very difficult for patients to get an appointment to see their physician—waits of up to 3-4 weeks are the norm. For complex problems, the difficulty is far greater. It's not possible for the general doctor to even choose the specialist, whom to refer the patient to. He is forced to send the patient to an approved specialist on the HMO's panel—and this specialist may not be the best for the patient's particular problem. However, the effects of HMOs on doctors are much worse. Most HMO doctors in the US are compelled by the HMO efficiency experts to see "x" number of patients per day. They are treated as mindless machines, who have to process one patient in 10 minutes, no matter how complex the problem. Doctors who spend too much time on a patient actually get pulled up, because the bottom line is no longer the quality of care, but rather its cost.

Often, payments are too little and too late, with the result that doctors get squeezed—and in fact, doctors in the US today often end up losing money by seeing patients (since the reimbursement from the HMO does not cover their overheads. One of the most harmful effects of HMOs has been the poisoning of the physician-patient relationship. To add insult to injury, the HMO applies constraints as to what the doctor can do and cannot do—but if something goes wrong, then it is the doctor who has to bear the full brunt of the patient's wrath—after all, how can an HMO clerk be held responsible for medical decisions?

Role of Indian Healthcare Federation

Indian Healthcare Federation is an independent non-statutory body comprising non-government hospitals, diagnostic centers, medical equipment manufacturers and pharmaceutical industries. The main objective of the Federation is to promote and encourage healthcare industry in the country; it seeks to function as a liaison medium between Government, health providers, medical equipment manufacturers and other medical institutions. The Federation also provides a common platform for its members to discuss and thrash out various issues related to healthcare industry and ensure organized action wherever necessary. It endeavors for a disease-free India by providing accessible quality healthcare every single citizen at affordable cost and transform India into a healthy and vivacious nation. IHCF has a membership of around 300 members from across India. It is affiliated to the Confederation of Indian Industry (CII) and works closely with the CII National Committee on Healthcare.

Government spending on Healthcare in India is low, compared to countries like China, Thailand, Korea and Brazil. Currently it stands at 0.52% of the GDP and it should be increased to at least 6%.

1. Government should focus on rural primary care

- Concentrate efforts and introduce programmes to prevent cardiovascular diseases, mental health, injuries and more importantly HIV and AIDS.
- Reduce centrally sponsored schemes and transfer resources to States.
- Reinvest heavily in public health systems—public health institutions, Management Information Systems, surveillance. Fund allocation should vary by state depending on needs and level of performance.

2. Spur private investments in under-served areas

Central and State Governments should identify areas that need additional Healthcare Delivery capacity based on assessment of number of beds per '000, quality of existing beds, affordability levels of residents. Then incentivise the Industry:

- Accord "Infrastructure Status" to Healthcare Industry with ten year tax holidays and carry forward of losses.

- Provide land at subsidized rate.
- Remove Customs duty on imported Medical Equipment, Consumables and disposables. This will make high quality healthcare affordable.
- Create public-private partnerships in terms of contract of services, private management of public facilities, compliment PHCs in delivery of care through organizing regular camps by private organizations.
- Increase availability of qualified practitioners in rural areas including nurses and paramedics. Create incentives in terms of:

3. Monetary incentives

i. Monthly incentive allowance.
ii. Tax deduction of 40% on incomes of doctors practicing in rural areas.

4. Non-Monetary incentives

i Mandatory rural service for doctors who qualify for PG Courses.
ii. Reservations of select PG seats for in-service rural doctors.
iii. Central and State Governments to create incentives to attract investments in medical colleges and nursing schools in under-served areas to check the imbalance in capacity of medical education.
iv. Government should stimulate the growth of private, social and community health insurance to improve affordability.
v. Give greater autonomy to hospitals.

5. Set-up of more hospitals in the lines of AIIMS and upgrade existing Medical Colleges to the level of AIIMS to have an evenly spread Healthcare system across India.

6. Affordable Medicines

Government should provide cheaper and quality

medicines to the needy by enlarging the scope of many schemes aimed at providing relief to lower economic groups. Essential Drugs for "below the poverty line" population should be dispensed at subsidised rates through the local Primary Healthcare Centre.

7 Technology in the centre-stage

Technology has greatly aided patients and providers alike by enhancing the quality of delivery, reduction in turn around time of workflows, besides bringing in higher accountability into the system. As a typical example, a 100 bedded hospital could decrease its time for discharge by 50% to less than 60 minutes leading to an approximate increase in revenue of over 25%, on an average investment of only 2% of its annual revenue by an appropriate hospital information system.

The Indian medical equipment and consumable market which is presently valued at over US$ 2 billion is largely made up of imports which account for over 90% of this share. The whole medical equipment market is witnessing a CAGR of 15%.

Medical equipment takes the biggest share as 52% followed by consumables 26%, orthopedic products 19% and medical furniture 3%. With the additional infrastructure requirements it could reach over US$ 18 billion dollars in the next five years.

How Medical tourism can finance our healthcare?

Having endured intractable pain caused by osteoarthritis of the hip for two years, a 44 year old woman from Norwich had two options—wait for her turn in the NHS or seek treatment in India. She took a 10 hour flight to India and checked into Apollo Hospital in the southern Indian city of Chennai. An orthopedic surgeon performed a Birmingham hip resurfacing procedure on her. She went back home in three weeks—but not before a visit to a traditional Indian herbal medicine centre, arranged by the hospital. This all at a 10% of cost as compared to the cost in her country.

In the process she saved a lot of money for herself, while providing valuable revenue for our healthcare.

Large hospitals in Mumbai, Chennai, and New Delhi have long been receiving patients from neighbouring South Asian and Gulf countries. Now they are trying to attract patients from Africa, Europe, and North America, marketing themselves as centers, capable of delivering world class medical services at low cost.

In recent months, hospitals have treated a French patient with occluded arteries, a Canadian patient with an orthopaedic problem, and patients from North America looking for cosmetic surgery. Some hospitals also arrange tours to sites of interest and lessons in yoga or traditional medicine as "perks" in the health package.

Currently the NHS does not fund British patients to go to India. It has told Indian hospitals that it cannot refer UK patients because flying time to India exceeds the three hours limit set for transferring patients. "Most Western patients we get, pay out of their own pocket," says George Eapen, chief executive officer of the Apollo Hospital. But hospitals hope the situation will change in the coming years through arrangements with insurance companies and governments. "Canadian patients now get 75% of their expenses reimbursed after treatment here," says Mr. Eapen. The Escorts Heart Institute is among the hospitals approved by the UK medical insurance company BUPA. The Indian Healthcare Federation is urging Western insurance companies to introduce products with lower premiums for patients willing to travel to India for treatment. Hospitals say low cost is only one factor that makes India an attractive destination for British and North American residents. "Doctors here speak excellent English and patients can look forward to highly personalised care," said Mr. Eapen.

Some enterprising hospitals offer greet-and-treat services with an all-inclusive health-tourist package, including the desired medical procedure, hotel, air travel, bookings and admissions to popular tourist attractions. Even England's cranky, leftwing Guardian newspaper has reported on India's success as an alternative to dying-while-u-wait on the British National Health. It cites 73-year-old George Marshall, a violin repairer who was diagnosed with coronary disease and told he would have a six month wait for an operation. He considered private treatment, but it would have cost £19,000 (approx. $35,000). Instead, he flew to Bangalore, "where surgeons at a specialist hospital and heart institute took a piece of vein from his arm to repair the thinning arteries of his heart." The cost was $9,000, including the flight. Marshall said he would not hesitate to come back.

From the US, 64-year-old San Francisco real estate consultant Robert Walter Beeney, who had been unable to walk due to a stiff hip, underwent a successful hip replacement surgery using an anatomic surface replacement at an Apollo hospital. Despite the fact that the device used was manufactured in the US, its use hadn't yet been cleared by the FDA. Beeney had considered going to Britain or Belgium for treatment, where it had been cleared for use, but the costs were too high. The cost for this advanced treatment was $6,600 in India.

Enhancing Quality, Safety and Affordability

'India needs to focus on preventive healthcare and information on healthcare must be provided by the Indian healthcare sector, with special emphasis given to women and children'. This was stated by Smt. Sheila Dikshit, Chief Minister of Delhi, at the 2nd India Health Summit—Emerging Healthcare Opportunities in India: Enhancing Quality, Safety and Affordability, organized by the Confederation of Indian Industry (CII). She sought suggestions from the healthcare sector on infrastructural facilities like communication, power, law and order, etc. in the spread of medical facilities so that the government could chalk out a policy in this regard. She announced that a Liver Institute in Delhi would be set-up in the next couple of years in collaboration with the US. Mrs. Dikshit specially mentioned empowerment of women through health and expressed concern on prevention and treatment of HIV/AIDS, again with women and children being the special targets. She talked about the use of tele-linking in rural healthcare so that minor health problems could be taken care of locally, and only those with major health problems needed to come to the metros. She added that 30% of patients in Delhi came from outside. In addition, she pointed out that adequate information on costs incurred on treatment, should be readily available. In his address, Dr. Naresh Trehan, Chairman, CII National Committee on Healthcare said the CII along with the Indian healthcare sector had succeeded in the important task of price branding of different procedures and quality to build global confidence.

Talking on similar lines, Mr. Harpal Singh, Conference Chairman and CMD Fortis India Ltd. said India is becoming an international health destination, not just for modern medicine but also for holistic healing. He said several procedures like heart by-pass, knee-operations, dentistry and cosmetic surgery, etc. were available at credible quality and competitive rates in India, attracting international interest.

Earlier in his special address, Dr. Prathap C. Reddy, Chairman Apollo Hospitals mentioned that health insurance still did not accrue sufficient importance in India. Citing examples of Korea and Malaysia, he said health insurance must be separate from general insurance. In his vote of thanks, Mr. Habil F. Khorakiwala, Chairman Wockhardt Group and Chairman, CII IPR and Patents Committee, appealed for exemption of all taxes in the healthcare sector to make healthcare more affordable and widespread.

Sources

Fairfield Gillian, Hunter David J., Mechanic David, and Rosleff Flemming, Managed care: origins, principles, and evolution, BMJ, 1997; 314: 1823.

Fairfield Gillian, Hunter David J., Mechanic David, and Rosleff Flemming, Managed care: Implications of managed care for health systems, clinicians, and patients. BMJ 1997; 314: 1895.

Rodwin, M.A., Conflicts in managed care, *N Engl J Med* 1995; 332:604-607.

Kassirer, J.P., Managed care and the morality of the marketplace, *N Engl J Med* 1995; 333: 50-52.

Kassirer, J.P., Managing care—should we adopt a new ethic?, *N Engl J Med* 1998; 339: 397-398.

Stocker, K., Waitzkin, H., Iriart, C., The exportation of managed care to Latin America, *N Engl J Med* 1999; 340:1131-1136.

Relman, A., Criticizing the takeover of public hospitals by commercial businesses, *New York Times*, January 25, 1985, Simpson's Contemporary Quotations.

Raja, V. and Singh, Shubnum, *Economic Times of India*, Nov. 2007.

Improving Rural Healthcare

Enhanced Allocations is Priority

The reality of easily accessible quality healthcare in rural India remains a myth. Gaps exist in several areas of healthcare. Some of the most important gaps include an understanding of the burden of disease and what causes ill-health, the availability and use of appropriate technology in the management of diseases, and health systems that impact upon service delivery. The National Rural Health Mission (NRHM) is an example of an initiative aimed at achieving the Millennium Development Goals (MDGs). The NRHM seeks to provide effective healthcare to the rural population, especially the disadvantaged groups including women and children, by improving access, enabling community ownership and demand for services, strengthening public health systems for efficient service delivery, enhancing equity and accountability and promoting decentralization. Five of the eight goals and one of the two prongs of the strategy for development concern health. These observations were made at the third International Knowledge Millennium Conference, IKMC 2006, 'Improving Public Health in India: Need for Innovative Solutions in Healthcare Delivery' on December 19-20, 2006 at Hyderabad organized by ICICI Knowledge Park and the ICICI Centre for Technologies.

Rural Healthcare in doldrums

In addition to income, several factors influence health outcomes including age, ethnicity, gender, social status, religion and residence. Girls in India are 30 to 50 percent more likely to die between the ages of one to five years than boys. Services such as education, water, food security, communication, electrification and transportation assume great importance. 74% of rural women are anemic even today. Only 8% of rural population has access to a toilet. Only 21% of the rural population has access to safe and sustained source of drinking water. Only 3.9% of them have a pucca house with drinking water and electricity connection. Only 6 out of 100 children who join first standard actually complete the 10 standard. Strangely, there is an influx of advanced tertiary care into rural areas even as primary healthcare services are dwindling. Expensive technology-oriented solutions like telemedicine are offered where finances could have been placed for simpler cost effective preventive and primary care measures. There are several examples in India where simple solutions focused on optimal utilization of local resources including human resources have resulted in dramatic improvements of healthcare indicators. Additionally, rural India now has to compete with the urban disadvantaged for a share of the healthcare allocations. This is a tragedy because the displaced rural poor often make up the urban poor.

Several challenges to improve rural health have been planned. For instance, how can we ensure that we get a correct diagnosis of malaria within 24 hours? The difficulty of reaching a sample to a lab, and getting the report back in a reasonable time is real for a rural person who may already have traveled long distances. Other issues of concern include, how do we improve the yield of sputum in diagnosing tuberculosis with an inexpensive test and potentially avoid radiographs? How do we know the drug resistance pattern in patients with tuberculosis early enough to decide treatment choices? Several innovative solutions developed to help community health workers with the diagnosis of urinary tract infections, vaginitis or cervicitis, and anemias have been discussed. Lack of accessibility to health centers, lack of information and erroneous treatment from health staff remain major issues. The relatively lower rates of literacy and enrolment into technical streams and technology diffusion are areas of concern. Issues like lower priority for healthcare, lack of information and family support, lack of transportation, lack of money and social taboos or beliefs still influence the uptake of healthcare.

There are several technological innovations developed by research institutes in India like detection kits for filariasis, leishmaniasis, dengue fever, west nile virus, typhoid, HIV, and kits for the detection of pregnancy. Many of the diagnostic tests that are marketed and available in primary healthcare settings in developing countries are sold and used with little or no evidence of their effectiveness. This is because unlike drugs, diagnostics are not subject to strict regulatory approval standards.

Mother and child need maximum attention

Ensuring safe motherhood is one of the biggest challenges facing India today. WHO estimates that out of 529,000 maternal deaths globally each year, 136,000 (25.7%) is contributed by India. This is the highest burden for any single country in the world. As per National Family Health Survey estimates, the Maternal Mortality Rate in India is 540 per 100,000 live births. Adding to the problem is the fact that only 33% of deliveries occur in health institutions. It is indeed a great challenge to meet the target of NPP, i.e., to increase the institutional deliveries to 80% by 2010. Essential obstetric care is sill not available in most primary healthcare centers. For example, there are 1786 Primary Health Centers in Karnataka, but as per the Health Task Force Report, only 8% of them conduct deliveries round the clock. Impacting maternal mortality needs the provision of care 24 × 7 in an institutional setting. The likely solution: add more doctors or people with skills to conduct deliveries. Alternatively, improving the referral system, transport and communication facilities could be a completely new non-medical solution to this problem. There are initiatives in a tribal belt of Karnataka that has trained and used human resources from within the tribal communities. Wireless handset to improve communication and a small lump sum to cover emergency travel has helped to increase institutional deliveries from 2% to 36% in an 18 month period of time.

Today, only 42% of children in India are completely immunized. The point of first contact of the healthcare delivery system is the Auxiliary Nurse Midwife (ANM). If only she could forge an 'effective partnership' with the local Integrated Child Development Service (ICDS) worker, the coverage could be increased significantly. Maintaining cold chain is yet another challenge. Despite advances in the field of solar power, provision of refrigerators to our PHCs and sub-centers is still a dream. Planning and prioritizing health interventions often use patterns of mortality data. In India, half the IMR today is because of 4 states. 72% of IMR comes from 8 states alone. 74% of rural women are anaemic even today. Only 8% of rural population has access to a toilet. Only 21% of the rural population has access to safe and sustained source of drinking water. Only 3.9% of them have a pucca house with drinking water and an electricity connection. Only 6 out of 100 children who join first standard actually complete the 10 standard. Good health is strongly associated with good education.

Financing Rural Healthcare

The cause for the failure of the public sector to reach the poor can often be traced back to the way the public sector spends money. Public sector expenditure management is a tough task especially when accountability is weak. If the public sector spends more than it can sustain, services deteriorate. Public sector expenditure will exceed available funds in the absence of transparent systems to resolve competing claims of politicians, policy-makers, ministries and regional governments. The resulting unsustainable fiscal deficits lead to tightening of expenditures. Unfortunately, it is usually basic services that get trapped within the drive to reduce expenditure. The key question is: How should funds be allocated to improve health outcomes? How do we ensure that these funds are utilized appropriately for the purpose they were meant for?

Infant mortality rates has much to do with how

expenses for clean water and education (especially female literacy) are managed simultaneous to health focused expenses. Worldwide, every minute, 380 women become pregnant, 190 women face unplanned or unwanted pregnancy, 110 women experience a pregnancy-related complication, 40 women have unsafe abortions, and 1 woman dies from a pregnancy-related complication. The highest burden of maternal death (25.7%) is in India. This burden is inequitably distributed regional differences; however, the poor have the maximum burden. The NFHS reports that maternal mortality rates have reduced in urban India over a decade but actually increased in rural India over the corresponding period. The lifetime risk for maternal death is 1 in 140 for South East Asia compared to 1 in 2800 for the developed countries. Approximately 75% of deliveries among the richest in India are attended by qualified personnel as compared to less than 20% for the poor. Nearly 60% of maternal deaths occur *postpartum*, and nearly one-fourth of deaths can be attributed to hemorrhage. The time from onset of complication to death ranged from 2 hours to 1 week. There appears to be a relationship between having skilled attendants at childbirth and a reduction in maternal mortality. So far, it appears to be the most effective intervention. 73.3% of babies die within the first week of delivery. Neonatal mortality also shows an association with skilled attendance at birth. Once major obstetric complication develops—even a trained TBA or a nurse cannot do much at home. These complications require surgical interventions, injections of antibiotic, blood transfusion and other aggressive treatments. There are three major delays that contribute to maternal death—(a) Delay in deciding to seek care (Individual and family), (b) Delay in reaching care (Community and System), and (c) Delay in receiving care (System). There are several options that maybe considered. (A) Improve Government Health Service with competent staff, adequate infrastructural facilities and user friendly, good quality competitive services and marketing of services, (B) Public Private Partnership including outsourcing of curative services, and (C) Health Insurance.

Below the poverty line

More than 30% of hospitalized Indians fall below the poverty line (IHR, 2003). The safety net of health insurance present in developed countries is often not there, existing health insurance schemes are skewed in favour of non-poor in organized sector. The vast majority in the unorganized/ informal sector remains vulnerable. When State as well as Market has failed, some NGOs are trying to protect the poor through Micro Health Insurance (MHI). MHI schemes are not-for-profit targeting the poor with community participation in scheme design and management, usually NGO managed, low premium-low benefit schemes. There are about 15 MHI in India and three primary models: (a) provider owned models, (b) NGO owned models, and (c) NGO mediated models. The schemes are diverse in nature but pre-payment is a common thread. The premium and benefits too vary between schemes. There are several issues with MHI and other schemes including the difficulty of the concept for the poor, low awareness levels (membership and exclusions) and low coverage, non-financial barriers, utilization barriers, poorest of the poor, regressive premium, skewed utilization (Equity Impact) and supply side moral hazard. Other issues include the high out of pocket expenses, the care that is accessible, financial sustainability, and the dearth of empirical database (documenting new scheme, analysing access and protection).

The bottom quintile, poorest 20% of the population spends a larger part of theirincome on healthcare which is more than 12% whereas the top quintile spends approximately 3%. There are several issues with healthcare in India that often result in no choice treatment including:

(a) Customer attitude—often see a doctor only when it is absolutely unavoidable,
(b) Providers—quality a major concern, care unilaterally decided by the doctor,
(c) Outcomes, and
(d) Cost of treatment, loss of income, travel expenses, indirect expenses related to healthcare still too high most often causing indebtedness.

The Arogya Rakshana Yojana partnering with Biocon and Narayan Hrudalaya in rural Karnataka is an example to be emulated. 60,000 lives in Anekal Taluka in Karnataka are provided cover for all kinds of common and complex surgeries and medical admission with co-payment for medical admission, drugs and diagnostics at discounted price, free outpatient consultation and preventive and promotive activities. Partnership provider models also exist with the Apollo and Manipal group of hospitals, Dharamsthala Trust, Microfinance institutions.

India's poor need a radical package: Amartya Sen

India spends a lower percentage of GDP on *public health* than almost any other country. The neglect here is massive, particularly because this has led to both the substandard delivery of public health and the development of an immensely exploitative private enterprise in healthcare that survives on the deficiencies—and sometimes absence—of public health attention. Surveys in West Bengal, Jharkhand, Punjab found; when patients go to many of the primary health centres, they find no one there. Sometimes, when they find someone, they will be referred to private doctors. Also, the medical system in the public sector offers no diagnostics, even of malaria or TB. Patients are usually told to go to private practitioners for testing. Sometimes the testing isn't very good and, in any case, the economic cost could be ruinous. On top of that, the care that is often provided by the private sector comes from quacks. The modern quacks are very expensive. So they have the effect of making the illnesses linger while whatever meager economic assets the poorer families have may be lost in the process. This is a dreadful situation. There are many areas where more privatization might make sense—hotels, tourism, a number of industries—but this is not one of them. And the high private share in the provision of healthcare in rural areas is a major deficiency of the Indian system.

Private medical treatment can work quite well when, as in Kerala, the public health sector provides a minimum care for all. On the basis of that, you can then get special care on a private system. But that's quite different from relying primarily on a private health system, especially when the patient has no idea who is a quack. . . . There are three different deficiencies here. First, there is an awfully inadequate amount of investment, so that the amount of public resources going in to providing healthcare for all is extraordinarily little. Secondly, the monitoring of the performance of public health centers is often totally absent or thoroughly defective. Thus, the absenteeism of doctors is quite high and the incidence of doctors trying to recommend that patients go and see them in their capacity as private practitioners is distressingly high. Third, there is no way the Government helps patients diagnose who is a quack and who is not. That requires a monitoring not just of the public health service but of medical services as a whole.

All three things act together to ruin the rural poor who, from their meager resources, must spend whatever they can to deal with that which is of greatest importance to them—namely their health. And they get hit both by the continuation of illness and economic ruination. Corruption is there in the sense that a doctor in a public health service asks patients to go to himself or a friend in private care, instead of providing treatment.

There are a lot of rich people in the country and there is no way you can prevent them from having state-of-the-art medical attention within India if they can pay for it. But public sector resources have to provide basic medical care for all, basic medicine, basic diagnosis, blood and urine tests, x-rays and so on, which go with the normal practice of medicine, and providing treatment for well known ailments and doing the best that the doctors can to help the patient, without going into an extremely expensive system of medical care. 'I think specialized healthcare, including sophisticated medicine and surgery, should be available. I would strongly recommend that we spend a lot more on public healthcare. But along with that, we have to introduce a better monitoring system for the delivery of public health services, and we also have to introduce a system of weeding out quackery.'

In India the elderly face a number of problems, such as poverty, illiteracy, and inadequate healthcare. Most of the elderly in India are dependent on their children. The elderly have an important place in the healthcare system of a nation. However, a large number of the elderly people in India are uninsured. The elderly in the rural areas are a neglected lot. Besides, many of the elderly in India are too poor to have access to basic healthcare. The distribution of healthcare resources is closely associated with the notion of human person, for health is a very important concern of him/her. Since the human person is endowed with intelligence and free will, he/she has a specific dignity that cannot be violated. The country must work in unison to ensure proper care and security for the elderly so that they live a proper community life.

Justice Jain's recommendation

Justice N.C. Jain, presently Mhairman Admission Committee, Medical Educational Institutions, Haryana Government is concerned about the non-availability of doctors and other staff in villages. He opines and recommends that there should be a dedicated rural cadre of doctors. The recruitment should be made for serving in specified rural areas and their services should be utilized only in the villages. If they wish to leave the village they can resign/services terminated. He feels that the salaries of rural doctors can be substantially higher than the doctors working in urban areas of the state.

Government funding is critical

There is clear evidence that public financing is critical for good healthcare and health outcomes in any country. Yet in India, only 15% of the Rs. 1,500 billion healthcare sector is publicly financed. Investment and expenditure in the public health sector is shrinking. As a result, the public health system is on the brink of collapse, and there's been a 30% decline in the use of public healthcare facilities. Reliance on private health financing can create adversities for health not only for poorer sections of society but also the middle classes. In most developed countries, where healthcare access is near-universal, public financing accounts for around 80% of all health expenditure, whether through state revenues and/or social insurance, has been the critical component in realizing

	Total health expenditure as% of GDP	*Public health expenditure as% of total*	*U-5 mortality*	*Life expectancy*	
				Male	*Female*
India	5	17	95	59.6	61.2
China	2.7	24.9	43	68.1	71.3
Sri Lanka	3	45.4	19	65.8	73.4
Malaysia	2.4	57.6	14	67.6	69.9
South Korea	6.7	37.8	14	69.2	76.3

Source: Changing the Indian Health System—Draft Report, ICRIER, 2001.

universal access with equity. In contrast, in India the reverse is true—70-80% of health expenditure is met by individuals from their private resources. With greater dependence on the market for healthcare, access becomes more difficult for an increasing number of people.

Health outcomes in relation to health expenditure patterns

The tragedy is that in India, as elsewhere, those who have the capacity to buy healthcare from the market most often get healthcare without having to pay for it directly, and those who are below the poverty line or living at subsistence levels are forced to make direct payments, often with a heavy burden of debt, loans and sale of assets are estimated to contribute substantially towards financing healthcare. This further underlines the need for insurance and social security.

Financing healthcare in India (2003)

About 80% of public financing of healthcare comes from state government budgets, 12% from the Union government and 8% from local governments. Private financing is mostly out-of-pocket, with a large proportion, especially for hospitalization, coming not from current incomes but from savings, debt and sale of assets. Insurance contributions, whether for social insurance schemes or as private insurance premiums, constitute a very small proportion.

	Estimated users in millions	Expenditure (Rs. in billions)
Public sector	**250@**	**252 (17)***
Of which social insurance	*55*	*30 (2)*
Private sector	**780@**	**1,250 (83)****
Of which social insurance	*30*	*24 (1.6)*
Private insurance	*11*	*11.5 (0.8)*
Out-of-pocket	*739*	*1,214.5 (80)*
Total	**1,030**	**1,552 (100)**

The dichotomy

The most obvious hierarchy is the rural-urban dichotomy in public health investment and expenditure. Rural areas across the country have public health services that largely focus on preventive and promotive aspects. Thus, immunisation for children and pregnant women, antenatal care, surveillance of selected diseases and family planning services constitute the key focus of the primary healthcare system provided for rural India. In contrast, the focus in urban healthcare is largely curative, with dispensaries and

Source for Funds for Healthcare in India, 2001-02

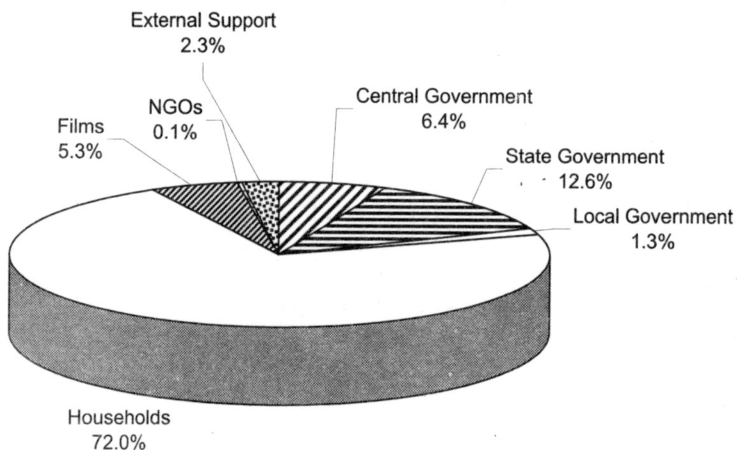

hospitals taking away most of the health resources. Since India lacks a national health accounting system, disaggregating of public spending across rural and urban areas, for the country as a whole, is difficult to compile. The rural-urban distribution of resources at one level favours urban health facilities with over 60% of allocations for urban areas where 40% of the population resides. In contrast, in urban areas, resource distribution shows a good mix of curative, preventive and promotive services, with curative services comprising nearly half the urban health budget.

Public expenditure on healthcare today is a dismal 0.9% of GDP, and growth is gradual. Of the private healthcare expenditure, 97% comes out-of-pocket. Only countries like Myanmar, Cambodia, Armenia, DR Congo and Azerbaijan, rank higher in terms of private health expenditure as a percentage of total health expenditure. Government expenditure on health as a percentage of total health expenditure in countries like Sri Lanka and Malaysia is almost twice that in India. The Centre/State contributions to expenditure on health as of 2001-02 National Health Accounts were 6.4% and 12.6%. The ideal scenario, is to get government funding of healthcare up to nothing less than 60% of total health expenditure, with a 35-65 split between the Centre and the State. The rest would be borne by the organized sector and other sources.

Investment in software is even more essential

There have been huge investments on infrastructure but much remains to be done to produce highly qualified and well trained surgeons and medical teachers. Unless this software of manpower training in healthcare is developed the hardware in the form of buildings and equipment will remain unutilized. Beautiful buildings have been built with World Bank and other donor funds, but many of them have not been occupied. The location of the infrastructure is mostly decided by the political system. There is no organized mapping of the health facilities. Decision-making should be based on objective parameters. Governments should take the courage to relocate or close down under-utilized Primary health centres (PHCs). The NFHS survey clearly indicates that 76% of the health infrastructure belongs to the state but only 34% of the people access it. This necessarily means that the private sector, having just 24% of infrastructure is catering to 66% of the population. Most of the qualified human resource today is in the public sector. The private sector is functioning with a significant amount of non-qualified or under-qualified human resources.

Paradoxically, top 20% of the country's elite (in terms of wealth) has access to 85% of resources and the bottom 20% has access to just 1.5% of India's resources. Ensuring that bottom 20% get access to healthcare is a major challenge. 52% of our population is below 25 years but there is no program to address the healthcare needs of the adolescents. 411 million children today are around 14 years and 131 million of them belong to socially and economically disadvantaged groups. These are the groups which have also been traditionally denied access to care. These adolescents need special attention and a healthcare program for the adolescents is a matter of priority. In our country traditional and indigenous systems of medicine are a good resource. AYUSH however, has become just a slogan, a matter of convenience without conviction. Ayurvedic doctors are being looked at as a cheap replacement for allopathic doctors in the public health system. This attitude has to change. AYUSH should be respected for what it is and given the place it deserves.

The relative importance given to HIV/AIDS as a public health problem is a little disturbing. Malaria kills more people than HIV in a year in India and so does TB. In fact, TB kills more people in a day than HIV does in a year. Though there is a Global Fund for Action against Malaria, Tuberculosis and HIV/AIDS (GFATM), the focus is more on HIV than the other two. Vector borne diseases are making a huge comeback in this country, whether it is chikungunya, dengue, malaria or kala-azar.

The key questions are:

(a) How do we get the government and the not-for-profit or profit sectors active in healthcare to work together towards a common end? How do we supplement efforts in each sector without competing with each other?

(b) Are the models of apparent success in the not-for-profit or profit sectors replicable on a national scale given the magnitude of the scale up needed in India?

(c) Are the models of success in the not-for-profit or profit sectors sustainable after discounting potential subsidies provided by the government?

(d) Do the indirect benefits of such models span the MDG even though the primary focus of the models may be narrowed down to one priority area or Disease?

Public healthcare sector not adequate

Studies have documented that persons accessing the public sector encounter longer waiting times, experience a lack of confidentiality and communication. A high proportion of the Indian population still suffers and dies from preventable infections, pregnancy and childbirth-related complications, and malnutrition. As per UNICEF's observation 2007, public health is deteriorating in India. High percentage of 56.2% women in the age group 15-49 are anemic. While Assam is at 72%, Haryana is 69.7%, Jharkhand at 68.4%. 79.1% children in the age group 3-6 were anemic in 2006 as compared to 74.2% in 1999. Even in Delhi 63.2% children and 43.3% women were anemic. HIV/AIDS is one of the most important of new threats. Since the first reported case of HIV in India in 1986, the disease has rapidly spread. As of December 2005, an estimated 5.21 million Indians are living with HIV, making India the world's second largest HIV burden after South Africa. With an annual per capita income of $620, only those Indians are able to afford the costs of treatment who can access the public healthcare facility.

On the basis of 1991 Indian census data, they created a Household Misery Index (HMI), which reflected the extent of deprivation in basic need of safe drinking water, toilet and electrical facilities, and the availability of fuel for cooking. Not only are there environmental factors influencing morbidity and mortality, India has a higher burden of disease in the area of communicable diseases. Sixty percent of children under five are malnourished. The majority of homes do not have a flush toilet. Women are not valued in India. Women's low decision-making power in the early ages of marriage, their poor health leading to miscarriages, social pressures against contraception before completion of the desired family size, general son-preference, secondary infertility due to reproduction tract infections, and so on are barriers to the use of contraception by women or limiting their family size.

The private healthcare sector is largely unregulated with little control as to what kinds of services can be provided by whom, in what manner, and at what cost. It highlights how the private sector has reneged on its commitments to provide subsidized care to those in need while having received and benefited from considerable government subsidies.

Public/private health partnerships (PPP)

Reasons for promotion of PPP include insufficient government resources and poor performance on the part of the public sector. There is a growing realization that involving the private sector in rural health services provision could lead to improved systems efficiency. In India given the extent of private sector dominance in the healthcare system the Government of India has laid various strategies under the NRHM 2005 for partnerships with the private sector in meeting national public health goals.

Recently the Planning Commission constituted a Working Group on PPP to improve healthcare delivery for the 11th Five-Year Plan (2007-12). There has been significant shift in the Government of India's approach to involve private sector in delivery mechanism to achieve desired output and improve upon macro-health indicators. It envisages partnerships with the private sector. A wide range of PPP have been initiated. Noticeable examples are contractual appointment of healthcare personnel for providing services in Primary Health Centres (PHCs)/Community Health Centres (CHCs), handing over management of public sector health facilities to private sector/NGOs, contracting for providing a variety of services in major hospitals. In addition, there is growing involvement of the corporate sector, partnership with professional organizations, Community Based Organisations (CBOs)/Non-Government Organisations (NGOs), social franchising and social marketing.

Gujarat Government has taken a policy decision to entrust management of 23 district level civil hospitals, with about 4,100 beds, and six medical colleges associated hospitals to the private sector. Rajasthan Government has contracted out the installation, operation and maintenance of CT-scan and MRI services to a private agency at SMS Hospital at Jaipur. The agency is paid a monthly rent by the hospital and the agency has to render free services to 20% of the patients belonging to the poor socio-economic categories. Rest of the patients are charged as per pre-agreed tariff, which is considerably less than the market. Chandigarh administration has also introduced PPP in the matter of several services in the government-run hospitals.

WHO has formally encouraged strategies that involve a public/private mix as a way of improving health, particularly in resource-limited settings. In the case of leprosy control, an organized strategy of information, education and communication (IEC) between public and private providers has greatly improved referrals of patients for leprosy treatment. Public-private partnerships to stem blindness due to cataracts is another success story where PPP strategy has led to more than 30% of the cataract surgeries being done in the private sector. Tuberculosis control has also benefited from recent public-private partnerships, but this is only after many years of failure. The TB Control Program of India has used a diverse group of strategies for engagement of community private providers to participate in the referral, diagnosis, or treatment of patients with TB.

Mobilizing and partnering with local NGOs have also been very useful. NGOs have disseminated key information regarding where to seek care and treatment. They have also played a role in actual referrals, follow-up and communication between public and private providers. Such strategies have led to increased case detection and improved clinical outcomes. The key features of successful PPP programs involve a combination of: (1) mobilization of private healthcare providers via one-to-one or group IEC,

(2) establishment of referral networks that provide either monetary incentives or non-financial incentives for referrals, (3) ongoing access to free continuing medical education, (4) access to free or low-cost, quality-assured diagnostics, (5) provision of free or low-cost quality-assured drugs, (6) access to continued treatment by private providers but with the guidance of local experts, and (7) ongoing feedback about the progress of the program. An example of apparently successful public-private partnerships to combat HIV is in the realm of community-based voluntary testing and counseling (VCT) through the help of NGOs. Care and treatment, however, have not been coordinated. Some of the recent success documented with TB control provides hope that mixed public-private strategies for HIV care and treatment are likely to be beneficial on both a macro and micro-economic as well as health perspective.

Singapore role model

Singapore was explored as a potential role model for health financing. Singapore is ranked 6th in terms of effectiveness (World Health Report, 2000) amongst 191 member countries. While in terms of health expenditure per capita it is ranked 38th. Singapore spends 3.8% of GDP on health compared to 15.3% spend by US and 7.7% spend by UK. The principles used in Singapore model include: (a) Health is the personal responsibility of the individual, (b) Mandatory savings scheme, and (c) Funding is based on co-payment scheme that keeps basic healthcare affordable. There is an increasing incidence of lifestyle diseases like diabetes, cancer and heart disease due to rising affluence and urbanization. Cancer and Heart disease are likely to constitute 37% of inpatient spends by 2012 compared to 27% in 2001. Critical Illness is impacting people at younger ages-30% of heart attack patients are below 40 years.

The chance of being diagnosed with the 3 Critical Illnesses in a particular year is about 3 times the chance of dying. Lifestyle diseases can be managed. Technological advancements enable preventive care and better chronic management with easier and more reliable monitoring tools and predictive testing. There is an opportunity to leapfrog the health spend evolution cycle, by moving directly to prevention-based approach. The way forward is to invest in customer education and provide them financial incentives to manage health costs, focus on pro-active management of health through regular preventive care and diagnosis, pattern recognition to assess likelihood of complications, evidence-based treatment of complications. This may enable us allow larger financing through efficient use of resources, achieve risk pooling and achieve overall cost reduction through preventive care and early detection to reduce incidence of disease and cost of treatment.

The ICICI Centre for Technologies in Public Health

The centre is planned as a research centre that aims at contributing to improvement of the health of poor populations by focusing on designing, developing and delivering innovative solutions in healthcare concerning India and the developing world. This would be done through an inclusive process that scientifically integrates knowledge of factors influencing health and diseases in India, regular evaluation and impact assessment of existing health systems and integration of appropriate technology for optimal healthcare delivery. ICTPH will adapt and translate learning from these experiences to other developing countries. The key objectives of the centre are to:

(a) Design and implement surveys of healthcare systems and healthcare technology gaps through field sites in 4 to 5 identified districts or clusters in India and develop recommendations for better healthcare delivery strategy.
(b) To evaluate existing service delivery models for replication.
(c) To design and implement an impact assessment of existing technologies.
(d) To design innovative technology and health systems research in collaboration with Centers of Excellence. The complementary role of the Public Health Foundation of India was presented on human resource development and research. The

aim is to establish 7 institutes of PHFI in India, providing Masters level, diploma level, and 3 year BSc programs in public health. PHFI will be a center of excellence developing a network of researchers, international partners, policy development, reaching civil society and governments, setting standards and accreditation mechanisms. Dr. Reddy emphasized that "Science discovers, technology develops, public health delivers" and the role of collaboration between PHFI and ICTPH are on an even keel and complementary to each other.

One major thrust of the health movement has been to generate public awareness regarding the commercialized, and to an extent, the exploitative nature of healthcare.

How to campaign for health movement?

Campaigns for awareness and policy change These initiatives have often been spearheaded by comparatively small groups of activists with some professional training in health or related fields. They have formed networks of concerned activists, have often used media and judiciary to press for policy changes and have often succeeded in creating awareness or sometimes even bringing about policy change on key health issues.

Some exdmples:

- Trade unions have built alternative healthcare services for their members and also to give low-cost and rational care to people from nearby villages. The most well-known and pioneering initiative in this regard has been Shahid Hospital, built in 1983 and sustained by the workers of CMSS (Chhattisgarh Mines Shramik Sangh) in Durg, MP. Similar such attempts are Maitri Swasthya Kendra run by the organised workers of Kanoria Jute Mills, and a hospital run by volunteer doctors in collaboration with the workers of Indo-Japanese Steel Labour Union—

both in West Bengal. These healthcare facilities have demonstrated the ability of organised workers to run an enterprise as complex and skilled as a hospital, in a rational way with minimal costs of care, with the help of inputs from committed doctors and health workers.

- A few attempts have also been made by rural organizations to build alternative healthcare initiatives. One example is in Thane, Maharashtra, where in the context of a tribal people's organization, Kashtakari Sanghatna, where women health workers have been trained at the village level to treat simple illnesses at minimal cost. Some attempts have also been made to make the local health system more accountable in its functioning.
- In certain situations, organizations have responded to events or influences, which have had major impact on people's health. The various initiatives and groups which have come up in the aftermath of the Bhopal gas disaster, attempting to study, treat and also demand justice regarding the terrible health effects of this catastrophe are one notable example. Attempts by trade unions and support groups to take up occupational health problems of workers and by groups of affected people to highlight environmental degradation as a cause of ill-health fall in the same category.

Sources

National AIDS Control Organization, Ministry of Health and Family Welfare, and Government of India, HIV/AIDS Epidemiological Surveillance and estimation report for the year 2005.

National Commission on Macroeconomics and Health, Ministry of Health and Family Welfare, Government of India, and New Delhi, Burden of Disease in India, 2005.

Hogg, R.S., Heath, K.V., Yip. B., Craib, K.J., O'Shaughnessy, M.V., Schechter, M.T., Montaner, J.S., Improved survival among HIV-infected individuals following initiation of antiretroviral therapy. JAMA 1998; 279:450-454.

Palella, F.J., Jr., Delaney, K.M., Moorman, A.C., Loveless, M.O., Fuhrer, J., Satten, G.A., Aschman, D.J., Holmberg, S.D., Declining morbidity and mortality among patients with advanced human immunodeficiency virus infection, HIV Outpatient Study Investigators, *N Engl J Med* 1998;338:853-60.

National Commission of Macroeconomics and Health Ministry of Health and Family Welfare and Government of India. Financing and Delivery of Healthcare Services in India, 2005.

Peters, D.H., Yazbeck, A.S., Sharma, R.R., Ramana, G.N.V., Pritchett, L.H., and Wagstaff, A. Better Health Systems for India's Poor: Findings, Analysis, and Options. The World Bank, Washington D.C., 2002.

Mahal, A., Yazbeck, A.S., Peters, D.H. and Ramana, G.N.V. The Poor and Health Service Use in India, August 2001, World Bank Report, Washington DC., 2001.

Bal, A.M., Private Health Sector in India: line between profit and profiteering is often thin, *BMJ* 2005; 331:1339.

Baru, R.V., Reproductive technologies and the private sector—implications for women's health, Health Millions, 1993; 1:6-8.

Bhat, R. Regulation of the private health sector in India, *Int J Health Plann Manage*, 1996;11:253-74.

Bhatia, J., Cleland, J., Healthcare of female outpatients in south-central India: comparing public and private sector provision, Health Policy Plan, 2004; 19:402-9.

Deshpande, K., Ravi Shankar, Diwan, V., Lonnroth, K., Mahadik, V.K., Chandorkar, R.K.

Spatial pattern of private healthcare provision in Ujjain, India: a provider survey processed and analysed with a Geographical Information System, Health Policy, 2004; 68:211-22.

Duggal, R., Healthcare utilisation in India, Health Millions, 1994; 2:10-12.

George, R., Abraham, R., Private health in India, Lancet, 2002; 359:1528.

Kamat, V.R., Private practitioners and their role in the resurgence of malaria in Mumbai (Bombay) and Navi Mumbai (New Bombay), India: serving the affected or aiding an epidemic? *Soc Sci Med*, 2001; 52:885-909.

Kielmann, K., Deshmukh, D., Deshpande, S., Datye, V., Porter, J., Rangan, S., Managing uncertainty around HIV/AIDS in an urban setting: private medical providers and their patients in Pune, India, *Soc Sci Med*, 2005; 61:1540-1550.

Sheikh, K., Rangan, S., Deshmukh, D., Dholakia, Y., Porter, J., Urban private practitioners: potential partners in the care of patients with HIV/AIDS, *Natl Med J India*, 2005; 18:32-36.

Uplekar, M., Juvekar, S., Morankar, S., Rangan, S., Nunn, P., Tuberculosis patients and practitioners in private clinics in India, *Int J Tuberc Lung Dis*, 1998; 2:324-29.

Uplekar, M., Pathania, V., Raviglione, M., Private practitioners and public health: weak links in tuberculosis control, *Lancet*, 2001; 358:912-16.

Uplekar, M.W., Cash, R.A., The private GP and leprosy: a study, *Lepr Rev*, 1991; 62:410-419.

Rao, S., Section II Delivery of health services in the private sector in Financing and Delivery of Health Services in India, National Commission on Macroeconomics and Health, 2005, pp. 89-124, New Delhi, 2005.

Dandona, R., Dandona, L., Mishra, A., Dhingra, S., Venkatagopalakrishna, K., Chauhan, L.S., Utilization of and barriers to public sector tuberculosis services in India, *Natl Med J India*, 2004; 17:292-99.

Ogden, J., Rangan, S., Uplekar, M., Porter, J., Brugha, R., Zwi, A., Nyheim, D., Shifting the paradigm in tuberculosis control: illustrations from India, *Int J Tuberc Lung Dis*, 1999; 3:855-61.

Mertens, T.E., Smith, G.D., Kantharaj, K., Mugrditchian, D., Radhakrishnan, K.M., Observations of sexually transmitted disease consultations in India, *Public Health*, 1998; 112:123-28.

Mudur, G., Inadequate regulations undermine India's healthcare, *BMJ*, 2004; 328:124.

Sengupta, A., Nundy, S., The private health sector in India, *BMJ*, 2005; 331:1157-58.

Bhat, R., Characteristics of private medical practice in India: a provider perspective, *Health Policy Plan*, 1999; 14:26-37.

Uplekar, M., Juvekar, S., Morankar, S., Rangan, S., Nunn, P., Tuberculosis patients and practitioners in private clinics in India, *Int J Tuberc Lung Dis*, 1998; 2:324-29.

Sudha, G., Nirupa, C., Rajasakthivel, M., Sivasusbramanian, S., Sundaram, V., Bhatt, S., Subramaniam, K., Thiruvalluvan, E., Mathew, R., Renu, G., Santha, T., Factors influencing the care-seeking behaviour of chest symptomatics: a community-based study involving rural and urban population in Tamil Nadu, South India, *Trop Med Int Health*, 2003; 8:336-41.

Bhatia, J.C., Cleland, J., Health-care seeking and expenditure by young Indian mothers in the public and private sectors, *Health Policy Plan*, 2001; 16:55-61.

Peters, D.H., The role of oversight in the health sector: the example of sexual and reproductive health services in India, *Reprod Health Matters*, 2002; 10:82-94.

Buse, K., Waxman, A., Public-private health partnerships: a strategy for WHO, *Bull World Health Organ*, 2001; 79:748-54.

Shepard, D.S., Public-private collaborations in healthcare: lessons from India, *Int J Qual Healthcare*, 2001; 13:277-78.

Subbanna, J., Public-private mix in the National Leprosy Elimination Programme, *Indian J Lepr*, 2004; 76:179-80.

Arora, V.K., Sarin, R., Lonnroth, K., Feasibility and effectiveness of a public-private mix project for improved TB control in Delhi, India, *Int J Tuberc Lung Dis*, 2003; 7:1131-38.

Rangan, S.G., Juvekar, S.K., Rasalpurkar, S.B., Morankar, S.N., Joshi, A.N., Porter, J.D.

Tuberculosis control in rural India: lessons from public-private collaboration, *Int J Tuberc Lung Dis*, 2004; 8:552-59.

Dewan, P.K., Lal, S.S., Lonnroth, K., Wares, F., Uplekar, M., Sahu, S., Granich, R., Chauhan, L.S., Improving tuberculosis control through public-private collaboration in India: literature review, *BMJ*, 2006; 332:574-78.

Murthy, K.J., Frieden, T.R., Yazdani, A., Hreshikesh, P., Public-private partnership in tuberculosis control: experience in Hyderabad, India, *Int J Tuberc Lung Dis*, 2001; 5:354-59.

World Bank 'South Asia Region (SAR)—India', Regional Updates, www.worldbank.org/ungass/India.htm accessed 22/4/06).

Nagelkerke, N.J., Jha, P., de Vlas, S.J., Korenromp, E.L., Moses, S., Blanchard, J.F., Plummer, F.A., Modelling HIV/AIDS epidemics in Botswana and India: impact of interventions to prevent transmission, *Bull World Health Organ*, 2002;80:89-96.

Population Division of the Department of Economic and Social Affairs of the United Nations Secretariat (2003) 'World population Prospects: the 2002 revision', *Highlights*, New York, February, pp. 78-90, 2002.

Mahal, A., Rao, B., HIV/AIDS epidemic in India: An economic perspective, *Indian Journal of Medical Research*, 2005; 121:582-600.

Ramachandani, S., Mehta, S., Saple, D.G., Vaidya, S., Pandey, V., Vadrevu, R., Rajasekaran, R., Bhatia, V., Chowdhary, A., Bollinger, R.C. and Gupta, A., Knowledge, attitudes, and practices of antiretroviral therapy among HIV-infected persons attending public and private clinics in India, *AIDS Patient Care and STDs*, 2006. In press.

International Labour Organization (ILO), Assessing the Socio-economic Impact of HIV/AIDS on People Living with HIV/AIDS (PLWHAs) and their families in India, New Delhi, India: ILO; 2004.

National AIDS Control Organization, *HIV Annual Report*, 2002-2004. New Delhi, 2005.

Over, M., Heywood, P., Gold, J., Gupta, I., Hira, S. and Marseille, E., HIV/AIDS Treatment and Prevention in India, *World Bank Report*, Washington, DC, 2004.

Brugha, R., Antiretroviral treatment in developing countries: the peril of neglecting private providers, *BMJ*, 2003; 326:1382-84.

Shah, B., Walshe, L., Saple, D.G., Mehta, S., Kharkar, J.P., Ramnani, J.P., Bollinger, R.C. and Gupta, A., Adherence to Antiretroviral Therapy Among Indian HIV Infected Persons Seeking Care in the Private Sector in Mumbai, India, Submitted for publication.

Kumarasamy, N., Generic antiretroviral drugs—will they be the answer to HIV in the developing world?, *Lancet*, 2004; 364:3-4.

National AIDS Control Organization. Annual Report, 2002-2004, 2005, New Delhi.

Kamat, V.R., Nichter, M., Pharmacies, self-medica.

Ramanathan, M., Krishnan, S., Bhan, A., Reporting on the First National Bioethics Conference, *Ind J Med Ethics*, 2006; 3:27-30.

Sen, G., Iyer, A., George, A., Structural reforms and health equity: a comparison of NSS surveys, 1986-87 and 1995-96.

CHAPTER

5

Investment in Healthcare can Spur Growth

Hospital Industry can Surpass even IT Sector!

Building brand India in healthcare sector is essential, not only to promote medical tourism, but also to provide adequate healthcare to the people of India. The factors governing the building of healthcare brand India are several. Besides the growing population, these include a rise in income levels across all strata of society, the commensurate increase in lifestyle diseases, deeper penetration and growing involvement of health insurance, newer treatment modes and finally the inadequacy of the public healthcare delivery systems. However, healthcare development can act as an engine of economic growth in several ways. During 2002, India's healthcare industry contributed 5 percent to the GDP and employed approximately 4 million people. By 2012, this industry is projected to contribute 8.5 percent of GDP. Healthcare spending is expected to double over the next 10 years. It is expected that private healthcare will form a large chunk of this spending, rising from US$ 14.8 billion to US$ 33.6 billion in 2012. No doubt, India is marching ahead.

- India has achieved impressive demographic transition owing to the decline of crude birth rate, crude death rate, total fertility rate and infant mortality rate.
- The rural primary public health Infrastructure has recorded an impressive development during the last 50 years of independence. The network consists of 1,45,000 sub-centers, 23,109 primary health centers and 3222 community health centers, catering to a population of 5000, 30,000 and 1,00,000 respectively (and 3000, 20,000 and 80,000 population in tribal and desert areas).
- The government is committed to raise public spending on health from the current 0.9 percent to 2-3 percent of GDP over the next five years with focus on primary healthcare. In line with this objective, the plan allocation for 2005-06 was US$ 630.35 million. A further step is visualized in the allocation budgeted for 2006-07 at US$ 721.38 million.
- There are about 200 recognized medical colleges spread throughout the country and approximately 20,000 medical graduates pass out each year. Medical institutions admit more than 6,000 post-graduate trainees in their programs.
- In the last five years, the number of foreign patients visiting India for medical treatment has risen from 10,000 to about 200,000. With an annual growth rate of 30 percent. More and more people have started traveling to India for Medical Treatment and Medical Tourism is finally coming of age. The reason for India being a favourable destination is because of its excellent health infrastructure and technology. Most common treatments are heart surgery, organ transplants, eye surgery, knee transplant, cosmetic surgery and dental care.
- The term AYUSH covers Ayurveda, Yoga and Naturopathy, Unani, Siddha and Homeopathy. A Department was established as Department of

Indian Systems of Medicines and Homoeopathy (ISM and H) in Ministry of Health and Family Welfare in March 1995 and was renamed as Department of AYUSH in Novembers 2003.

- A recent McKinsey study on healthcare says medical tourism alone can contribute Rs. 5,000-Rs. 10,000 crore (Rs. 50-100 billion) additional revenue for up market tertiary hospitals by 2012, and will account for 3-5% of the total healthcare delivery market.
- The Ministry of Tourism has taken several initiatives, in partnership with the private sector, to promote India as a destination for medical tourism. The Ministry is also considering setting up of a National Accreditation Board for Hospitals.
- Measures for rationalizing the flow of tourist traffic have already been taken. Government has decided that there should be a fast track clearance for the patients at the airport.

National Health Policy (2002): Universal healthcare a mirage

Way back in 1946, a very forward looking Health Survey and Development Committee, headed by Joseph Bhore, outlined a universal healthcare plan. Anticipating that large sections of the population may be unable to pay for healthcare, the committee recommended that no person should be denied medical care because of an inability to pay for it. It also recommended that health workers be on the public payroll, limiting the need for private practitioners. The committee also laid special emphasis on preventive methods and communicable diseases. Moreover, recognizing urban-rural disparities, it laid out an infrastructure plan for a comprehensive three-tier healthcare system at the district level in order to provide preventive and curative healthcare to everyone. Six decades after the recommendations of the Bhore Committee were put forward, the nation's actual delivery of healthcare is among the worst in the world, and the benchmarks for healthcare set then are still very far from being achieved. Here is one quick measure of how India is tracking, as of 1998, with respect to specific infrastructural recommendations: while the committee recommended 567 hospital beds for every 100,000 people, the country actually has 70, only a little more than a tenth of the recommended ratio. The investment required then to achieve the recommended levels of healthcare services was under 1% of GDP; implementing the Bhore committee recommendations then could have been the recipe for a robust healthcare system in India today, with a recurring cost of just 1.33% of GDP, according to one estimate. The social welfare ethos of the committee has long been left in the dust, and instead India has allowed the private sector in healthcare to take its place. As a result, accessible, quality universal healthcare today is simply a dream for most citizens.

(See Appendix I, National Health Policy 2002 for details).

Policy Initiatives

- Infrastructure status conferred on the healthcare industry (under Section 10(23G) of the Income Tax Act); allows private hospitals to raise cheaper long-term capital.
- Reduction in import duty on medical equipment from 25 percent to 5 percent.
- Depreciation limit on such equipment raised to 40 percent from 25 percent, to encourage medical equipment imports.
- Customs duty reduced to 8 percent from 16 percent for medical, surgical, dental and veterinary furniture.
- Customs duty on as many as 24 medical equipments, which include X-ray, goniometer and teletherapy stimulator machines has been reduced to 5 percent.
- The Government has announced income tax exemption under Section 80(1B) of the Income Tax Act for the first five years, to hospitals (with 100 beds or more) set-up in rural areas.
- Budgetary allocation to healthcare is 2 percent of

the Gross Domestic Product (GDP) at US$ 1.51 billion, up from from US$ 1.26 billion.

- Customs duty exemption on items like talking books, Braille computer terminals, braille writers and typewriters, hearing aids and devices, cochlear implants and stair lifts. These items will also be exempt from excise duty and CVD.
- Crutches, wheel-chairs, walking frames, artificial limbs, etc. for the disabled will also be fully exempt from customs duty. Ambulances used by all hospitals will now be eligible for concessional duty.
- Launch of a new group health insurance scheme through public sector non-life insurance companies. As per the scheme, the insured will be the members of self-help groups and other credit linked groups who avail of loans from banks or co-operative institution.
- US$ 56 million will be earmarked for the HIV/ AIDS control programme through the use of primary health centres, prevention of drug abuse, etc.

80,000 to 100,000 additional hospital beds will be required every year for the next three to four years to adequately meet growing healthcare demands. With the public healthcare system adding 8000 beds per year, the private healthcare companies have a huge business opportunity to fill the gap.

With changing consumer preferences and attributes, coupled with greater liberalization and reform, the role of the private sector is likely to enhance significantly. The Confederation of Indian Industry's (CII) Indian Healthcare Federation estimates that fresh investments of US$ 25 billion over the next 8-10 years to establish facilities will put the sector on the global healthcare map. With US$ 12-15 billion expected in domestic investments, the Indian healthcare sector represents a US$ 10 billion opportunity for foreign investors.

100 percent FDI is permitted for all health-related services under the automatic route.

Global healthcare: $ 4 trillion industry

Globally, healthcare is a $ 3 trillion industry, and if you add the cosmetics and beauty segment, it is another one trillion dollars. This also makes it the largest employer across the world. But there is an acute shortage of highly trained manpower and facilities. In the West, they have one bed for 250 people. In India, we have one bed for 1,200 people, when it should be at least one bed for 600 people. We need to double and triple the beds. When countries like the US and the UK want to expand their healthcare system, they are short of manpower. And the biggest advantage India has is its skilled manpower. But India is also woefully short of highly skilled manpower and trainers. Over the last two years, foreign investors have been keen to invest in the Indian healthcare sector. Will it do the same as it has done for IT? And then there is the special economic zone (SEZ) policy. Can it work in the healthcare sector as well? With great difficulty, industry status was given to healthcare. This gave some relief on interest rates but not on taxation. Now it is time to consider the infrastructure status to healthcare for overall economic growth and a healthy nation. There is a huge waiting list in countries like the UK and Canada, so they can come to us for medical treatment. The question is how can we accelerate this? The governments in Thailand, Singapore and Malaysia have pitched in by taking over the advertising budgets for the healthcare industry. We should develop an Indian healthcare brand. It will not be too long before Indians take over the global healthcare industry. Healthcare employs 4 million people at present, by 2012 India would be spending $45 billions or 8% of GDP and the sector would employ 9 million people. Massive investment in private as well as government sector is required for it to surpass the information technology (IT) sector.

Pockets of opportunities

The **healthcare** industry is all set to become a vehicle of Indian economy with 'pockets of opportunity' in the area of Medical Infrastructure, Health Insurance, Telemedicine, Medical Equipment, Medical Textiles, Clinical Trials, Medical Value Travel and Training and Education. However, there are serious gaps in India's **healthcare** system we need to address them upfront, said Onkar S. Kanwar, past President, FICCI, while addressing the Global Healthcare conference, held at new Delhi in Jan. 07.

The key issues outlined were:

1. Our current bed to thousand population at 1.11, compares poorly even with our neighbouring countries. For example China, Korea and Thailand have about 4.3 beds per thousand population. To reach that level, we will need over 3 million beds with a requirement to invest US$ 240 Billion. Given the low level of government spending on medical infrastructure, the bulk of this increase will have to come from private investment. Currently the private sector meets over 75% of India's **healthcare** demand that actually comes to the market. In the future, even if there is a substantial increase in public spending, it is evident that the private sector will have to mobilize US$ 15 Billion per annum over the next 10 years to reach the capacity of our neighbour. We need to create a policy framework that can facilitate and attract huge doses of investment in healthcare.
2. **Healthcare** sector should be given the tax breaks given to other infrastructure sectors. Although, the government has announced income tax exemption for first 5 years for 100 bed hospitals to set-up in rural areas. This is not enough as break-even periods are long and therefore the tax breaks must be increased to at least 10 years.
3. There is lack of availability of land for hospitals and medical colleges in cities. Apart from creating land banks for hospitals, the government must also increase the FAR to allow more beds to be built per sq. yard of land. The Delhi government

has moved in this direction and other State governments need to be motivated to do the same.

4. The government has given custom duty exemption to some equipments and drugs. We need to extend these exemptions to more life-saving drugs and essential drugs not manufactured in India.
5. We need a regulatory framework for ensuring credible players and in implementing an accreditation mechanism in the **healthcare** facilities. Quality Council of India is making efforts in this direction; however, the process needs to be expedited.
6. Although government hospitals have good infrastructure in terms of land and building, majority of them are marked with inefficiency in managing these facilities, which results in poor quality of **healthcare** service delivery. It is now becoming imperative that **public-private partnerships** are the solutions to augment resources for growth of secondary and tertiary **healthcare** systems in the country.
7. There is an urgent need to facilitate investment in **Medical Education and Training**. There is a projected shortfall of about 45,000 doctors by 2012 and 350,000 nurses just for primary and secondary care by 2015. For tertiary care a large number of highly skilled persons are required, which are in short supply.
8. **Health Insurance** is another area that needs to be given urgent priority as only 0.9% of the vast population in India is covered by Health Insurance.
9. India has the potential to become a **global healthcare** hub with its offering of most competent doctors, world class Medical Facilities and lowest charges for treatment. However, it will require massive investment in hospitals, before medical tourism picks up.

CII's role in Healthcare

CII is playing a major role in taking initiative in healthcare. It released a guide to select cities and corresponding hospitals on November 17, 2004. Besides, it is working on formulating Price Bands corresponding to various specialized areas of services. One of the major initiatives is providing accreditation to hospitals. The Government of India, along with CII, is working on Accreditation of Hospitals. CII is also working on developing the Minimum Quality Standards for all hospitals. This will give comfort to patients seeking treatment in India. Ministry of Health and Family Welfare as well as Ministry of Tourism have formed Task Forces to take this initiative forward. Major corporations have made significant investments in setting up state-of-the-art private hospitals in cities, using the latest technical equipment and the services of highly skilled medical personnel. These services are available at extremely competitive prices, encouraging patients not only from developing countries but even from a number of developed ones to come to India for specialized treatment. In the next ten years, Tertiary Care in India will be predominantly Private Healthcare and extensive Public and Private partnerships. The Secondary Care would be Private and Public Healthcare and selective public and private partnerships. The Primary Care would be predominantly public, especially in the rural areas.

Investment Opportunities

- Health Insurance
- Medical Tourism
- Hospital Management
- Curative and Preventive Services
- Infrastructure Facilities like Hospitals and Diagnostic Centre
- Training Manpower (doctors, nurses, technicians)

Centers of Excellence

Since liberalization in 1991, a growing number of Indian companies have formed alliances with foreign firms.

Most have aimed at leveraging the international partners' skills, knowledge and experience in devising and implementing improved medical care services; not relying only on capital invested. India's first geriatric hospital, the Heritage Hospital of Hyderabad has formed a joint venture with US-based United Church Homes to recruit, train and provide placement to registered Indian nurses in USA. To cater to this demand they have formed 2 legal entities, namely, UCH Heritage Healthcare Inc. and UCH Heritage Healthcare India Private Limited. Max Healthcare and Singapore General Hospital (SGH) have entered into collaboration for medical practice, research, training and education in healthcare services. Apollo-Gleneagles Hospitals Ltd., a 50:50 joint venture between Apollo Hospitals Ltd. and Parkway Group of Singapore. The joint venture is also looking at business opportunities overseas in West Asia and North Africa. Apollo Hospitals has also entered into a partnership with Yemen's Hayel Saeed Anam Group to provide advisory services to the latter's hospital project. Apollo will provide consultancy to set-up a 160-bed super specialty hospital at Taiz, Yemen. Other alliances are: Wockhardt and Harvard Medical International Inc., USA Fortis Healthcare and Partners Healthcare System, USA Birla Heart and Research Centreand Clevel and Clinic Foundation, USA. Some other hospitals are: Piramal, Duncan, Ispat, Cipla, etc.

Some details regarding the best hospitals of India is given in chapter 2.

Healthcare BPO

Healthcare BPO could potentially be a US$ 4.5 billion opportunity for India, offering employment to about 200,000 people. It includes offshoring of processes such as medical billing, disease coding, forms processing and claims adjudication. Already, over a dozen companies are either consolidating operations or have kicked-off pilots in this space.

These include Indian companies such as Apollo Health Street (AHS), iHealthcare, Paramount Healthcare, Hinduja TMT, Ajuba, Affiliated Computer Services, Cognizant

Technology Solutions and Vision Healthsource. As healthcare BPO players mature, other businesses like claims repricing, medical diagnosis and actuarial work are expected to gain momentum. The opportunity is being driven by the US$ 1.4 trillion US healthcare industry, trying to rationalise costs. The American Healthcare Association estimates that the profitability of US hospitals fell from 6.1 percent, six years ago to 2.8 percent in 2002. Almost 40 percent of the US hospitals make losses. State-owned insurer Medicare has US$ 20 million in liabilities. Hospitals need to offshore the US$ 350 billion administrative functions and US$ 50 billion billing and coding tasks to be able to bring down their costs.

Telemedicine can improve accessibility

Telemedicine is a method by which patients can be examined, monitored and treated, while the patient and doctor are geographically distant. Potentially, the next big success story in the healthcare sector, several examples already offer an insight into this emergent opportunity that is changing the lives of over 600 million people in rural India. Gujarat The Online Telemedicine Research Institute (OTRI) provided telemedicine links for teleconsultation, thereby establishing 750 sessions in a period of 30 days in Bhuj after the earthquake in January 2001. Telemedicine services in India are also expected to grow, which in turn, are creating a demand for diagnostic medical equipment such as X-Ray machines, CT Scanners, dopplers ultrasound scanners, electrocardiographs and the like. Leading international companies such as General Electric, Siemens, Hitachi, Bayer.

Boston Scientific, Wipro-GE, Phillips Medical Systems and Toshiba market most of the high value equipment and have local support, while only consumables and disposable equipments are made locally. These companies have expanded their operations in the Indian market and established manufacturing facilities to assemble equipment such as ultrasound scanners and mobile X-ray units for the domestic market and export sales.

Karnataka Asia Heart Foundation, Bangalore has successfully been practising Telecardiology between Bangalore and cities in eastern India. Paramedics are guided to save patients suffering from Acute Myocardial Infarction by performing life-saving procedures as per doctors' directions over video conferencing. Tamil Nadu Apollo Hospital, Chennai is providing expert opinion from its tertiary level hospitals in bigger cities to those in far-flung towns of India. Over a period of 27 months, over 4,000 patients benefitted from teleconsultations and over 75 percent of those teleconsulted were treated in their respective cities.

Budget 2007–08: Highlights

- GDP growth rate estimated at 9.2% in 2006-07.
- Manufacturing growth rate estimated at 11.3%.
- Saving rate of 32.4%, investment rate of 33.8% will continue.
- Tax as % of GDP at 11.4%
- Gross domestic capital formation up 23%.
- Fiscal deficit to be 3.7% in the current year and revenue deficit 2%.
- Fiscal deficit for 2007-08 pegged at 3.3% of GDP and Revenue deficit at 1.5%.
- Bank credit rate grew by 29% during first ten months of 2006-07.
- E-Governance expenditure hiked to Rs. 719 crore.
- Inflation during 2006-07 estimated at between 5.2 and 5.4% against 4.4% during the previous year.
- Total expenditure during 2006-07 estimated at Rs. 6,80,521 crore.
- Defence Budget hiked to Rs. 96000 crore.
- Overseas investment to be allowed by individuals via Mutual Funds.
- Government to allow short selling by institutions.
- Mutual Funds to be allowed to launch infrastructure funds.
- PAN to be made sole identity for participants in the security markets to strengthen capital market.
- Foreign exchange reserves stand at 180 billion dollars.
- Tourism infrastructure to get an allocation of Rs. 520 crore as against Rs. 423 crore last year.

- Northeastern region to get Rs. 405 crore for highway development. Road-cum-rail project over Brahmaputra in Bogibil, Assam.
- New industrial policy for the Northeast.
- Technology Upgradation Fund to be continued during the 11th Plan. Rs. 911 crore to be provided for this.

Social Sector

- Allocation on Healthcare to increase by 21.9 percent.
- Allocation for education to be enhanced by 34.2 percent.
- Allocation under Rajiv Gandhi Drinking Mission stepped up from Rs. 4680 crore to Rs. 5850 crore.
- Annual target of 15 lakh houses under Bharat Nirman Programme to be exceeded.
- Allocation for National Rural Health Mission stepped up from Rs. 8207 crore to Rs. 9947 crore.
- Allocation for Integrated Child Development Scheme (ICDS) to be increased from Rs. 4087 crore to Rs. 4761 crore.
- 130 more districts under National Rural Employment Guarantee Act (NREGA). Additional allocation of Rs. 12,000 crore for it.
- Rs. 800 crore for Sampoorna Gram Rozgar Yojana in districts not covered by NREGA.
- Swarna Jayanti Swarozgar Yojana allocation increased from Rs. 250 crore to Rs. 344 crore.
- Allocation for schemes only for SCs and STs to be increased to Rs. 3271 crore.
- Allocation for SC/ST scholarships enhanced from Rs. 440 crore to Rs. 611 crore.
- Rs. 63 crore for share capital for National Minorities Development Finance Corporation following Sachar Committee recommendations.
- To prevent high rate of school dropout, a National Means-cum-Merit scholarship to be implemented, with an allocation of Rs. 6,000 per child.

- Rs. 1290 crore to be provided for elimination of polio.
- Allocation for AIDS control programme to be raised to Rs. 969 crore.
- Computerisation of PDS and integrated computerisation programme for FCI.
- Rs. 22,282 crore allocated for women development.
- Death and disability cover for rural landless families to be introduced, known as 'Aam Aadmi Bima Yojana'.
- Health insurance cover for weavers to be enlarged to ancillary industries. Allocation increased from Rs. 241 crore to Rs. 321 crore.
- The ceiling of loans for weaker sections under differential rate of interest scheme will be raised from Rs. 6500 to Rs. 15,000 and in housing loan from Rs. 5000 to Rs. 20,000.
- Reverse mortgage scheme for senior citizens announced.
- Rs. 73.24 billion allocated for mid-day meal scheme.
- Two lakh more teachers to be employed and five lakh more classrooms to be constructed.
- Government to provide 1 lakh jobs for physically disabled with a salary limit of Rs. 25,000 a month.
- Backward Regions Grant Fund to be raised to Rs. 5800 crore.

Ministry of Health and Family Welfare

The ministry was allocated $3.4 billion for this year's budget, an increase of $886 million from last year, to expand healthcare services in the country, including HIV/AIDS programs. In addition, Finance Minister P. Chidambaram has proposed allocating $219 million from the health ministry's budget to the third phase of the National AIDS Control Organizations. The third phase of NACP is scheduled to launch on April 1. About $466 million was allocated to the second phase of the National AIDS Control Program. Chidambaram said that the government has brought HIV/AIDS "out of the closet" and promised to make efforts to stop the spread of HIV in the country. He added that more hospitals in India will provide access to HIV/AIDS treatment to prevent mother-to-child HIV transmission. Appreciating the increase in allocation for healthcare by 21.9 percent and enhanced funding for the National Rural Health Mission, AIDS control programme and elimination of polio, he said the emphasis on rural healthcare and communicable diseases would help reduce the disease burden on the lower socio-economic groups.

He also hailed the reduction in customs duty from 12.5 percent to 7.5 percent and removal of service tax on clinical trials. "The latter will help in developing new treatment modalities for patients suffering from varied conditions. Coupled with our wide gene pool and excellent resources in the healthcare, IT sectors, India's chances in becoming a favoured destination for clinical research will certainly receive a big boost."

Striking the right balance

What might be the most effective way to stimulate demand in the most rational manner? According to a recent assessment of China's healthcare system in *The Economist* magazine, "What China needs most is a health-insurance system that works." The same prescription could be applied equally well to Mexico and India. A well-designed national insurance program spreads the financial risk of healthcare across an entire population, vastly reducing the likelihood of catastrophic loss for families with serious health problems.

One potential strategy for improving affordability would be to establish a social insurance program that is "sponsored" by the government but incorporates contributions from the private sector and from individual beneficiaries. Coverage would need to be universal in order to prevent the problem of adverse selection, but premiums could be set on a sliding scale that reflects ability to pay. This public-private support would not only protect patients from potentially catastrophic expenses related to high-tech/high-cost care but also help free up government resources to fund prevention initiatives and public health and safety measures that benefit all citizens. Even if this program were partially publicly funded and nationally organized, there would be an important role for the private sector, since competitive market forces would be expected to promote efficiency and innovation.

Prevention is better than cure

J.K. Arrow, the Nobel Prize winning economist laid the foundation of health economics. The Principles are relevant for India's healthcare research and policy-making. The growth in per capita income, increasing urbanization, availability of modern biomedical technology, education and overall awareness indicate that demand for healthcare is bound to increase in the country. Greater investment in healthcare leads to longer life expectancy, less morbidity and increasing work productivity that result in economic progress. Over the last two decades, life expectancy at birth in India has increased by approximately double the increase in life expectancy in middle income and high-income countries.

Though the budget resources are scarce, there is certainly a need to double the public expenditure on health, given the long-term benefits. The emphasis should be on prevention and making essential public health services available to the poor. About 88 percent of the pregnant women are anemic. Other aspects such as low birth weight babies and child malnutrition are close to the poverty line numbers. While deadly diseases such as Tuberculosis and HIV are receiving public attention, the long-term consequences of in utero problems have been neglected. "It may well be that a very large increase in expenditures on ante-natal care and pediatrics care in infancy and early childhood is the most effective way to improve health over the entire life cycle, by delaying the onset of chronic diseases, alleviating their severity if they occur, and increasing longevity."

Research has shown substantial medical expenditure occurs during the last two years of a person's life. A broad-based hospitalization catastrophic insurance must be offered to protect individuals in their old age. Last but not the least, more collaboration is needed between doctors and economists to jointly pursue research and make health economics a robust discipline for specialization. A healthy India is certainly a precondition for a wealthy India. Until there is a radical change in the paradigm, healthcare costs will continue to escalate, whether the bill is paid at the doctor's office or in the form of taxes. As long as the demand for drugs, along with drug prices, continues to rise, the pharmaceutical companies will get paid and you will be left paying for the extra costs.

NRIs: India's brain bank

Solutions for the challenge of overcoming India's health deficit were suggested in the working session on Health at the Pravasi Bharatiya Divas (PBD), 2007, held at New Delhi by the Ministry of Overseas Indian Affairs in partnership with the Delhi government and the Confederation of Indian Industry. Similar sentiments were echoed at PBD, 2008 in Delhi and Non-Resident Punjabis (NRPs) conference held at Chandigarh.

1. Dr. Sayeda Hameed, Member (Health), Planning Commission, gave an overview of the health challenge in India. While India has made significant advances in life-expectancy, maternal mortality and eradication of some diseases, in indicators such as infant mortality, malnutrition and others, the country lags even other developing nations. 70% of India's population is rural with 19 crores still under the poverty line. Access to clean drinking water, sanitation, and nutrition is difficult, and 30% of the population is estimated to suffer from malnutrition.

   Dr. Hameed stated that health is a priority for the 11th Plan. She said that the National Rural Health Mission for the period 2005-12 is expected to be extended to the urban areas. Primary health access will be measured through traveling time to reach primary health centres, which will considerably benefit women in particular. NRHM will require strong policies and institutions, and interventions must be evidence-based and area-specific. She urged the Indian community overseas to pay particular attention to malnutrition and anemia among adolescent girls. Indian systems of medicine such as ayurveda, unani, siddha, and homeopathy and their practitioners form a good resource base. Training can help use this base for local health delivery. Communities must also be involved with large scale replication of successful civil society models, said Dr. Hameed.

2. Dr. Naresh Trehan, Chairman, CII National Committee on Healthcare, and the then Executive Director, Escorts Heart Institute Research Centre, moderated the session saying that steps need to be taken for doubling infrastructure in healthcare, necessitating investments of $25-30 billion in the next ten years. Access to basic healthcare facilities requires 750,000 more hospital beds, 540,000 more doctors, a large number of super specialist surgeons, and 750,000 additional nurses. The Indian Healthcare Federation has taken initiatives in the sector. Among its recommendations is to have more mobile health clinics through which remote or small villages can be provided medical facilities without needing a doctor permanently stationed. Responding to a question, Dr. Trehan said that the government is considering registration of medical practitioners of Indian origin who may have overseas qualifications, in order that they may contribute their services to the country as well.
3. Dr. Subramaniam Balasubramaniam, President, American Association of Physicians of Indian Origin (AAPI) gave an overview of its operations in India. AAPI is currently celebrating its silver jubilee and represents 45,000 physicians in the USA. He stated that the organization can best contribute by way of knowledge, skills and experience in India. Knowledge transfer needs a proper system set-up, training of the trainers, and ongoing monitoring in a cost efficient manner.

AAPI has worked in several fields in India. In Pune it has contributed to emergency medical services and helped reduce mortality rates by 35%. It has also instituted pilot projects in diabetes, deafness in children, and cancers of the cervix and prostate. It is operating 17 free clinics for many years and also running two burn centers. A recent initiative to adopt villages has already received commitments from 25 people. The Confederation of Indian Industry and AAPI are entering into a partnership for carrying forward initiatives in the health sector.

4. Commenting on the incidence of kidney and renal problems, Dr. Georgi Abraham, Consultant Nephrologist, Sri Ramchandra Medical College and Research Institute, Chennai, said that increasing diabetes and heart disease, even among rural populations, is leading to greater kidney problems. He pointed out that 20% of nephrologists in USA are of Indian origin, yet the number of doctors in the specialty was not increasing. Challenges at the local, national and international levels needed to be addressed. Non-profit organizations could utilize funds from medical tourism for the purpose. Training of highly skilled workforce and epidemiological studies are needed.
5. Dr. Sant P. Chawla, an oncologist in USA, stressed the importance of drug development, research and development and clinical trials. Drug companies are ready to spend money on free patient healthcare and provide money to hospitals for undertaking clinical research. India with its large population and good trained personnel has not yet reaped the advantages of this. Problems relate to poor records, lack of good clinical practices, lack of hospital and ethical boards, etc. He suggested the establishment of an institution for drug development, research and clinical trials.
6. Dr. Rajeev Venkayya, Adviser to the President on

Biodefence, USA, emphasized that while pandemics do not appear to be of immediate concern, there is a history of such pandemics occurring thrice in every century. The last epidemic in 1918 had 20-40 million casualties. Such pandemics can have magnified impact on countries such as India. Lauding India for its leadership in international forum on pandemics, he said that India will be hosting the next international meet this year. Dr. Venkayya said that strong leadership control to manage pandemics is needed, along with, close collaboration between ministries of agriculture and health, and robust public-private partnership in vaccine and antiviral drug development.

7. NRIs can mitigate the sufferings of the native Indians not only by improving water supply but can well assist in the development of other areas viz. agriculture, infrastructure, education, women and youth and above all health was observed by Montek Singh Ahluwalia, Deputy Chairman Planning Commission. Prime Minister Manmohan Singh called upon 30 million strong Indian Diaspora to invest in the country of their origin, not just financially, but intellectually, socially, culturally and emotionally as well. Infrastructure in particular needs $ 384 billions of investments in next five years, of which 25 billions need to come from overseas every year. 'Investment in healthcare infrastructure will yield rich dividends' most of the speakers opined. Since the remittances from abroad are to the tune of $27.2 billions annually, the investment requirements in infrastructure in general and health sector in particular can be met from our extended family; the NRIs settled all over the globe.
8. Chandigarh delegation led by Vivek Atray and Dr. R. Kumar mooted massive investment in hardware as well as software of the healthcare industry to benefit the people of India as well as

> from elsewhere in this global village. The single largest challenge to India's developmental aspirations is in the space of healthcare. From infections to lifestyle diseases, India has the dubious distinction of being the leader in a number of these including HIV/AIDS. These pose special challenges to the Indian policy-makers, as well as to the global community. We should explore ways in which NRIs can connect with India through their participation in making the India healthier and in turn India contributing to redress the surgical and wellness needs of the global community.

The other areas where the NRIs can contribute are:

(i) Quality medical research; financial as well as intellectual inputs.
(ii) Pharmaceutical industry; research and development of new drugs in India.
(iii) Medical equipment; supply of life saving equipment to our public hospitals, free of cost.
(iv) Medical education and manpower training; setting up NRI sponsored centers of excellence, medical colleges, institutes as well as arranging skill transfer to our doctors from abroad.
(v) Setting up of modern convention centers; bidding for international conferences for India.
(vi) Providing Consultancy services in area such as clinical waste management, telemedicine and medical transcription centers.

NRIs have been playing a significant role by remitting billions of US $ per annum to India. Apparently this money is improving the living conditions of millions of Indians at home, but the same is also finding way to improve the infrastructure for the nation and health of the people, as well. This will open vistas for medical tourism for the benefit of global community. This will also entitle the NRIs to share the dividend out of the profits thus earned.

SOURCES

M. Barraza-Llorens, S. Bertozzi, E. Gonzalez-Pier and J. Gutierrez, "Addressing Inequity in Health and Healthcare in Mexico," *Health Affairs*, 2002, 21 (3): 47-56.

World Bank Country Data Profile:. The figures cited represent the percentage of children aged 12 and 24 months who had been immunized against measles.

M. Lim, H. Yang, T. Zhang, W. Feng and Z. Zhou, "Public Perceptions of Private Healthcare in China," *Health Affairs*, 2004, 23 (6): 222-234; "Where are the Patients? China's Healthcare," *The Economist*, August 21, 2004; "China's Growing Pains," *The Economist*, August 21, 2004.

World Health Organization, The World Health Report 2000—Health Systems: Improving Performance (Geneva: WHO, 2000).

G. Leather, "China — Government Unveils Rural Healthcare Plan," WMRC Daily Analysis, October 30, 2002.

World Health Organization, The World Health Report 2000—Health Systems: Improving Performance, (Geneva: WHO, 2000).

"Where are the Patients? China's Healthcare," *The Economist*, August 21, 2004.

S. Leeder, S. Raymond, H. Greenberg, H. Lui and K. Esson, "A Race Against Time: The Challenge of Cardiovascular Disease in Developing Countries" (New York: Columbia University, 2004).

"Where are the Patients? China's Healthcare," *The Economist*, August 21, 2004.

Organisation for Economic Co-operation and Development, The OECD Health Project: Towards High-Performing Health System (Paris: OECD, 2004).

C. Smith, C. Cowan, A. Sensenig, and A. Catlin, "Trends: Healthcare Spending Growth Slows in 2003," *Health Affairs*, January 11, 2005,

N. Sekhri, "Managed Care: The U.S. Experience," *Bulletin of the World Health Organization*, 2000, 78 (6); D. Cutler, Your Money or Your Life: Strong Medicine for America's Healthcare System (Oxford: Oxford University Press, 2004).

L. Zendle, "An Innovative Approach to Population Health: Kaiser Permanente Southern California," in Consumer-Driven Healthcare: Implications for Providers, Payers and Policymakers (R. Herzlinger, editor) (San Francisco: Jossey-Bass, 2004).

Deloitte Research, "Clinical Transformation: Cross Industry Lessons for Healthcare" (New York: Deloitte Consulting, 2002).

J. Wilkerson, K. Devers and R. Given, "The Potential and Limits of Competitive Managed Care," in Competitive Managed Care: The Emerging Healthcare System (J. Wilkerson, K. Devers and R. Given, editors) (San Francisco: Jossey-Bass, 1997).

Alkire, Sabina and Lincoln Chen, June 2004, "Medical Expectations in International Migration: Should Doctors and Nurses Be Treated Differently?" Paper presented at "Global Migration Regimes" Workshop, Stockholm, Sweden.

Bach, Stephen, July 2003, "International Migration of Health Workers: Labour and Social Issues", International Labour Office, Geneva.

Buchan, J., T. Park and J. Sochaiski, April 2003, "International Nurse Mobility: Trends and Policy Implications." World Health Organization, Geneva.

Dovlo, Dela and Tim Martineau, January 2004, "A Review of the Migration of Africa's Health Professionals," Paper Commissioned by the Joint Leaning Initiative on Human Resources for Health, Africa Working Group.

Joint Learning Initiative, 2004. "Human Resources for Health: Overcoming the Crisis."

Martineau, Tim, K. Decker and P. Bundred, 2002, "Briefing note on international migration of health professionals: Leveling the playing field for developing health systems, International Health Division," School of Tropical Medicine, Liverpool.

Lowell, B. Lindsay and Stefka Gerova, November 2004. "Immigrants and the Healthcare Workforce: Profiles and Shortages", *Work and Occupations,* Vol. 34 (no. 4): 1-25.

Regional Network for Equity in Health in Southern Africa (EQUINET), Health Systems Trust (South Africa) and MEDACT (UK), 2003, "Health Personnel in Southern Africa: Confronting Maldistribution and Brain Drain."

OECD, 2004, "The International Mobility of Health Professionals: An Evaluation and Analysis Based on the Case of South Africa," Trends In International Migration: SOPEMI 2003 Edition.

Physicians for Human Rights, June 2004, "An Action Plan to Prevent Brain Drain: Building Equitable Health Systems in Africa."

United Nations Development Programme, 2004, Human Development Report, 2004.

CHAPTER

6

Better Environment can Reduce Healthcare Costs

World Health Organization

A good environment is conducive to better health is a well known fact, which in turn can reduce healthcare costs. Environmental health addresses all the physical, chemical, and biological factors external to a person, and all the related factors impacting behaviours. It is targeted towards preventing disease and creating health-supportive environments. The ability to avoid exposure to disease or to treat it depends among other things on environmental conditions, including such factors as access to clean air, safe water, housing conditions and sanitation.

The rationale for government expenditure is that public spending will have a positive impact on economic growth and GDP, if the benefits exceed the marginal cost of public funds. While there is a clear case for improved public health, education and other infrastructure services, there is also the need for holistic policy design. Take health, for instance. International experience suggests that better housing can significantly improve health indicators. A recent World Bank paper finds that simply replacing dirt floors with cement flooring considerably improves family health, especially of children. Specifically a study of Mexico finds that complete substitution of dirt floors by cement leads to as much as 78% reduction in parasitic infection, 49% drop in diarrhoea, 81% decrease in anaemia and 36 to 96% improvement in cognitive development. It also improves adult welfare, as measured by increased satisfaction with housing and quality of life, and also lowers depression and perceived stress levels.

Holistic policy design is critical for the most optimal public expenditure outcomes and delivering welfare gains across the board. For instance, replacing dirt floors with cement flooring may be less effective when households do not have access to safe water supplies. The lack of such supplies would mean that the major cause for parasite infections would remain, despite the improved living environment. Also, malnourishment would imply heightened susceptibility to ill health. The big picture needs to be kept sight of, while improving secroral allocations. Otherwise, public spending can be both more costly and much less effective. (Jaideep Mishra)

The World Health Organization (WHO) released the first ever analysis of the impact environmental factors has on health on 13 June 2007. The data demonstrates that people's health could be improved by reducing environmental risks including pollution, hazards in the work/living environment, UV radiation, noise, agricultural risks, climate and ecosystem change. The data shows that 13 million deaths worldwide could be prevented every year by making environments healthier. In some countries, more than one-third of the disease burden could be prevented through environmental improvements. In 23 countries worldwide, more than 10% of deaths are due to just two environmental risk factors: unsafe water, including poor sanitation and hygiene; and indoor air pollution due to solid fuel used for cooking. Around the world, children under five are the main victims and make up 74% of deaths due to diarrhoeal disease and lower respiratory infections. Low income countries like India suffer the most from environmental health factors, losing about 20 times more healthy years of life per person per year than high income countries. Even in countries with better environmental conditions, almost one sixth of the disease burden could be prevented, and efficient environmental interventions could significantly reduce heart disease and road injuries. "It is important to quantify the burden of disease from unhealthy environments. This information is key to help countries select the appropriate interventions." For the purposes of assessment, environmental factors include pollution, occupational factors, UV radiation, noise, agricultural methods, climate and ecosystem change. Using cleaner fuel such as gas or electricity, using better cooking devices, improving the ventilation or modifying people's behaviour (such as keeping children away from smoke) could have a major impact on respiratory infections and diseases among women and children. Interventions at the community or national level would involve promoting household water treatment and safe storage, and introducing energy policies which favour health. For example, reducing levels of air pollution as set out in WHO's Air Quality Guidelines would save an estimated 865,000 lives per year.

Improve environment; prevent cancers

One of the hopeful messages from cancer research is that most of the cases of cancers are linked to environmental causes and, can be prevented. Environment includes both lifestyle factors such as diet, tobacco, and alcohol, as well as radiation, infectious agents, and substances in the air, water, and soil. A review of recent scientific studies finds compelling evidence linking cancer with specific exposures, namely: (i) Breast cancer from exposure to the pesticide DDT before puberty, (ii) Prostate cancer from exposure to pesticides and metal working fluids, (iii) Non-Hodgkin's lymphoma from exposure to pesticides and solvents, (iv) Brain cancer from exposure to non-ionizing radiation, (v) Leukemia from exposure to 1, 3-butadiene, and (vi) Lung cancer from exposure to air pollution and so on.

We know with considerable certainty that tobacco is a major contributor to cancer. We also know a lot about the cancer risks associated with exposure to ionizing radiation. This includes radiation from many sources—cosmic rays, radon, X-rays, atomic bombs, and above ground nuclear bomb tests. However, the quantum of contribution from all the other causes of cancer, such as diet, occupational exposures, or air and water pollution, is less certain. The estimate that diet may contribute 30-35 percent is probably right. So, tobacco and diet are major contributors. There are a number of occupational exposures where the scientists have been successful in decreasing harmful exposures to toxic substances—arsenic, asbestos, and benzidine, and there is some evidence that rates are decreasing for some cancers that are related to these exposures. We now know that HIV and HPV are significant risk factors for certain cancers, and the bacterium H. pylori is an important risk factor in stomach cancer. Another area where strong information has emerged are the health effects of physical activity and obesity—two environmental conditions also tied to diet. For example, physical inactivity is now pretty clearly related to cancers of the colon, breast, and prostate, and associations with additional cancer sites are likely to be made in the future. It's very clear that colorectal and breast cancers are linked to physical activity, and prostate, lung, ovarian, and endometrial cancers are probably linked, too.

The way we and other animals are being fed and made to inhale chemicals in our environment, We can assume that every Indian has some level of these chemicals in their body. That shows that they are at risk to suffer health risks including cancers. The problem with most of the 80,000 chemicals used in the production of consumer goods is that no one knows the threshold for humans A recent acrimonious debate between the environmentalists and the cold drinks lobby, on the presence of toxic substances, is a case in point.

Phthalates (industrial chemicals) are found in Shower curtains, garden hoses, table clothes, vinyl flooring, swimming pools, plastic clothing, childrens toys, automobile upholstery, carpets, capsules, soap, shampoo, hair spray, nail polish, deodorants and fragrances. They are Associated with lower sperm counts, the feminization of male genitalia in male fetuses, childhood asthma, reduced lung capacity. Avoid plastics and eat fresh food grown without pesticides, i.e. organic foods.

Similarly BPA chemicals are found in some water bottles, baby bottles, food storage and heating containers, the lining of metal food cans, dental sealants and toys. BPA has been known to simulate estrogen and is associated with cancer and diabetes. To reduce exposure use glass, stainless steel or polyethylene bottles instead of polycarbonate bottles; avoid heating food in polycarbonate containers; cut back on canned foods.

Polybrominated diphenyl ethers is another class of chemicals found in furniture foam, textiles, kitchen appliances, electronics like TVs and computer monitors, and in the fat of some food animals. These are Associated with birth defects, cancer neonatal exposure affects learning and memory. To avoid Wash hands frequently; dust with a damp cloth; choose vegetarian food and cooking methods that needs no fat.

Proportion of Cancer Deaths Caused by Different Avoidable Cancers (1998, UK)

Causes	*Percent*
Tobacco	29-31
Diet	20-50
Medicines	<1
Infection: parasites, bacteria, viruses	10-20
Ionizing and UV light	5-7
Occupation	2-4
Pollution: air, water, food	1-5
Physical inactivity	1-2

This shows how can we prevent dreadful diseases like cancer by improving our environment.

The environmental health issues for children and their mothers

The environment is one of the most critical contributors to the global toll of more than ten million child deaths annually. It is also a very important factor in the health and well-being of their mothers. Polluted indoor and outdoor air, contaminated water, lack of adequate sanitation, toxic hazards, disease vectors, ultraviolet radiation, and degraded ecosystems are all important environmental risk factors for children and in most cases for their mothers as well. Particularly in developing countries, environmental hazards and pollution are major contributors to childhood deaths, illnesses and disability from acute respiratory disease, diarrhoeal diseases, physical injuries, poisonings, insect-borne diseases and perinatal infections. Childhood death and illness from causes such as poverty and malnutrition are also associated with unsustainable patterns of development and degraded urban or rural environments.

Environment-related killers in children under five:

- Diarrhoea kills an estimated 1.6 million children each year, caused mainly by unsafe water and poor sanitation.
- Indoor air pollution associated with the still-widespread use of biomass fuels kills nearly one million children annually, mostly as a result of acute respiratory infections. Mothers, in charge of cooking or resting close to the hearth after having given birth, are most at risk of developing chronic respiratory disease.
- Malaria, which may be exacerbated as a result of poor water management and storage, inadequate housing, deforestation and loss of biodiversity, kills an estimated one million children under five annually, mostly in Africa.
- Unintentional physical injuries, which may be related to household or community environmental hazards, kill nearly 300,000 children annually: 60,000 are attributed to drowning, 40,000 to fires, 16,000 to falls, 16,000 to poisonings, 50,000 to road traffic incidents and over 100,000 are due to other unintentional injuries.

Lead in air, mercury in food and other chemicals can result in long-term, often irreversible effects, such as infertility, miscarriage, and birth defects. Women's exposure to pesticides, solvents and persistent organic pollutants may potentially affect the health of the fetus. Additionally, while the overall benefits of breastfeeding are recognized, the health of the newborn may be affected by high levels of contaminants in breast milk. Small children, whose bodies are rapidly developing, are particularly susceptible—and in some instances the health impacts may only emerge later in life. Furthermore, children as young as five years old sometimes work in hazardous settings. Pregnant women living and working in hazardous environments and poor mothers and their children are at a higher risk, as they are exposed to the most degraded environments, are often unaware of the health implications, and lack access to information on potential solutions.

Filtration and disinfection of water at the household level dramatically improves the microbial quality of water, and reduces the risk of diarrhoeal disease at low cost. Improved stoves reduce exposures to indoor air pollution. Better storage and safe use of chemicals at community level reduces exposures to toxic chemicals, especially among toddlers, who explore, touch and taste the products found at home. Personal protection from malaria through the use of insecticide-treated mosquito nets has a proven track record of saving lives. Education is also key-mothers who receive the information they need to understand the environmental risks present in their homes and communities are better equipped to take appropriate action to reduce or eliminate exposure.

WHO and its partners lead and coordinate research and global knowledge-sharing about the long-term impacts of major environmental hazards on child health.

Shelter and water supply: Inadequacies can jeopardize health

Even though the number of dwelling units is increasing, the rate does not keep pace with the rate of population increase. The housing gap has increased steadily from 23 million in 1981 to 31 million dwelling units in 1991 and it will become worse by 2001. This widening gap though has been a middle-class concern, with the vast acute need of slum and pavement dwellers hardly entering the calculation. In rural areas, the shortage of shelter is both less visible and harder to assess. Sanitation is linked closely to both shelter and water supply. According to government estimates, in

1981 only 25.1% of the urban population and 0.5% of the rural population had access to basic sanitary facilities. This coverage increased by 1985 to 28.4% and 0.7% respectively. The chances of reaching the reduced goals of the International Drinking Water Supply and Sanitation of 50% urban and 5% rural coverage appear very remote. A study on water sources was carried out by NSSO during 1986-1987. The results showed that only 16% of rural and 72% urban population use a tap as a major source of drinking water. The problem villages are those with excessive salinity, iron, fluoride, etc. in water. As of April 1989, there were nearly 21,000 problem villages, which required drinking water (GOI 1989). The UNDP reports that the population with access to safe water in 1985-87 was 57%, compared to 31% in 1975. Supply of drinking water is the primary responsibility of the State Government. The Accelerated Rural Water Supply Programme (ARWSP) is supported fully by the Central Government in order to provide safe drinking water to the population. By 2000 AD the Government had set its goal in the National Health Policy document to provide 100% population with a protected water supply. The goals are yet to be met. Scarcity of water or polluted water can give rise to a host of infective ailments, which can increase morbidity and mortality in the populations.

Air quality determines the level of health

Air pollution, both indoors and outdoors, is a major environmental health problem affecting all countries alike. The new WHO Air quality guidelines (AQGs) are designed to offer global guidance on reducing the health impacts of air pollution. The new guidelines apply worldwide and are based on expert evaluation of current scientific evidence. They recommend revised limits for the concentration of selected air pollutants: particulate matter (PM), ozone (O_3), nitrogen dioxide (NO_2) and sulfur dioxide (SO_2), applicable across all WHO regions.

Several recent key findings merit special mention:

- Currently there are serious risks to health from

exposure to PM and O_3 in many cities of developed and developing countries. It is possible to derive a quantitative relationship between the pollution levels and specific health outcomes (increased mortality or morbidity). This allows invaluable insights into the health improvements that could be expected if air pollution is reduced.

- Even relatively low concentrations of air pollutants have been related to a range of adverse health effects.
- Poor indoor air quality may pose a risk to the health of over half of the world's population. In homes where biomass fuels and coal are used for cooking and heating, PM levels may be 10–50 times higher than the guideline values.
- Significant reduction of exposure to air pollution can be achieved through lowering the concentrations of several of the most common air pollutants emitted during the combustion of fossil fuels. Such measures will also benefit programmes for the reduction of greenhouse gases.

Particulate matter (PM)

PM affects more people than any other pollutant. It consists of a complex mixture of solid and liquid particles of organic and inorganic substances suspended in the air. The particles are identified according to their aerodynamic diameter, as either PM 10 (particles with an aerodynamic diameter smaller than 10 µm) or PM 2.5 (aerodynamic diameter smaller than 2.5 µm). The latter are more dangerous since, when inhaled, they may reach the peripheral regions of the bronchioles, and interfere with gas exchange inside the lungs. As no threshold for PM has been identified below which no damage to health is observed, the recommended value should represent an acceptable and achievable objective to minimize health effects in the context of local constraints, capabilities and public health priorities.

The major components of PM are sulfate, nitrates, ammonia, sodium chloride, carbon, mineral dust and water. Particles may be classified as primary or secondary, depending on how they are formed. Primary particles are emitted into the atmosphere through man-made and natural processes including combustion of fuels in vehicle engines or in households; industrial activities; erosion of road surfaces by road traffic and abrasion of brakes and tyres; and work in caves and mines. Particles produced by outdoor sources (industry and traffic) penetrate easily into indoor spaces and add to the burden of PM emitted indoors. Chronic exposure to particles contributes to the risk of developing cardiovascular and respiratory diseases, as well as of lung cancer. In developing countries, exposure to pollutants from indoor combustion of solid fuels on open fires or traditional stoves increases the risk of acute lower respiratory infections and associated mortality among young children; indoor air pollution from solid fuel use is also a major risk factor for chronic obstructive pulmonary disease and lung cancer among adults. The mortality in cities with high levels of pollution exceeds that observed in relatively cleaner cities by 15–20%.

Ozone (O_3)

Ozone at ground level—not to be confused with the ozone layer in the upper atmosphere—is one of the major constituents of photochemical smog. It is formed by the reaction with sunlight (photochemical reaction) of pollutants such as nitrogen oxides (NOx) from vehicle and industry emissions and volatile organic compounds (VOCs) emitted by vehicles, solvents and industry. The highest levels of ozone pollution occur during periods of sunny weather. The previously recommended limit, which was fixed at 120 μg/m3 8-hour mean, has been reduced to 100 μg/m3 based on recent conclusive associations between daily mortality and ozone levels occurring at ozone concentrations below 120 μg/m3. Excessive ozone in the air can have a marked effect on human health. It can cause breathing problems, trigger asthma, reduce lung function and cause lung diseases. Several studies have reported that the daily mortality rises by 0.3% and that for heart diseases by 0.4%, per 10 μg/m3 increase in ozone exposure.

Nitrogen dioxide (NO_2)

The current WHO guideline value of 40 µg/m3 (annual mean) set to protect the public from the health effects of gaseous NO_2 remains unchanged from the level recommended in the previous AQGs.

- At short-term concentrations exceeding 200 µg/m³, it is a toxic gas which causes significant inflammation of the airways.
- NO_2 is the main source of nitrate aerosols, which form an important fraction of PM 2.5 and, in the presence of ultraviolet light, of ozone.

The major sources of emissions of NO2 are combustion processes (heating, power generation, and engines in vehicles and ships). Epidemiological studies have shown that symptoms of bronchitis in asthmatic children increase in association with long-term exposure to NO_2. Reduced lung function growth is also linked to NO_2 at concentrations currently observed in cities.

Sulfur dioxide (SO_2)

SO_2 concentration of 500 µg/m³ should not be exceeded over average periods of 10 minutes duration. Studies indicate that a proportion of people with asthma experience changes in pulmonary function and respiratory symptoms after periods of exposure to SO_2 as short as 10 minutes.

- Health effects are now known to be associated with much lower levels of SO_2 than previously believed.
- A greater degree of protection is needed.
- Although the causality of the effects of low concentrations of SO_2 is still uncertain, reducing SO_2 concentrations is likely to decrease exposure to co-pollutants.

The main source of SO_2 is the burning of sulfur-containing fossil fuels for domestic heating, power generation and motor vehicles. The use of tall chimneys at power stations has caused widespread dispersion of SO_2 affecting populations located far away from the sources. In many developing countries, the usage of coal high in sulfur is increasing.

SO_2 can affect the respiratory system and the functions of the lungs, and causes irritation of the eyes. Inflammation of the respiratory tract causes coughing, mucus secretion, aggravation of asthma and chronic bronchitis and makes people more prone to infections of the respiratory tract. Hospital admissions for cardiac disease and mortality increase on days with higher SO_2 levels. When SO_2 combines with water, it forms sulfuric acid; this is the main component of acid rain which is a cause of deforestation. Exposure to air pollutants is largely beyond the control of individuals and requires action by public authorities at the national, regional and even international levels. Emission of pollutants into the atmosphere should be addressed by relevant regulatory instruments, such as national emission ceilings, *ad hoc* limits for specific sources of emission (e.g. enterprises, cars and heating stations) and regulations limiting the use of polluting technologies.

Electromagnetic fields and health

A common concern about base station and local wireless network antennas relates to the possible long-term health effects that whole-body exposure to the Radio-frequency (RF) signals may have. To date, the only health effect from RF fields identified in scientific reviews has been related to an increase in body temperature (> 1°C) from exposure at very high field intensity found only in certain industrial facilities, such as RF heaters. The levels of RF exposure from base stations and wireless networks are so low that the temperature increases are insignificant and do not affect human health. Further, radio and television broadcast stations have been in operation for the past 50 or more years without any adverse health consequence being established. Studies have not provided evidence that RF exposure from the transmitters increases the risk of cancer. No consistent evidence of altered sleep or cardiovascular function has been reported. From all evidence accumulated so far, no adverse short- or long-term health effects have been shown to occur from the RF signals produced by base stations. Since wireless networks produce generally lower RF signals than base stations, no adverse health effects are expected from exposure to them. Though use of mobile phone has created a lot of anxiety about harmful rays, no actual harm has been established.

Sun beds, tanning and UV exposure

The desire to acquire a tan for fashion or cosmetic purposes has led to a large increase in the use of artificial tanning sun beds in, mostly, developed countries. Use of sun beds for tanning continues to increase in popularity, especially among young women. Sun beds used in solariums, and sun tanning lamps, are artificial tanning devices that claim to offer an effective, quick and harmless alternative to natural sunlight. However, there is growing evidence that the ultraviolet (UV) radiation emitted by the lamps used in solariums may damage the skin and increase the risk of developing skin cancer. Most skin cancers are attributable to over-exposure to natural UV radiation.

Exposure to UV, either naturally from the sun or from artificial sources such as sunlamps, is a known risk factor for skin cancer. Short-wavelength UVB (280-315 nm) has been recognized for some time as carcinogenic in experimental animals, and there is increasing evidence that longer-wavelength UVA (315-400 nm) used in sunbeds, which penetrates more deeply into the skin, also contributes to the induction of cancer. A study conducted in Norway and Sweden showed a significant increase in the risk of malignant melanoma among women who had regularly used sunbeds.

Any excessive exposure to UV, not just from sunbeds, can result in structural damage to human skin. In the short- term this damage can be due to burning, fragility and scarring and in the longer-term as photoageing. Photoageing, caused by the breakdown of collagen in the skin by UV, manifests itself as wrinkling and loss of elasticity. The effects of UV on the eye include cataracts, pterygium (a white coloured growth over the cornea) and inflammation of the eye such as photokeratitis and photoconjunctivitis. Furthermore, excessive UV exposure can suppress the immune system, possibly leading to a greater risk.

Particular attention is required to ensure children and adolescents do not use sunbeds.

There is a widespread false belief that a tan acquired using a sunbed will offer good skin protection against sunburn for a holiday in a sunny location. In reality, a tan acquired using a sunbed offers only limited protection against sunburn from solar UV. It has been estimated that a sunbed tan offers the same protective effect as using a sunscreen with a sun protection factor (SPF) of only 2-3.

Impact of temperature, rains, floods and other climatic factors

Marked fluctuations in weather can cause adverse health effects:

- Extremes of both heat and cold can cause potentially fatal illnesses, e.g. heat stress or hypothermia, as well as increasing death rates from heart and respiratory diseases.
- In cities, stagnant weather conditions can trap both warm air and air pollutants—leading to smog episodes with significant health impacts.
- These effects can be significant. Abnormally high temperatures in Europe in the summer of 2003 were associated with at least 27,000 more deaths than the equivalent period in previous years.

Other weather extremes, such as heavy rains, floods, and hurricanes, also have severe impacts on health. Approximately 600,000 deaths occurred world-wide as a result of weather-related natural disasters in the 1990s; and some 95% of these were in poor countries. Some examples:

- In October 1999, a cyclone in Orissa, India, caused 10,000 deaths. The total number of people affected was estimated at 10-15 million; and
- In December 1999, floods in and around Caracas, Venezuela, killed approximately 30,000 people, many in shanty towns on exposed slopes.

In addition to changing weather patterns, climatic

conditions effect diseases transmitted through water, and via vectors such as mosquitoes. Climate-sensitive diseases are among the largest global killers. Diarrhoea, malaria and protein-energy malnutrition alone caused more than 3.3 million deaths globally in 2002, with 29% of these deaths occurring in the Region of Africa.

Global Warming

About two thirds of solar energy reaching Earth is absorbed by, and heats, the Earth's surface. The heat radiates back to the atmosphere, where some of it is trapped by greenhouse gases, such as carbon dioxide. Without this 'greenhouse effect' the average surface temperature would make the planet uninhabitable for human populations. Human activities, particularly burning of fossil fuels, have released over the last 50 years, sufficient quantities of CO_2 and other greenhouse gases to affect the global climate. The atmospheric concentration of carbon dioxide has increased by more than 30% since pre-industrial times, trapping more heat in the lower atmosphere.

According to the Third Assessment Report (2001) of the Intergovernmental Panel on Climate Change (IPCC), some effects include:

- The global average surface temperature has increased by 0.6°C+0.2°C over the last century;
- Globally, 1998 was the warmest year and the 1990s was the warmest decade on record;
- Many areas have experienced increases in rainfall, particularly mid to high latitude countries;
- In some regions, such as parts of Asia and Africa, the frequency and intensity of droughts have increased in recent decades; and
- Episodes of El Niño have been more frequent, persistent and intense since the mid-1970s compared with the previous 100 years.

Global emissions of carbon dioxide are still increasing. They have made the following predictions for the next century:

- Global mean surface temperature will rise by 1.4°-5.8°C. Warming will be greatest over land areas, and at high latitudes;
- The projected rate of warming is greater than anything humans have experienced in the last 10,000 years;
- The frequency of weather extremes is likely to change leading to an increased risk of floods and drought. There will be fewer cold spells but more heat waves;
- The frequency and intensity of El Niño may be affected; and
- Global mean sea level is projected to rise by 9—88 cm by the year 2100.

How the health may be affected?

Health effects of a rapidly changing climate are likely to be overwhelmingly negative, particularly in the poorest communities, which have contributed least to greenhouse gas emissions. Some of the health effects include:

- Increasing frequencies of heat waves.
- Compromising the supply of freshwater, increasing risks of water-borne diseases.
- Rising temperatures are likely to decrease the production of staple foods, increasing risks of malnutrition.
- Rising sea levels increase the risk of coastal flooding, and population displacement.
- Changes in climate are likely to lengthen the transmission seasons of important vector-borne diseases, and to alter their geographic range, potentially bringing them to regions which lack either population immunity or a strong public health infrastructure.

Well-designed urban transport systems can reduce greenhouse gas emissions, while simultaneously reducing the major health impacts of urban air pollution and physical inactivity. Housing with efficient insulation can cut energy consumption and associated greenhouse gas emissions, reduce deaths from both cold and heat, and in poor countries, reduce the need for burning of biomass fuels and the impacts of indoor air pollution.

Hospital's polluted environment and HAI

Hospital-acquired infection (HAI) is an infection that first appears between 48 hours and four days after a patient is admitted to a hospital. About 5–10% of patients admitted to hospitals in the United States develop a hospital-acquired, with an annual total of more than one million people. HAIs are usually related to a procedure or treatment used to diagnose or treat the patient's initial illness or injury. About 36% of these infections are preventable. What can make these infections so troublesome is that they occur in people whose health is already compromised by the condition for which they were first hospitalized. HAI can be caused by bacteria, viruses, fungi, or parasites. These microorganisms may already be present in the patient's body or may come from the environment, contaminated hospital equipment, healthcare workers, or other patients. Depending on the causal agents involved, an infection may start in any part of the body. A localized infection is limited to a specific part of the body and has local symptoms. For example, if a surgical wound in the abdomen becomes infected, the area around the wound becomes red, hot, and painful. A generalized infection is one that enters the bloodstream and causes systemic symptoms such as fever, chills, low blood pressure, or mental confusion. This can lead to sepsis, a serious, rapidly progressive multi-organ infection, sometimes called blood poisoning that can result in death.

"Today over 1.4 million people worldwide are suffering from infections acquired in hospitals," said Dr. Rosenthal. Figures coming from India are alarming with hospital infections rate at over 25 percent. Here hospital acquired infections kill more people than any other form of accidental death. The estimated annual economic cost is more than US$4.5 billion. Nosocomial infections account for about 50% of all major complications of hospitalization, with the remaining being medication errors, patient falls, and other non-infectious adverse events. Most importantly, HAI are often caused by drug resistant organisms which pose a great problem to efforts at management. If these resistant microorganisms gain entry into the community they could cause havoc.

The most common types of hospital-acquired infections are urinary tract infections (UTIs), ventilator-associated pneumonia, and surgical wound infections. Most common sources of infection in their hospital are urinary catheters, central venous (in the vein) catheters, and endotrachial tubes (tubes going through the mouth into the stomach). Catheters going into the body allow bacteria to walk along the outside of the tube into the body where they find their way into the bloodstream. Death has been shown to occur in 4–20% of catheter-related infections. Any type of invasive procedure can expose a patient to the possibility of infection. Some common procedures that increase the risk of hospital-acquired infections include:

- urinary bladder catheterization,
- respiratory procedures such as intubations or mechanical ventilation,
- surgery and the dressing or drainage of surgical wounds,
- gastric drainage tubes into the stomach through the nose or mouth, and
- intravenous (IV) procedures for delivery of medication, transfusion, or nutrition.

Pneumonia is the second most common type of hospital-acquired infection. Bacteria and other microorganisms are easily introduced into the throat by treatment procedures performed to treat respiratory illnesses.

Invasive surgical procedures increase a patient's risk of getting an infection by giving bacteria a route into normally sterile areas of the body. An infection can be acquired from contaminated surgical equipment or from the hands of healthcare workers.

An infection is suspected any time a hospitalized patient develops a fever that cannot be explained by the underlying illness. Some patients, especially the elderly, may not develop a fever. In these patients, the first signs of infection may be rapid breathing or mental confusion.

Prevention

- Adopt an infection control program such as the one sponsored by the U.S. Centers for Disease Control (CDC), which includes quality control of procedures known to lead to infection, and a monitoring program to track infection rates to see if they go up or down.
- Employ an infection control practitioner for every 200 beds.
- Identify high-risk procedures and other possible sources of infection.
- Strict adherence to hand-washing rules by healthcare workers and visitors to avoid passing infectious microorganisms to or between hospitalized patients.
- Strict attention to aseptic (sterile) technique in the performance of procedures, including use of sterile gowns, gloves, masks, and barriers.
- Sterilization of all reusable equipment such as ventilators, humidifiers, and any devices that come in contact with the respiratory tract.
- Frequent changing of dressings for wounds and use of antibacterial ointments under dressings.
- Remove nasogastric (nose to stomach) and endotracheal (mouth to stomach) tubes as soon as possible.
- Use of an antibacterial-coated venous catheter that destroys bacteria before they can get into the blood stream.
- Prevent contact between respiratory secretions and healthcare providers by using barriers and masks as needed.
- Use of silver alloy-coated urinary catheters that destroy bacteria before they can migrate up into the bladder.

- Limitations on the use and duration of high-risk procedures such as urinary catheterization.
- Isolation of patients with known infections.
- Sterilization of medical instruments and equipment to prevent contamination.
- Reductions in the general use of antibiotics to encourage better immune response in patients and reduce the cultivation of resistant bacteria.

Sources

ICNIRP (1998) www.icnirp.org/documents/emfgdl.pdf. IEEE (2006) IEEE C95.1-2005 "IEEE Standard for Safety Levels with Respect to Human Exposure to Radio Frequency Electromagnetic Fields, 3 kHz to 300 GHz"

Andreoli, T.E., J.C. Bennet, C.C. Carpenter, and F. Plum, Cecil Essentials of Medicine. Philadelphia: W.B. Saunders Co., 1997.

Schaffer, S.D., et al. Infection Prevention and Safe Practice, New York: Mosby-Year Book, 1996.

U.S. Center for Disease Control and Prevention (CDC), 1600 Clifton Road, Atlanta, GA 30333, 404-639-3311.

"Safer Hospital Stay, and Reducing Hospital-Born Infections." Health Scout News, 2003 [cited July 7, 2003].

1Air quality guidelines for Europe. Copenhagen, World Health Organization Regional Office for Europe, 1987 (WHO Regional Publications, European Series, No. 23), 2 Air quality guidelines for Europe, 2nd ed. Copenhagen, World Health Organization Regional Office for Europe, 2000 (WHO Regional Publications, European Series, No. 91).

World Health Organization Statistical Information (WHOSIS) WHO (2002) Healthy Environments for Children—Initiating an Alliance for Action. World Health Organization, Geneva.

Healthy Environments for Children—Initiating an Alliance for Action 2002 World Health Organization, Geneva.

Agar, N.S., Halliday, G.M., Barnetson, R.S., et al. (2004), The basal layer in human squamous tumors harbors more UVA than UVB fingerprint mutations: a role for UVA in human skin carcinogenesis, 101(14):4954-9.

AGNIR (2002), Advisory Group on Non-ionising Radiation Health. Effects from Ultraviolet Radiation. Documents of the NRPB 13(1).

ICNIRP (2003) International Commission on Non-Ionizing Radiation Protection. Health Issues of Ultraviolet Tanning Appliances Used for Cosmetic Purposes, Health Physics, 84:119-127.

IEC (1995) International Electrotechnical Commission. Safety of household and similar electrical appliances. Part 2: Particular requirements for appliances for skin exposure to ultraviolet and infrared radiation. Geneva: IEC 335-2-27.

McKinlay, A. and Repacholi, M.H. (2000), Ultraviolet Radiation Exposure, Measurement and Protection, Radiation Protection Dosimetry 91 (vols. 1-3).

United States Department of Health and Human Services (2004) 11th Report of Carcinogens. National Institute of Environmental Health Sciences, Research Triangle Park, NC. p. III-266-267.

Veierød, M.B., Weiderpass, E., Thörn, M., et al. (2003), A prospective study of pigmentation, sun exposure, and risk of cutaneous malignant Melanoma in women, J Nat Cancer Inst 95:1530–1538.

WHO (1994), World Health Organization. Environmental Health Criteria 160. Ultraviolet Radiation Geneva.

WHO (2003), World Health Organization. Artificial tanning sunbeds—risks and guidance. Geneva.

Young, et al. (2003), UV-induced pigmentation in human skin. In: P.U. Giacomoni, ed. Sun Protection in Man. Amsterdam: Elsevier; pp. 357-375.

Young, A. (2004), Tanning devices—Fast track to skin cancer?, Pigment Cell Res, 17: 2-9.

Mishra, Jaideep, Effective Spending, *Economic Times of India*, Nov. 13, 2007.

Meenal Kumar, Improve environment, prevent cancers, *The Tribune*, Jan. 9, 2008.

Aspects of Preventive and Promotive Healthcare

Palliative Care is an Emerging Concept

India has been striving to achieve its goals of health, i.e. to prevent various ailments through better immunization, nutrition, environmental improvements and increasing awareness through various educational means. It has also been making provisions for healthcare to its populations by setting of hospitals in rural as well as urban areas. The concept of providing palliative care to those who cannot be cured or where the prevention of ailments was not possible is relatively a new concept. There have been loopholes in all the areas. Similarly the aspects of proactive promotion of health through yoga, sports, and gyms have been rather sketchy. Today's India needs the human power, infrastructure, financial resources and appropriate healthcare know-how to ensure quality healthcare for all its citizens.

Preventive healthcare

India is a victim of double whammy in the field of healthcare. While lifestyle diseases are invading the health scenario in a big way, infectious diseases have continued to show their ugly head. Environmental degradation combined with weakening public health systems have contributed to the resurgence of Diarrhoea, dysentery, acute respiratory infections and asthma. Around 6 lakh children die each year from an ordinary illness like diarrhoea. While diarrhoea itself could be largely prevented by universal provision of safe drinking water and sanitary conditions, these deaths can be prevented by timely administration of oral rehydration solution, which is presently administered in only 27% of cases. Cancer claims over 3 lakh lives per year and tobacco-related cancers contribute to 50% of the overall cancer burden, which means that such deaths might be prevented by tobacco control measures. Estimates of mental health show about 10 million people suffering from serious mental illness, 20-30 million having neuroses and 0.5 to 1 percent of all children having mental retardation. The Infant Mortality Rate in the poorest 20% of the population is 2.5 times higher than that in the richest 20% of the population. In other words, an infant born in a poor family is two and half times more likely to die in infancy, than an infant in a better-off family. A child in the 'Low standard of living' economic group is almost four times more likely to die in childhood than a child in the better off 'High standard of living' group. A girl is 1.5 times more likely to die before reaching her fifth birthday, compared to a boy! The female to male ratios for children are rapidly declining, from 945 girls per 1000 boys in 1991, to just 927 girls per 1000 boys in 2001. This decline highlights an alarming trend of discrimination against girl children, which starts well before birth (in the form of sex selective abortions), and continues into childhood and adolescence (in the form of worse treatment to girls). Dalit women are one and a half times more likely to suffer the consequences of chronic malnutrition (stunted height) as compared to women from other castes. The delivery of a mother, from the poorest quintile of the population is over six times less likely to be attended by a medically trained person than the delivery of a well-off mother, from the richest quintile of the population. An adivasi mother is half as likely to be delivered by a medically trained person. Thus, preventive health and public health spending are closely related.

Only five other countries in the world are worse off than India regarding public health spending (Burundi, Myanmar, Pakistan, Sudan, and Cambodia). The W.H.O. standard for expenditure on public health is 5% of the GDP. The average spending today by Less Developed Countries is 2.8% of GDP, but India presently spends only 0.9% of its GDP on public health, which is merely one-third of the less developed countries' average. The consequence of this dismally low allocation, which stands at the lowest levels in the last two decades, (in contrast to 1.3% of GDP achieved in 1985), is deteriorating quality of public health services. Over 2 crores of Indians are pushed below the poverty line every year because of the catastrophic effect of out of pocket spending on healthcare. Irrational medical procedures are on the rise. According to just one study in a community in Chennai, 45% of all deliveries were performed by Cesarean operations, whereas the WHO has recommended that not more than 10-15% of deliveries would require Cesarean operations.

Cigarette smoking

One million Indians die every year from tobacco-related diseases. Cigarette smoking is the primary cause of lung cancer, chronic obstructive pulmonary diseases (COPD), coronary artery disease and a major risk factor for coronary heart disease. It is also the primary cause of chronic bronchitis and emphysema. "Passive smoking also called environmental smoke exposure is the phenomenon where non-smokers involuntarily inhale the smoke of nearby smokers. Wives, children and friends of smokers are a highly risk-prone group. Passive smoking is associated with an overall 23 percent increase in risk of coronary heart disease (CHD) among men and women who had never smoked. A lot of harm is caused due to the inhaling of the side stream smoke." "Sidestream smoke is the smoke issued from the burning end of a cigarette between puffs. Mainstream smoke, as distinguished from side-stream smoke, is the one that is exhaled by the smoker after inhalation. Sidestream smoke contains three times more nicotine, three times more tar and about 50 times more ammonia. Inhalation of sidestream smoke by a non-smoker is definitely more harmful to him than to the actual smoker as he inhales more toxins."

Supreme Court directed all states and Union Territories to immediately issue orders banning smoking in public places and public transports, including railways." "The order banning smoking in public places would include hospitals, health institutes, public offices, public transports including railways, court buildings, educational institutions, libraries and auditoriums, the court said. How practical is it to regularly pick up people seen smoking on the road or in other public places and take them to court? Does our police force have the time, manpower and infrastructure to concentrate on smoking offenders, unless they institute a separate 'anti-smoking squad'?

Fluorosis

It occurs due to excessive flourine in drinking water, which is endemic in several areas. Our bones are brittle, our teeth come in colour, we seem to age faster and our babies do not have normal childhood—all works out to a different lifestyle. All of this we owe it to Flouride. We also owe it to several successive central and state administrations, local and other leaders that conveniently forgot about our drinking water problems. We stand corrected! They remind us constantly at every five years or sooner at every election cycle. Our drinking water problem was an election agenda for 4 decades and unfortunately it still is!

Commercialization in medical education

Medical education is commercialized by opening private colleges and making a business out of it. Most of these colleges are not in rural places. Some of the medical colleges do not have enough infrastructure—the hospital, number of beds, and most important, the faculty. According to the report, out of 172 medical colleges and 123 dental colleges in the country, 23 medical and 38 dental colleges are in Karnataka alone. There is 30 to 40 percent of the shortage in teachers in all the health science institutions in the state, resulting in substandard professional education in healthcare. According to a report, commercialization and corruption are two important issues that need to be tackled firmly. Corruption in medical education has raised its head at various levels, and a mechanism should be evolved to root out this cancerous growth, as otherwise it will erode the credibility of the healthcare system in the country. Corruption is visible at every stage, including that of examinations at the undergraduate and postgraduate levels. Starting from joining the medical college—you can buy a seat, you can buy the examiner, the corrupt examination system, you can get question papers in the viva-voce and practicals, many people have paid and it is still continuing. Can we expect better treatment from the doctors who graduated in these circumstances? What are the steps we need to suggest to the government?

There is a need to focus on the following observations:

(1) Metros and cities are becoming crowded; there is plenty of contaminated water, poor sewage system, poor drainage system, new form of living style in the house without using mosquito nets, lack of adequate public healthcare facilities.

(2) It is not possible to check outbreak of any febrile illness like Dengu in crowed cities and metro despite the large number of hospitals.

(3) Present day hospital system dictates maximum bed strength up to 300/350 beds only with more emphasis on ambulatory care, day care treatment, advanced technology with minimal post-procedure stay in the hospital, promotion of home care treatment with family, with more emphasis on utility and supportive services unit of hospital system, more emphasis on preventive and rehabilitative care, integration and innovation of various other technology with healthcare technology and recently new form of medical education system separated from patient care system under single roof with the use of telemedicine, virtual communication technology, more emphasis on use of computers in medical education, more awareness of advanced

technology in education with emphasis shifting to research division in education sector.

(4) If we observe our strength in nursing care, which is most important, it is insignificant. The present ratio with doctor is 1 nurse to 4 doctors. But it should be 4 nurses to one doctor.

(5) If we observe the history and geography of epidemics, we can see maximum outbreak of febrile and communicable diseases were seen in cities, metros except nutritional-related epidemics in rural areas.

Telemedicine and healthcare

(1) The two-way communication in distant medical education, training in new technology, patient referral, and distant follow-up of care,

(2) Integration of clinical, experimental and research data in a multi-centric study all over the country in a single theme.

(3) Clinical marketing for the top dedicated clinicians and surgeons (who can not be made available in various parts of the country).

(4) Feedback information network for clinical, administrative management of one sector, may be government, private, for organizational and policy matters of healthcare at a distance.

(5) Accreditation for qualifying doctors as present scenario dictates not-only recognized qualification, recognized training, but also utilization of qualification and training and the performance through tele network.

(6) Help lines for rural-based doctors for the management of complicated cases.

(7) Future progress of satellite surgery in the country.

(8) Increases awareness among the receivers of healthcare regarding modern treatment and removes the age old taboos from the minds of people.

Health Promotion

Health promotion is "the process of enabling people to increase control over their health and to improve health". It is not directed against any particular disease, but is intended to strengthen the host through a variety of approaches. Health promotion implies general measures undertaken to improve the health of community at large. Health promotion generally refers to broad measures undertaken in pre-pathogenesis phase, i.e. before the occurrence of disease. Providing safe water supply is not directed towards cholera or jaundice only rather provision of safe water is a general measure and a part of quality of life. Similarly ensuring provision of safe blood transfusion facilities as a health promotion measure is neither directed towards a particular individual or community nor towards a specific disease (HIV/AIDS). Health promotion measures address the whole society, large scale ventures and hence are very costly.

The well-known interventions in this area are:

(i) health education,
(ii) environmental modifications,
(iii) nutritional interventions, and
(iv) lifestyle and behavioural changes.

The Ottawa Charter for Health Promotion (WHO, 1986) has led to the development of a series of health promotion initiatives based on settings. The pressures for hospitals to broaden their role from the focus on treating diseases towards health promotion have been felt for a long time.

Hospitals are in a strong position within the healthcare system to be advocates for health promotion. The hospitals are seen as credible sources of advice and expertise on health issues beyond their responsibilities for sick care services.

The key elements of a health promotion programme should include:

- strong leadership at different levels of the organization (especially from the Board of Management, Chief Executive Officer, Assistant Chief Executive Officer, Health Promotion

Consultant and several champions from corporate and clinical areas);

- incorporation of health promotion into the hospital's vision and strategic role statements, policies, service agreements with divisions, and job descriptions for staff, as well as a specific health promotion policy;
- strategic, operational and evaluation plans for health promotion;
- staff development and education; and
- resources allocated (human, physical facilities and financial).

Delegating health promotion

This approach has been observed in hospitals that have a health promotion unit, have designated health promotion workers, or have established community-oriented visions or departments who 'do health promotion' or 'have a community orientation' for the hospital. A common phenomenon observed in organizations with this orientation is that staff working in these roles, departments or divisions often became limited in the impact they can have on re-orientation of the broader hospital, as health promotion was often seen as 'their job'. Hospitals in the United States are increasingly positioning themselves as the leading provider of health promotion services within the community. Traditionalists argue that hospitals should maintain their long-established role as centers for acute care, relegating the responsibility for public health education to other community agencies. Progressive hospital leaders, however, are establishing integrated healthcare systems as a strategy for long-term survival.

In today's health-conscious environment, physicians continue to be perceived as the primary source of useful and reliable health information, but few people are satisfied with the information they receive from their physicians. Most people associate hospitals with physicians and transfer this perceived reliability and credibility to hospital-based activities. In many communities the hospital is identified as a centre for health. It seems likely, therefore, that people would want hospitals to take a leading role in health promotion.

Patient Education

One of the earliest health promotion initiatives within a hospital was the establishment of formal programmes for patient education. Many social factors led to the increased interest in patient education observed in the late 1960s and 1970s including: the increased prevalence of chronic diseases requiring long-term and continuous management, often self-administered; a growing social concern about containing costs, the utilization of health services, and quality care; the consumer movement, public demand for influence in medical care decisions, and frustration with the complexities of the healthcare delivery system; documented evidence that patient education helps attain treatment goals; legislation related to informed consent; and malpractice issues. In response to these factors and others, supportive documents, mandates and guidelines have evolved to further entrench patient and family education as an integral component of quality care and professional practice in hospitals.

Many studies have demonstrated the benefits that patients realize from a planned and coordinated approach to patient education. Reductions in length in stay, reductions in complications, and reductions in admissions and readmissions to hospital are the benefits to patients most widely documented in research on patient education.

Clinical rehabilitation programmes that incorporate exercise therapy and health education enhance the continuity of care and treatment of people moving from the inpatient unit to the outpatient unit or home treatment. Following the treatment and stabilization of an illness, a rehabilitation programme is designed to return the person to a level of health equal to or greater than the level before the illness. The goal of clinical rehabilitation programmes is to improve stamina and strength, return people to their homes and activities of daily living, and at the same time prevent recurrence of the illness or injury.

Clinical rehabilitation programmes. typically provided by hospitals include: cardiac rehabilitation and pulmonary rehabilitation; exercise therapy to rehabilitate mental health patients and those suffering from substance abuse and eating disorders; and sports medicine. Self-directed, home rehabilitation programmes are prudent alternatives to structured hospital-based programmes. Typically, the guide for the home programme is provided on discharge from the hospital. Rehabilitation professionals carefully educate people in exercise and lifestyle modification. Home programmes require frequent follow-up to evaluate progress, encourage adherence, and provide support.

Community and Corporate Wellness

Wellness programmes are designed to educate and motivate individuals to reduce their risk of preventable diseases. By adopting healthy lifestyle practices, the individual decreases the risk of premature death and disability, and the costs associated with medical care. The enhanced community relations and direct revenue resulting from providing health promotion services can justify entry into the wellness arena for many hospitals. Hospital-based programmes are typically directed at three audiences: apparently well groups or individuals within the community, employees of local businesses and industries (and their dependants), and the health professionals and other staff employed by the hospital. The programmes encompass a broad spectrum of activities and services, and are planned to address the health-related needs and interests of the target population.

It is a truism to say that education and counseling are most effective provided as near as possible to the time when need arises. In a study by Wallace (1988) patients expressed a consistent preference for preparation (including booklets) prior to hospitalization rather than after admission. With the use of individualized care plans and the encouragement of active participation of patients in their care, there ought to be a continual monitoring of educational need and organization of appropriately timed response. Much of this response may take place on a one-to-one basis in association with other ongoing activities. In addition, there may be needs which could usefully, and cost effectively, be met through group methods.

A model of health promotion

Tannahill has developed an elegant model in which health promotion is viewed as a number of different combinations of prevention, health protection and health education (Downie, Fyfe and Tannahill, 1992). The model however, differs in its concern to emphasize and explicate the contribution made by education; its structure represents a development of the familiar health field concept.

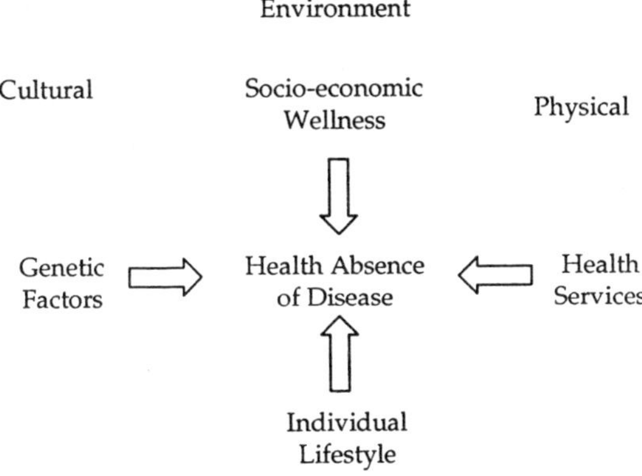

The contribution of health education

The Alma Ata and Ottawa declarations insist that neither people nor health should be seen in isolation. Each is nested in systems that profoundly affect behaviour and health. Health promotion must take this ecological fact into account. Such an ecological view represents a move away from the educationist tendency of biomedical science and some applications of health education in the service of centralized, categorical, and vertical programs, to a broader systems view. This view recognizes the interaction of life-style and environment when health is being considered. In this view, the individual and the context are of equal account. It legitimates both a life-style and a systems approach to health promotion.

An ecological model of health promotion says that health is the product of the individual's continuous interaction and interdependence with his or her ecosphere—

The Health Field Concept

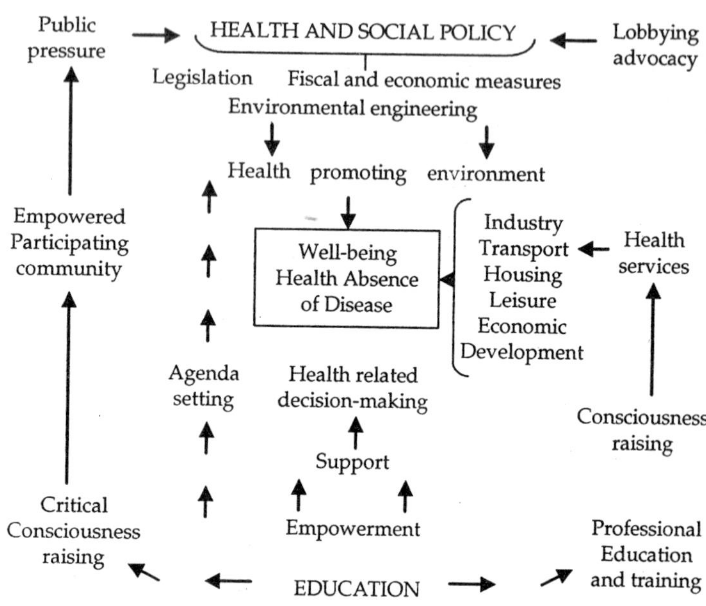

this is, the family, the community, the culture, the societal structure, and the physical environment. Characteristic modes of interacting over time constitute a life-style, as distinct from discrete acts or behaivour. The determinants of a life-style must be seen as a combination of intrapersonal and external environmental forces, continuously interacting. In some instances, health promotion programs need to emphasize the individual or behavioural side, in others, the environmental side needs emphasis as the point of intervention. If the individual has a sense of harmony with, or a degree of mastery over, the everyday environment, then his or her health is likely to be good. But with oppression, poverty, limited opportunity, and lack of mastery, health will suffer.

Health, in the Ottawa Charter, is still given the original WHO definition of a state of complete physical, mental, and social well-being, to reach which "an individual or group must be able to identify and to realize aspirations, to satisfy needs, and to change or cope with the environment" (WHO,

1986). Of special importance is inclusion of yoga in the management of illnesses. Sufficient evidence need to be collected on this aspect so that a scientific basis can be provided to yoga training in hospitals. Hospitals should be projected as role models for adopting HP practices e.g. hygiene, environmental cleanliness, food hygiene, safe water supply, provision of healthy food, clear air. People's religious sentiments may also be honoured by providing prayer facilities within the premise.

Palliative care is an emerging concept

According to the WHO, at least a million terminal cases of cancer are diagnosed in India every year. Now, there is some solace for them in the form of palliative care, some comfort in the form of love and care. Palliative care is any form of medical care or treatment that concentrates on reducing the severity of disease symptoms, rather than providing a cure. The goal is to prevent and relieve suffering and to improve quality of life for people facing serious, complex illness. A recent WHO statement calls palliative care "an approach that improves the quality of life of patients and their families facing the problems associated with life-threatening illness." The term "palliative care" is now increasingly being used with regard to diseases other than cancer as well, such as chronic, progressive pulmonary disorders, renal disease, chronic heart failure or progressive neurological conditions. Palliative care improves the quality of life of patients and families who face life-threatening illness, by providing pain and symptom relief, spiritual and psychosocial support to from diagnosis to the end of life and bereavement.

In nutshell Palliative care provides the following:

- provides relief from pain and other distressing symptoms;
- affirms life and regards dying as a normal process;
- intends neither to hasten or postpone death;
- integrates the psychological and spiritual aspects of patient care;

- offers a support system to help patients live as actively as possible until death;
- offers a support system to help the family cope during the patients illness;
- uses an approach to address the needs of patients and bereavement counseling;
- will enhance quality of life, and may also positively influence the course of illness; and
- conjunction with other therapies that are intended to prolong life, such as chemotherapy or radiation therapy, and includes those investigations needed to better understand and manage distressing clinical complications.

A relatively recent development is the concept of a dedicated healthcare team that is entirely geared toward palliative treatment, called a palliative care team. The goals of palliative treatment are extremely concrete: relief from suffering, treatment of pain and other distressing symptoms, psychological and spiritual care, a support system to help the individual live as actively as possible, and a support system to sustain the individual's family.

Hospice and palliative care

Hospice is a movement to improve care for people who were dying alone, isolated, in hospitals. In 2005 more than 1.2 million individuals and their family caregivers received hospice care. It is the Medicare benefit in U.S. that includes pharmaceuticals, medical equipment, twenty-four hour/seven day a week access to care and support for loved ones following a death. The majority of hospice care is delivered at home or in a home-like (hospice) residence. Hospice care is also available to people in nursing homes, assisted living facilities, veterans facilities, hospitals and prisons. In most countries, hospice and palliative care is provided by an interdisciplinary team consisting of physicians, registered nurses, social workers, hospice chaplains, physiotherapists, occupational therapists, complimentary therapists, volunteers and, most importantly, the family.

Dealing with distress

The key to effective palliative care is to provide a safe way for the individual to address their physical and psychological distress, that is to say their total suffering, a concept first thought up by Dame Cicely Saunders, and now widely used. Dealing with total suffering involves a broad range of concerns, starting with treating physical symptoms such as pain, nausea and breathlessness. The palliative care teams have become very skillful in prescribing drugs for physical symptoms, and have been instrumental in showing how drugs such as morphine can be used safely while maintaining a patient's full faculties and function. However, when a patient exhibits a physiological symptom, there are often psychological, social, or spiritual symptoms as well. The interdisciplinary team, which often includes a social worker or a counselor and a chaplain, can play a role in helping the patient and family cope globally with these symptoms, rather than depending on the medical/pharmacological interventions alone. Usually, a palliative care patient's concerns are pain, fears about the future, loss of independence, worries about their family, and feeling like a burden. While some patients will want to discuss psychological or spiritual concerns and some will not, it is fundamentally important to assess each individual and their partners and families need for this type of support. Denying an individual and their support system an opportunity to explore psychological or spiritual concerns is just as harmful as forcing them to deal with issues they either don't have or choose not to deal with. Alternative medical treatments such as relaxation therapy, massage, music therapy, and acupuncture can relieve some cancer-related symptoms and other causes of suffering.

Euthanasia as a palliative care

It is widely defined as "the intentional killing by act or omission of a dependent human being for his or her alleged benefit." Voluntary euthanasia refers to a situation where the person who is killed has requested to be killed. Involuntary Euthanasia refers to a situation where the person who is killed made an expressed wish to the contrary. Non-voluntary euthanasia refers to a situation where the person who is killed made no request and gave no consent. Assisted suicide refers to a situation where someone provides an individual with the information, guidance, and means to take his or her own life. When it is a doctor who helps another person, to kill themselves it is called 'physician assisted suicide' Euthanasia By Action refers to a situation of intentionally causing a person's death by performing an action such as by giving a lethal injection. Euthanasia is usually suggested as a measure of relief for 'terminally ill' persons, who are bound to face death in a short span of time. The measure is meant to alleviate suffering, by hastening the inevitable death. The argument that is usually raised is that in medicine, one cannot ever say for certain, what a person's life expectancy will be like, even if their medical condition is really hopeless. Increasingly, however, euthanasia activists have dropped references to terminal illness, replacing them with such phrases as 'hopelessly ill', 'desperately ill', 'incurably ill', 'hopeless condition', and 'meaningless life.'

Euthanasia has, so far been legalized in Northern Australia in 1995, the US state of Oregon in 1998, Netherlands in 2001 and Belgium in 2002. The Netherlands and Belgium have legalized euthanasia as well as assisted suicide, whereas Oregon has legalized assisted suicide. Both euthanasia and assisted suicide have been widely practiced in the Netherlands since 1973 although they were against the law until 2002.

Euthanasia has not been specifically covered in any Indian statute. The closest the issue has come to be addressed, is in section 309 of the Indian Penal Code,1860, which states that an attempt to suicide is a criminal offence. While it is considered as an offence under the same section, any person assisting an attempt to commit euthanasia, can be accused u/s 306 of IPC for abetment to suicide. A bench comprising Justice Y.K. Sabharwal and Mr. Justice P.P. Naolekar issued notice to the Centre on the PIL by NGO 'Common Cause', which argued that right to life under Article 21 of the Constitution included right to live with human dignity. Every individual should have a right to execute a 'Living Will' expressing his or her desire to have or not to have an extraordinary life prolonging measures when his or her recovery from any terminal illness is not possible. The petition argued that a person should be allowed to execute a 'Living Will' before getting into a state of permanent vegetative state, the petition said, adding that he should have a right to refuse treatments like feeding through hydration tubes, being kept on ventilators or other life supporting machines. Government of India has not enacted any legislation on this behalf.

Sources

SRS Bulletin, 'Government of India', 1998.

Planning Commission, Government of India, Tenth Five Year Plan 2002-2007. Volume II.

International Institute for Population Sciences and ORC Macro. National Family Health Survey (NFHS-II) 1998-99, India.

International Institute for Population Sciences, RCH-RHS India, 1998-1999.

National Crime Records Bureau. Ministry of Home Affairs. Accidental Deaths and Suicides In India, 2000.

World Health Organization. The World Health Report, 2003.

International Institute for Population Sciences, Facility Survey, 1999.

Misra, Chatterjee, Rao, India Health Report, Oxford University Press, New Delhi, 2003.

Morbidity and Treatment of Ailments, NSS Fifty second round, Government of India, 1998.

Changing the Indian Health System—Draft Report, ICRIER, 2001.

Shariff Abusaleh, India Human Development Report, Oxford University Press, New Delhi,

Duggal,Ravi, Operationalizing Right to Healthcare in India, Right to Healthcare, Moving from Idea to Reality.

CEHAT Mumbai, 2003.

National Coordination Committee for the Jana Swasthya Sabha, Health for All NOW, 2004.

Central Bureau of Health Intelligence, Directorate General of Health Services, Ministry of Health and Family Welfare, Health Information of India, 2000 and 2001.

National Sample Survey Organization, Department of Statistics, GOI, 42nd and 52nd Round.

Census of India 2001: Provisional Population Totals, Registrar General and Census Commissioner, GOI.

Pai, M. *et al.*, A high rate of Cesaerean sections in affluent section of Chennai, is it a cause for concern?, *Nat Med J India*, 1999, 12:156-158.

TB India 2003, RNTCP Stats Report,Central TB Division, DDHS GOI.

Health Survey and Development Committee, GOI, 1946 (Bhore Report).

Mahal, A. www.worldbank.org

Phadke, A. Drug Supply and Use, Towards a Rational Policy in India, Sage Publications, New Delhi.

Ministry of Chemicals and Fertilizers.

Matching Services to needs, Copenhagen, WHO Regional Office for Europe, 2002 (document EUR/RC50/10).

WHO Regional Office for Europe, Health Promoting Hospital, (http://www.euro.who.int/healthpromohosp), Copenhagen, WHO Regional Office for Europe, 2002 (accessed 4 March 2004).

Vienna Recommendations for Health Promoting Hospitals (http:/Iwww.euro.who.int/document/IHB/hphviennarecom.pdf) (accessed 4 March, 2004).

Ottawa Charter for Health Promotion (http://www.who/int/hpr/NPH/docs/ottawa_charter_hp.pdf). Ottawa, WHO, 1986 (accessed 4 March 2004).

WHO, Standards Working Group, Development of standards for disease prevention and health promotion, WHO, Meeting on standards for disease prevention and health promotion, Bratislava, 14 May 2002.

The International Society for Quality in Healthcare, Alpha and accreditation (http://www.isqua.org.au/isquaPages/Alpha.html). Victoria, Isqua, 2003 (accessed 4 March 2004).

WHO Definition of Palliative Care, World Health Organization, Retrieved on March 07, 2006.

Seymour, J.E; D. Clark, M. Winslow (2004), "Morphine use in cancer pain: from 'last resort' to 'gold standard', Poster presentation at the Third research Forum of the European Association of Palliative Care,", Palliative Medicine 18(4): 378.

Center to Advance Palliative Care, www.capc.org

Joanne Lynn (2004), Sick to death and not going to take it anymore!: reforming healthcare for the last years of life, Berkeley: University of California Press, 72, ISBN 0-520-24300-5.

Zerzan, J.; S. Stearns, L. Hanson (2000), "Access to palliative care and hospice in nursing homes", *Journal of the American Medical Association* 284: 2489-2494.

2007, Center to Advance Palliative Care.

Walsh, D., Gombeski, W., Goldstein, P., Hayes, D., Armour, M. (1994), "Managing a palliative oncology program: the role of a business plan", J. Pain Symptom Manage 9(2): 109, PMID 7517428.

Center to Advance Palliative Care, www.capc.org

See Existential pain—an entity, a provocation, or a challenge? in Journal of Pain Symptom and Management, Volume 27, Issue 3, pp. 241-250 (March 2004).

CLIP: Current Learning in Palliative Care. Online tutorials, Help the Hospices, Retrieved on March 07, 2006.

Integration of behavioural and relaxation approaches into the treatment of chronic pain and insomnia, NIH Technology Assessment Panel on Integration of Behavioural and Relaxation Approaches into the Treatment of Chronic Pain and Insomnia, *The Journal of the American Medical Association* (archives) (1996), Retrieved on March 07, 2006.

Walker, Walker *et al.* (1999), Psychological, clinical and pathological effects of relaxation training and guided imagery during primary chemotherapy (abstract), PubMed, National Center for Biotechnology Information (NCBI), Retrieved on March 07, 2006.

Grealish, L., Lomasney, A., Whiteman, B. (2000), Foot massage, A nursing intervention to modify the distressing symptoms of pain and nausea in patients hospitalized with cancer (abstract), PubMed, NCBI, Retrieved on March 07, 2006.

Cassileth, Vickers, Magill. (2003), Music therapy for mood disturbance during hospitalization for autologous stem cell transplantation: a randomized controlled trial (abstract), PubMed, NCBI, Retrieved on March 07, 2006.

David, Alimi *et al.* (2003), Analgesic Effect of Auricular Acupuncture for Cancer Pain: A Randomized, Blinded, Controlled Trial, *Journal of Clinical Oncology*, Retrieved on March 07, 2006.

Cassel, C.K. ICD-9 code for palliative or terminal care. N Engl J Med 1996; 335: 1232-4. 2. Sullivan, A.D., Hedberg, K., Hopkins, D., Legalized physician-assisted suicide in Oregon, 1998-2000, *N Engl J Med* 2001; 344:605-7.

Quill, T.E., Lo B, Brock, D.W., Palliative options of last resort: a comparison of voluntarily stopping eating and drinking, terminal sedation, physician-assisted suicide, and voluntary active euthanasia, *JAMA*, 1997; 278:2099-104.

Ganzini, L., Goy, E.R., Miller, L.L., Harvath, T.A., Jackson, A., Delrot, M.A., Nurses' experiences with hospice patients who refuse food and fluids to hasten death, *N Engl J Med* 2003; 349:359-65.

Women's Healthcare and Empowerment

Gender Budgeting may Help

Just as there is no one type of woman, there is no single strategy for promoting good health among all women, at all stages of their lives. Whether it's researching how to increase the survival of girl child, breastfeeding, immunization, reproductive complications, midlife crisis, mammogram usage, cardiovascular disease preventive behaviours, or promoting safer sex practices, you have to constantly look for new and innovative ways to have access to all the women from newborn babe to extreme old age. To truly have an impact on women's health, we must ask questions that address every aspect of a woman's life and at all the stages from birth to sunset. Does a young girl play sports? If she does, she's more likely to have good physical and psychological health. Does a young adult woman get regular screenings for cervical cancer? If so, cervical cancer can be prevented from developing almost 100% of the time. The lifelong interaction between a woman and her environment, cultural and social influences, personal and familial responsibilities, psychological and physical characteristics and lifestyle choices these are true indicators of how healthy a woman's life can be.

Women's health is best explored not as a series of isolated medical conditions but in terms of all the factors that affect a woman's health and quality of life, at various stages, throughout her lifespan. On the one hand we see a new age woman whose life is changing on every level. She's living in a different family structure than her mother did; she's marrying later, if at all; she's more likely to be the sole head of a household; she's working; she's getting older; and she's living longer. On the other hand, there is a woman living in traditional society, who is fully subjugated and powerless even to survive or thrive. We consider women's health as encompassing all functions that relate to women's mental and physical wellness from conception, neonatal period, infancy, childhood, puberty, youth, adult, midlife, old age, the factors that affect wellness and the activities and behaviours that promote it. Although lives are a continual process of learning, adapting and growing, women's lives involve several stages viz. newborn and neonatal period, infancy, childhood, puberty, adolescence, youthhood, marriage and pregnancy, antenatal period, childbirth and postnatal care, pre-menopausal stage, postmenopausal health problems, old age and so on. Each stage has to be studied in some detail to bring wellness, development and empowerment in her life.

At the level of ministry of women and child in the central government and as well as at the state level, we should work to promote healthful behaviours and practices by all women, across all the stages of their lives. Among other things, for all ages we want to encourage routine and appropriate immunization, physical activity, good nutritional habits, safe sexual choices, no tobacco use, healthy development and ageing. We also need to work with NGOs, business organizations, and state and local health departments, among others. America's office of women's health (OWH) can be used as a model to set-up a nodal agency to supervise all aspects of women's health, at all stages of their lives. We need to discuss the key issues that affect women at each stage of life, from birth through the end of life. We need to focus on promoting longevity coupled with better quality of life besides preventing disease, injury, and disability. Our message is that just by changing the mindset towards the girl child and women, over time—many of the diseases, injuries, and disabilities experienced by women can be prevented and thus women can be empowered.

In the first instance health of a girl child 'newborn to preschool' stage has to be taken care of. It deals with issues concerning the hostility, neglect and discrimination towards girls from pre-birth times through the stages of neonatal period, infancy and pre-school phase of her life. The emphasis is required on the psyche of Indian mothers and the aspects of female feticide, infanticide and the consequent unfavourable male to female ratio in our societies. It requires care of aspects like prematurity, birth defects, and parenting hassles during infancy.

The second stage comprises growth and development of girl children from 5-12 years of age. It highlights the feeding and nutrition, immunization, basics of different foods, common medical conditions, pre-pubertal zone, health problems of girls and various forms of violence unleashed on them.

Subsequent stages include aspects of health of teenager girls and female youths and how to solve their myriad of problems. Then comes the reproductive phase consisting of pregnancy and antenatal care and childbirth and postnatal care. One of the major challenges of Reproductive phase is addressing the barriers in communication and access and to improve dialogue between diverse stakeholders, particularly women in the community. Knowledge, tradition, stigma and accessibility of services are identified as the key primary factors affecting decision-making of women in the community, particularly on their health-related issues.

There is a special concern for the needs and healthcare concerns of women in their early midlife. The husbands, children and medical practitioners alike often overlook women, as soon as their reproductive phase is over and they enter in postmenopausal phase of their midlife. The next phase of life, i.e. old age brings more health problems and even more discrimination, neglect and violence. This phase can be dealt in two parts, one dealing with the general health and social problems and the other with the diseases that occur in old age. Besides health focus on the development and empowerment of women is constantly required at all ages. Women's healthcare is not merely a slogan; it is to provide facilities for better health, education, nutrition, job opportunities, legal rights, social status, and gender equality-sans discrimination or violence of any kind. Further the society has to provide for a comprehensive care of women's socio-economic development and entrepreneurship of women. A detailed insight into various issues can be had by referring to the set of 12 volumes entitled 'better health for all women: Asian women's wellness, development and empowerment'. By Dr. R. Kumar and Dr. Meenal Kumar.

The contents of each of the volumes are given below:

Volume 1

1. Female babies are vulnerable; let them not perish
2. Baby Girl is born: Celebrate it
3. Nurture your newborn: Shed prejudices
4. Challenges of neonatal period
5. Prematurity signals more risks
6. Growth and Development: commit to successful parenting
7. Love your infant girl; key to healthy emotional growth
8. Emotional development: take her tantrums in your stride

Volume 2

1. Girl child: Saga of Stunned growth and short life
2. Basics of good food: Nutritional journey through childhood to puberty
3. Simple and sure way to save children: Immunization
4. Common Medical conditions: childhood revisited in sickness
5. Pre-Pubertal Zone: A period of rapid march towards teen-age
6. Gynecological and other problems in childhood: specific to girl-child
7. Violence against girls: Son preference can unleash the devil.

Volume 3

1. Adolescent health and development
2. Determinants of teenager girl's health
3. Physical growth and mental development
4. Fitness for every teenager
5. Sex education is essential
6. Adolescent sexuality
7. Realities of premature reproduction
8. Accidents and teens: close encounters

Volume 4

1. Youth health and development
2. Health conditions specific to youth
3. Substance abuse among the youth
4. Physical health problems during youth-hood
5. Communicable diseases among youth
6. Non-communicable diseases among the youth
7. Mental health issues and problems in young females
8. The marriage, Sacrosanct vow to safe sex and planned progeny

Volume 5

1. Public policy: Women's health during reproductive years
2. Genetic counseling is essential
3. Anatomy and physiology of reproductive apparatus
4. Planning safer motherhood
5. High risk and complicated pregnancy
6. Healthy mother and healthy child: Good antenatal care

Volume 6

1. The normal childbirth and caesarean delivery
2. Mother needs critical care after childbirth

3. Abortions and miscarriages
4. Infertility can make life fruitless
5. Diseases and medical conditions in women's prime of life

Volume 7

1 Women's Diversity Knows No-bounds: health burdens in early mid-life
2 Trials and Tribulations to Wellness after 40: Poor and powerless women
3 Environment and health: women are on the receiving end
4 Love in the afternoon of life: Women, ageing and sexuality
5 Excess weight adds to health problems: Obesity in pre-menopausal period and after
6 Excessive menstrual bleeding: why lose uterus in mid life?

Volume 8

1 Devil of Menopause Strikes: Loss of womenhood or newfound freedom?
2 Heart disease high blood pressure: Pros and cons of prevention
3 Universal health problems: Osteoporosis, urinary incontinence
4 Cancers in mid-life: Major risks in menopausal
5 More health conditions specific to women: are you fit?
6 Mid life crisis: Study of mental health.

Volume 9

1. Gender bias get accentuated in old age
2. Chronic ailments come naturally in old age
3. Aches and pains are Inevitable with ageing
4. Ageing brings multiple losses: memory, hair, breath, balance, and confidence
5. Violence against senior women

Volume 10

1. Diseases of bones and joints
2. Diseases of Heart, brain, kidneys
3. Diseases of Lung and respiratory diseases
4. Diseases of Urogenital system
5. Diseases of Liver and pancreas
6. Diseases of vision and hearing
7. Diseases of mind in older women
8. Frequently asked questions (FAQs)

Volume 11

1. Health development and Women Empowerment
2. Healthcare systems in India and women
3. Violence against women and health problems
4. Discrimination and women
5. Women and human rights
6. Law: A powerful tool to empower women
7. Women and democracy

Volume 12

1. Socio-economic development and women
2. Entrepreneurship and women
3. Women and Industry
4. Women and Agriculture
5. Rural Women: More poor and powerless
6. Women and education

The Nobel laureate Amartya Sen's Hypothesis

Inequality and discrimination lead to compromised healthcare and disempowerment of women. Queen Victoria wrote "That . . . within each community, nationality and class, the burden of hardship often falls disproportionately on women". The afflicted world in which we live is characterized by deeply unequal sharing of the burden of adversities between women and men. Gender inequality exists in most parts of the world; it can take very many different forms.

(1) Mortality inequality

In some regions in the world, inequality between women and men directly involves matters of life and death, and takes the brutal form of unusually high mortality rates of women and a consequent preponderance of men in the total population, as opposed to the preponderance of women found in societies with little or no gender bias in healthcare and nutrition. India is one such country. This type of gender inequality need not entail any conscious homicide, and it would be a mistake to try to explain this large phenomenon by invoking the occasional cases of female infanticide that are reported from India; these are truly dreadful events when they occur, but they are relatively rare. Rather, the mortality disadvantage of women works mainly through a widespread neglect of health, nutrition and other interests of women that influence survival.

Indeed, female fetuses tend to have a lower probability of miscarriage than male fetuses have. Everywhere in the world, more male babies are born than female babies (and an even higher proportion of male foetuses are conceived compared with female foetuses), but throughout their respective lives the proportion of males goes on falling as we move to higher and higher age groups, due to typically greater male mortality rates. The excess of females over males in the population of Europe and North America comes about as a result of this greater survival chance of females in different age groups. Kerala in India provides a sharp contrast with many other parts of the country in having little or no gender bias in mortality. Indeed, not only is the life expectancy of Kerala women at birth above 76 (compared with 70 for men), the female-male ratio of Kerala's population is 1.06 according to the 2001 Census (possibly somewhat raised by greater migration for work by men, but certainly no lower than the West European or North American ratios, which are around 1.05 or so). Also Kerala's fertility rate around 1.7 or 1.8 is one of the lowest in the developing world (about the same as in Britain and France, and much lower than in the United States).

(2) Natality inequality

With the availability of modern techniques to determine the gender of the fetus, sex-selective abortion has become common in India. The female-male ratio for the 0-5 age group is 94.8 in Germany, 95.0 in the U.K., and 95.7 in the U.S., and perhaps we can sensibly pick the German ratio of 94.8 as the cut-off point below which we should suspect anti-female intervention. There are the States in the north and the west where the female-male ratio of children is consistently below the benchmark figure, led by Punjab, Haryana, Delhi and Gujarat (with ratios between 79.3 and 87.8), and also others, Himachal Pradesh, Madhya Pradesh, Rajasthan, Uttar Pradesh, Maharashtra, Jammu and Kashmir, and Bihar. On the other side of the divide, the States in the east and the south tend to have female-male ratios that are above the benchmark line of 94.8 girls per 100 boys: with Kerala, Andhra Pradesh, West Bengal and Assam (each between 96.3 and 96.6), and others.

(3) Basic facility inequality

There are many countries in Asia where girls have far less opportunity of schooling than boys do. India is struggling to come out of it.

(4) Special opportunity inequality

The opportunities of higher education may be far fewer for young women than for young men.

(5) Professional inequality

In terms of employment as well as promotion in work and occupation, women often face greater handicap than men.

(6) Ownership inequality

In many societies the ownership of property can also be very unequal. Even though traditional property rights have favoured men in the bulk of India, in what is now the State of Kerala, there has been, for a long time, matrilineal inheritance for an influential part of the community, namely the Nairs.

(7) Household inequality

The family arrangements can be quite unequal in terms of sharing the burden of housework and child care. It is, for example, quite common in many societies to take it for granted that while men will naturally work outside the home, women could do it if and only if they could combine it with various inescapable and unequally shared household duties.

Let us observe four substantial phenomena that happen in India.

(a) Undernourishment of girls

At the time of birth, girls are obviously no more nutritionally deprived than boys are, but this situation changes as society's unequal treatment takes over from nature's non-discrimination. Often enough, the differences may particularly arise from the neglect of healthcare of girls compared with what boys get. Undernourishment may well result from greater morbidity, which can adversely affect both the absorption of nutrients and the performance of bodily functions.

(b) High incidence of maternal undernourishment

Maternal under nutrition and anemia are more common than in most other regions of the world.

(c) Prevalence of low birth weight

In India, as many as 21 percent of children are born clinically underweight. In terms of weight for age, South Asia has around 40 to 60 percent children undernourished compared with 20 to 40 percent undernourishment even in Africa. The children start deprived and stay deprived.

(d) High incidence of cardiovascular diseases

India stands out as having more cardiovascular diseases than any other part of the third world. Researchers have shown that low birth weight is closely associated with higher incidence, many decades later, of several adult diseases, including hypertension, glucose intolerance, and cardiovascular hazards. What begins as a neglect of the interests of women ends up causing adversities in the health and survival of all—even at an advanced age? The extensive penalties of neglecting women's interests rebounds, it appears, on men with a vengeance.

Spiritual Health Empowerment

Sri Aurobindo Society has a Women's Wing, to awaken them through the valuable words of The Mother. The Mother gives special attention and force to women. Modern woman does not wish to remain 'just a house wife'. Woman is basically a 'shakti', the dynamic creative and executive energy of the divine Reality or Being. Unfortunately, a girl is treated as delicate and protected being. Let each parent remember to bring up a child as a human being, a soul with its own individual needs and aspirations. Nature has chosen woman as a medium for creation and has therefore bestowed her with a motherly instinct in which love, care, humility, harmony, beauty and grace predominate. What should be done to develop her as a shakti?

(a) Physical

She has to make her body healthy, agile, supple, strong, capable of endurance, beautiful, graceful, and above all conscious and receptive.

Woman has a great responsibility in bearing children. The child must be consciously prayed for. In ancient India, women used to undertake austerities and prepare themselves in order to give birth to a worthy soul.

Pre-Natal Education

(b) Vital

She has to cultivate her emotions, feelings and aspirations to be high, noble, pure, transparent, peaceful, powerful, bal selfless, full of flaming joy and fervour.

(c) Mental

She has to mould her thoughts to be calm, concentrated, clear, complex, wide, organized, positive, sharp and sensitive to the new knowledge that is ready to descent on earth.

(d) Psychic and Spiritual

She should aspire and strive to unfold the ever-perfect spirit within. She has to develop her intuition. The future race will be intuitive, a faculty beyond mind, which will give it certain knowledge at every moment, in each field and phase of life.

In the occult-spiritual view no human being is exclusively made of feminine or masculine qualities. There is a male aspect in every woman and a female aspect in every man. An educated and enlightened woman well-informed in child-education, health-care, sanitation, nutrition and population control can bring down infant-mortality, control birth-rate in the family, keep the environment clean, bring up a healthy child, supplement or support or even enhance the education given to the child at the school by her own educational inputs and if she is trained in a productive skill, can bring additional income to the family. Thus it is the educated and enlightened woman-power which has the greatest potentiality to enhance the quality of life of a community.

- She is symbol of divine shakti,
- All knowledge, all strength, all triumph and victory, all skill and works are in her hands and they are full of the treasures of the Spirit and of all perfection and siddhis,
- She is Maheshwari, goddess of the supreme knowledge,
- She is Mahakali, goddess of the supreme strength,
- She is Mahalakshmi, the goddess of the supreme love and delight,
- She is Mahasaraswati, the gooddess of divine skill and of the works of the Spirit,
- Elected Women Representatives (EWRs) and gender budgeting.

Gender Budgeting

Elected Women Representatives (EWRs) in Urban Self government Bodies have made their presence felt after the 74th amendments in the Indian constitution in 1994. Now, we have 33 percent women in municipal bodies. But when we do gender audit of municipal budgets, we realize that not much has been contributed for urban poor women. Gender Budgeting" is now recognized as a tool for empowering women. The Ninth Five Year Plan onwards provision of women component plan ensures that not less than 30% of development sectors funds and benefits flow to women. The declared objective is "Faster and More Inclusive Growth". The economy is in a stronger position than ever before. It therefore behoves us to set higher goals. The Approach Paper to the Eleventh Plan states that the Plan "will aim at putting the economy on a sustainable growth trajectory with a growth rate of approximately 10 percent by the end of its period." Among the other objectives of the Plan are growth of 4 percent in the agriculture sector, faster employment creation, reducing disparities across regions and ensuring access to basic physical infrastructure as well as health and education services to all. There is growing awareness of gender sensitivities of budgetary allocations. 50 ministries/ departments have set-up gender budgeting cells. For 2007-08, 27 ministries/departments and 5 Union Territories covering 33 demands for grants have contributed to a statement placed in the budget papers. The outlay for 100 percent women specific programmes is Rs. 8,795 crore and for schemes where at least 30 percent is for women specific programmes is Rs. 22,382 crore. We have made a sincere effort to remove the errors that were pointed out in last year's statement. Currently, 56 ministries and departments have set-up Gender Budget Cell and as per GR of Ministry of finance, they are expected to submit gender audit of allocation and actual expenditure on women. Budget is an important tool in the hands of state for affirmative action for improvement of gender relations through reduction of gender gap in the development process. It can help to reduce economic inequalities, between men and women as well as between the rich and the poor. Hence, the budgetary policies need to keep into considerations the gender dynamics operating in the economy and in the civil society.

There is a need to highlight participatory approaches to pro-poor budgeting, bottom up budget, child budget, SC budget, ST budget, green budgeting, budgeting for differently abled people, local and global implications of pro-poor and pro-women budgeting, alternative macro scenarios emerging out of alternative budgets and inter-linkages between gender-sensitive budgeting and women's empowerment. Serious examining of budgets calls for greater transparency at the level of international economics to local processes of empowerment. There is a need to provide training and capacity building workshops for decision-makers in the government structures, municipal bodies, parliamentarians and audio-visual media. Gender Commitments must be translated into Budgetary Commitment. Transparency/accountability for revenue generation and public expenditure need to be ensured. For Reprioritisation in public spending we must prepare our 'bottom up budgets' and lobby for its realization in collaboration with the elected representatives. Gender economists must lift the veil of statistical invisibility of the unpaid 'care economy' managed by poor women and highlight its equality and efficiency dimension and transform macro-policies so that they become women friendly. Right to information has proved to be an important tool in the hands of civil society for transparency in public expenditure on women's healthcare, development and empowerment. For the past 15 years, gender economists and women's groups are making efforts to answer the following questions:

- How to enable women to direct economy through designing and constructing fiscal policy?
- How to link economic governance to political governance?
- How to enable EWRs to participate in the budget-making efforts?

Gender concerns

1. Macro-economic Policies and Gender Audit of Municipal Budgets

Poor women have suffered the most due to drastic budgetary cuts in PDS and public health, public transport and child care facilities, food security, water and sanitation. Gender sensitive budget demands re-prioritization of financial allocations by municipal bodies in favour of:

- Working women's hostels, crèches, cheap eating facilities, public toilets,
- Housing-subsidized for single/deserted/divorced/ widowed women,
- Nutrition-strengthening PDS, mid day meals, and
- Health-Abolition of user fees for BPL population, one stop crisis centre in public hospital.

2. Girls survivors of violence linked with shelter homes

- Skill training centers for women and tailor made courses,
- Safe, efficient and cheap public Transport-bus, train, metro,
- Water—Safe drinking water in the community centers,
- Waste Management—Technological upgradation-Occupational health and safety of recycling workers/rag pickers,
- Proper electrification in the communities, and
- Multipurpose Community centres, half way homes for elderly and mentally disturbed women.

3. Method of Revenue Generation

Government of Maharashtra has allocated 5% of total revenues for women and children. Moreover, urban local self government (LSGs) bodies can raise revenues by heavy taxes on tobacco, alcohol, private vehicles and entertainment industry.

Portion of fine collected for causing damage to environment (introduction of Green Tax), high speed driving, wrong parking and breaking rules can be used for welfare of women and children.

Surcharge, earmarked charge for specific purpose such as Education Cess—2% of salary, income tax for disaster management has raised revenues for urban LSG. In Maharashtra, transport cess at the time of Bangladesh war in 1971, later on was diverted to EGS kitty.

4. Meetings with the stake-holders

Urban LSGs should organize discussion on needs

identified by EWRs with GOs, NGOs and SHGs. They should be made aware of Socio-economic Profile of the Municipality. The ward officers should ensure scrutiny of needs and perceived problems by impartial experts who can also suggest methods to fulfil needs (Labour, land, services). Financial aspects of programmes and projects should be discussed in a transparent manner.

5. Tasks of Citizens Associations

Civil society groups must be allowed to give their opinions on suitable budgetary allocations and generation of revenues from local sources. They can verify/cross check collected data and results of the surveys/interactive workshops and prepare a vision document. Sub-committees can work out details of different budget heads and it must have all stake groups of the ward. Presentation of reports of these sub-committees should be made through EWRs to the municipal authorities. Currently women's groups are lobbying for reprioritization of allocation to reflect women's interests. E.g. Financial allocation for implementation of DV act, PCPNDT Act, utilization of funds earmarked for Swadhar scheme for women in difficult circumstances and working women's hostels in urban centers.

6. Activity Mapping

Women's groups discussing of micro-economics involved in dealing with problems faced by women at ward levels such as drinking water, health centers, garbage-disposal and are moving beyond grievance redressal. Women's groups such as Anand (Ahmedabad), Alochana (Pune), Stree Mukti Sangathana (Mumbai), National Alliance of Women's Organisations (Bhubaneshwar), Sagamma Srinivas Foundation (Bangalore), Action India (Delhi) are organizing workshops for awareness about technicalities of budget, building knowledge about programmes, schemes, projects under different departments, gathering procedural information about critical issues/felt needs, skills of proposal writing. Stack groups in support of EWRs are Self Help Groups, gender sensitive administrators, corporators/councilors, individuals within political parties, NGOs and Women in the communities.

They make efforts to seek allocation under appropriate budget heads to identify streams of revenue, available revenue and the required expenditure.

7. Some unresolved Issues

Decision-makers in the urban LSG bodies need to address the following issues demanding urgent attention:

- How to bridge the gap between notional allocation and actual allocation?
- Accounting, auditing and record keeping of gender disaggregated data and allocation.
- How to achieve physical and performance/ achievement targets?
- Implementation of maternity benefits, Tribal Sub-Plan, Scheduled Caste Plan for the urban poor.
- Major departments claiming indivisibilities of allocation of resources.
- Notional allocation projected as real allocation.

8. Gender budgeting in Urban LSG Bodies

Process of gender budgeting demands special programmes targeting women based on enumeration of differential impact of expenditures across all sectors and services-gender disaggregated impact on literacy, school drop outs, mortality, morbidity, malnutrition, illnesses, safety and security. Hence, they need to ensure the review of equal opportunity policies and opportunities in the public sector—jobs, school education, wages, healthcare, skills, technical training, and computer education.

9. Allocation and expenses of resources for women in Panchayat Budgets

NIPFP has recommended the following classification of financial allocation on schemes and programmes for gender audit as well as gender budgeting—

- Women specific schemes where 100% of the allocation is required to be spent on women, targeted 100% to women by Ministry of Women and Child Development (MWCD).

- Pro-women schemes where at least 30% of allocation and benefits flow to women. E.g. All anti-poverty programmes.
- Gender Neutral Schemes meant for community as a whole (Employment generation programmes, Jawaharlal Nehru National Urban Renewal Mission (JNNURM).
- Residual schemes for disaster management.

All India Institute of Local Self Government (AIILSG) gives details of all schemes under these 4 categories through its publications, workshops and training programmes. Moreover, it also teaches the elected representatives the efficient ways of programme implementation through budgeting from below.

10. Budgetary allocation for Protective and Welfare Services

These are the schemes directly benefiting women for crisis management of situations arising out of economic and socio-cultural subordination and dehumanisation of women such as shelter homes, short stay homes, rehabilitation schemes for women survivors of violence, pensions for widows and destitute women.

11. Budgetary allocation for Social Services Expenditure for capacity building, reduction of domestic drudgery and better quality of life for girls and women

- Education
- Health
- Crèche
- Working women's hostels
- Housing
- Nutrition
- Water supply
- Sanitation—toilets, drainage
- Fuel
- Waste management
- Transport

12. Budgetary allocation for Economic Services to provide economic opportunities to women

- SHGs-credit, loans to self-employed women,
- Training programmes—Vocational training in Sunrise sectors, e.g. Biotechnology, IT, etc.,
- Physical infrastructure—transport, energy,
- Urban housing—10% reserved flats/tenements for single women,
- Marketing facilities for women entrepreneurs and self employed women—10% of shops reserved for businesswomen, women vendors/traders in municipal markets, women's haats/bazars,
- Public Toilets for women without userfees, and
- Safe and efficient transport for working women and women vendors.

13. Budgetary allocation for Regulatory Services to put in place institutional structures and mechanisms

- State Commission for Women/Municipal Commission for Women,
- Women Development Cell in municipal bodies,
- Budgetary allocation and space for ward-wise WDC for prevention of sexual harassment of women in the organized and unorganized sectors,
- Women's cell at the police stations, LSG bodies' offices, municipal hospital and schools, and
- Awareness generation programmes.

14. Financial Matters and PRIs

Elected representatives, ward officials and NGOs working in the area should act as facilitators in preparation of the plan for area development and social justice. The UN system has supported allocation of resources for women in PRIs, right from the beginning. "The evidence on gender and decentralization in India thus suggests that while women have played a positive role in addressing, or attempting to address, a range of practical gender needs. Hence, WERs deserve to be empowered to address the strategic gender needs. There is a need for provisions in the composite programmes under education, health and skill development to target them specifically at girls/women as the principal beneficiaries and disaggregated within the total allocation. It may also be necessary to place restrictions on their re-appropriation for other purposes.

Sources

William St. Clair, The Godwins and the Shelleys (New York: Norton, 1989), pp. 504-8.

Bina Agarwal, among others, has investigated the far-reaching effects of landlessness of women in many agricultural economies; see particularly her 'A Field of One's Own' (Cambridge: Cambridge University Press, 1994).

World Health Organisation, Handbook of Human Nutrition Requirement (Geneva: WHO, 1974); this was based on the report of a high-level Expert Committee jointly appointed by the WHO and FAO—the Food and Agriculture Organisation.

Development as Freedom (New York: Knopf, and Oxford: Oxford University Press, 1999), Chapter 1.

Presented in my "More Than a Hundred Million Women Are Missing," *The New York Review of Books*, Christmas Number, December 20, 1990, and in "Missing Women," *British Medical Journal*, 304 (March 1992).

The fact that I had used the sub-Saharan African ratio as the standard, rather than the European or North American ratio, was missed by some of my critics, who assumed (wrongly as it happens) that I was comparing the developing countries with advanced Western ones; see for example Ansley Coale, "Excess Female Mortality and the Balances of the Sexes in the Population: An Estimate of the Number of 'Missing Females'," *Population and Development Review*, 17 (1991). In fact, the estimation of "missing women" was based on the contrasts within the so-called third world, in particular between sub-Saharan Africa, on the one hand, and Asia and North Africa, on the other. The exact methods used were more elaborately discussed in my "Africa and India: What Do We Have to Learn from Each Other?," in Kenneth J. Arrow, ed., *The Balance between Industry and Agriculture in Economic Development* (London: Macmillan, 1988); and (with Jean Dreze), Hunger and Public Action (Oxford: Clarendon Press, 1989).

Stephan Klasen, "'Missing Women' Reconsidered," *World Development*, 22 (1994).

See Ester Boserup, Women's Role in Economic Development (London: Allen and Unwin, 1970); M.R. Rosenzweig and T.P. Schultz, "Market Opportunities, Genetic Endowments, and Intrafamily Resource Distribution," *American Economic Review*, 72 (1982).

On this see my "Women and Cooperative Conflict," in Irene Tinker, *Persistent Inequalities* (New York: Oxford University Press, 1990). See also J.C. Caldwell, "Routes to Low Mortality in Poor Countries," *Population and Development Review*, 12 (1986); Jere Behrman and B.L. Wolfe, "How Does Mother's Schooling Affect Family Health, Nutrition, Medical Care Usage and Household Sanitation," *Journal of Econometrics*, 36 (1987); Jean Dreze and Amartya Sen, Hunger and Public Action (Oxford: Clarendon Press, 1989).

I have discussed these factors in my "More Than a Hundred Million Women Are Missing" (1990). See also Jean Dreze and Amartya Sen, India: Economic Development and Social Opportunity (Delhi: Oxford University Press, 1995), and particularly V.K. Ramachandran, "Kerala's Development Achievements," in Jean Dreze and Amartya Sen, eds., *Indian Development: Selected Regional Perspectives* (Delhi: Oxford University Press, 1996).

See the literature on this cited in Development as Freedom (1999).

One of the earliest and pioneering studies was by Lincoln Chen, E. Huq and S. D'Souza, "Sex Bias in the Family Allocation of Food and Healthcare in Rural Bangladesh," *Population and Development Review*, 7 (1981).

See my joint paper with Sunil Sengupta, "Malnutrition of Rural Indian Children and the Sex Bias," *Economic and Political Weekly*, 19 (1983).

See my joint paper with Jocelyn Kynch, "Indian Women: Well-being and Survival," *Cambridge Journal of Economics*, 7 (1983), and also Resources, Values and Development (Cambridge, MA: Harvard University Press, 1984).

See Peter Svedberg, Poverty and Undernutrition: Theory and Measurement (Oxford: Clarendon Press, 2000), for an illuminating and thorough analysis of comparative nutrition in South Asia and sub-Saharan Africa.

See S.R. Osmani, "Poverty and Nutrition in South Asia," in ACC/SCN, Nutrition and Poverty (1997), and also Nutrition Policy Paper No. 16 (Geneva: WHO, 1997). This is the First Abraham Horowitz Lecture of the United Nations. See also the references to the literature cited by Osmani.

On this see Osmani, "Poverty and Nutrition in South Asia" (1997), and also the references cited there.

See D.J.P. Barker, "Intrauterine Growth Retardation and Adult Disease," Current Obstetrics and Gynaecology, 3 (1993); "Foetal Origins of Coronary Heart Disease," *British Medical Journal*, 311 (1995); Mothers, Babies and Diseases in Later Life (London: Churchill Livingstone, 1998). See also P.D. Gluckman, K.M. Godfrey, J.E. Harding, J.A. Owens, and J.S. Robinson, "Fetal Nutrition and Cardiovascular Disease in Adult Life," *Lancet*, 341 (1995).

Siddiq Osmani and Amartya Sen, "The Hidden Penalties of Gender Inequality: Fetal Origins of Ill-Health," mimeographed, Trinity College, Cambridge, 2001.

On the extensive role and reach of capabilities of women, see particularly Martha Nussbaum, Women and Human Development: The

Capabilities Approach (Cambridge: Cambridge University Press, 2000).

UNDP's Human Development Report, 1995 (New York: United Nations, forthcoming: 1995) presents an inter-country investigation of gender differences in social, political and business leadership, in addition to reporting on gender inequality in terms of more conventional indicators. See also Sudhir Anand and Amartya Sen, "Gender Inequality in Human Development: Theories and Measurement," in UNDP, Background Papers: Human Development Report, 1995 (New York: United Nations, 1996).

The complex influences that operate in fertility decline, including cultural adaptations, have been discussed by Alaka Basu and Sajeda Amin in "Conditioning Factors for Fertility Decline in Bengal: History, Language Identity, and Openness to Innovations," *Population and Development Review*, 26 (2000).

A recent study of local governmental decisions in India brings out the substantial nature of this change, as a consequence of women coming to occupy leadership positions in the "Panchayats" (local administrative bodies); see Raghabendra Chattopadhyay and Esther Duflo, "Women's Leadership and Policy Decisions: Evidence from a Nationwide Randomised Experiment in India," mimeographed, Department of Economics, MIT, 2001.

Note, however, that the Chinese and Korean figures cover children between 0 and 4, whereas the Indian figures relate to children between 0 and 6. However, even with appropriate age adjustment, the general comparison of female-male ratios holds in much the same way.

See, among other contributions, Irawati Karve, Kinship Organization in India (Bombay: Asia Publishing House, 1965); Pranab Bardhan, "On Life and Death Questions," *Economic and Political Weekly*, Special Number, 9 (1974); David Sopher, ed., An Exploration of India: Geographical, Perspectives on Society and Culture (Ithaca, NY: Cornell University Press, 1980); Barbara Miller, The Endangered Sex (Ithaca, NY: Cornell University Press, 1981); Tim Dyson and Mick Moore, "On Kinship Structure, Female Autonomy, and Demographic Behaviour in India," *Population and Development Review*, 9 (1983); Monica Das Gupta, "Selective Discrimination against Female Children in Rural Punjab," *Population and Development Review*, 13 (1987); Alaka M. Basu, Culture, the Status of Women and Demographic Behaviour (Oxford: Clarendon Press, 1992); Satish Balram Agnihotri, Sex Ratio Patterns in the Indian Population (New Delhi: Sage, 2000).

Patel, V. (2002), "Gendering the Budget at State and National Level and Gender Audit of the Union Budget—A Critical Approach", Urdhva Mula, Mumbai, Vol. 1, No. 1, pp. 30-57.

Patel, V. (2002), Women's Challenges of the New Millennium, Gyan Books, Delhi, p. 70. websites: www. cehat.org and www.humanscapeindia. net

Patel, V. (2003), "Gender Budget Initiatives in India", paper presented at Workshop on "Gender Budget Initiatives in Orissa" organised by

School of Women's Studies, Utkal University, Bhubaneshwar, Orissa on 22nd to 24th September 2003.

Patel, V. (2003), "Gender Budget- A Case Study of India", Centre for Advanced Study in Economics, Department of Economics, University of Mumbai, Working Paper UDE (CAS) 7(7)/2003, also published in *Vikalpa,* Vol. XI, No. 1, 2003 published by Vikas Adhyayan Kendra, Mumbai.

Patel, V. (2004), "Gender Budget: Media Concerns and Policy for India" in Kiran Prasad (Ed.) Communication and Empowerment of Women: Strategies and Policy Insights from India, The Women Press, Delhi.

Patel, V. (2005), "India's Economic Reform and Women" in Susheela Subramanya, Meera Chakravorty and N.S. Viswanath (Ed.s) (2005) Women in Nation Building—Perspectives, Issues and Implications, A Southern Economist Publication, Bangalore.

UNDP (2001), Decentralisation in India—Challenges and Opportunities, United Nations Development Programme, New Delhi.

Virmani, S. (1999), "Social Mapping, Modèlling and Other Participatory Methods", All India Institute of Local Self Government, Mumbai.

Injuries are a Major Challenge to Healthcare

Trauma Care Systems still Primitive

The planning and development of trauma care systems in India has yet to gain attention and priority from the government or NGOs, even though trauma is a major public health problem. Accelerated urbanization and industrialization have led to an alarming increase in the rate of accidental injuries, crimes, protests and violence in India. An unprecedented increase in the number of vehicles has outpaced the development of adequate roads and highways. Also, India has 1% of the motor vehicles in the world, but bears the burden of 6% of the global vehicular accidents. It is well recognized that our healthcare system is not fully equipped to meet the challenge of either prevention of accidents or care of the ever increasing number of trauma victims.

Perfect storm of medical errors

Trauma care creates a perfect storm of medical errors: unstable patients, incomplete histories, time-critical decisions, concurrent tasks, involvement of many disciplines, and often junior personnel working after-hours in busy emergency departments. Studies in several countries have identified adverse events, including death, that occur in trauma and emergency care. Various studies provide insights into the nature of preventable deaths, including the significance of failure to evaluate the abdomen, delays to treatment, and critical care errors. The estimates of preventable death rate ranges from 2% to 50%, indicating the variability of care provided and the need for standardized approaches. In trauma, as in all fields, it is likely that recognizable clinical situations create predictable vulnerability to human error, and the erroneous decision-making that occurs in response to these situations. To reduce errors, institutions need effective means of identifying errors and error-associated deaths. This is all the more difficult in trauma care, given high baseline mortality rates, often complicated in-hospital care, and the relative paucity of widely applicable management protocols, especially beyond the Golden Hour of initial resuscitation, to which Advanced Trauma Life Support (ATLS) protocols apply. Furthermore, errors that result in death may be relatively infrequent; therefore, opportunities to learn from them may be limited by infrequent attention and lack of institutional memory.

In tertiary care hospitals patients with multi-system injuries are admitted to emergency department under supervision of the general surgery service, as are unstable patients with isolated injuries for resuscitation and stabilization before transfer to other services. An in-house attending anesthesiologist and a full-time operating room staff are present 24 hours per day, 7 days per week. The CT scanner and the angiography suite are adjacent and easily accessible to the emergency department. All trauma deaths are discussed at weekly surgical morbidity and mortality (M&M) meetings. Those identified as being associated with possible or definite errors in care are subsequently reviewed by departmental and hospital quality assurance (QA) officers, and significant cases are presented for discussion at monthly multidisciplinary hospital trauma council meetings.

Delivery of trauma care

There is an urgent need to improve the delivery of trauma care for the injured. A chain of trauma care centers is essential in India, since ours is one of the most populous countries in the world, and one with a high incidence of disasters and consequent burden of trauma deaths and disability. Also there is gross disparity between trauma services available, *inter se* in various parts of the country. Rural India lacks trauma care services almost completely and in urban areas it is a part of emergency department, with inefficient services for trauma care, due to the varied topography, financial constraints and lack of appropriate health infrastructure. There is no national nodal agency to co-ordinate various components of a trauma care. Education in trauma life-support (TLS) skills is hardly available. The doctors trained in super-specialties like orthopedics, plastic surgery, neuro-surgery are not willing to be dumped in 'Trauma Centres', for the rest of their lives. There is a need to develop a specialty of traumatology to man the proposed centers. Although injury is a major public-health problem; responsible for a large number of deaths, the Government of India as well as state governments have failed to recognize it as a priority area. Some efforts to develop trauma-care systems across the country are seen mainly in the private sector. In the public health system the allocation of funds remains grossly inadequate for any significant impact on the outcome.

Chandigarh administration is in the process of setting up its first trauma hospital, though trained manpower in traumatology is a far cry. Presently PGI emergency department is the main stay of trauma management in and around the city of Chandigarh. Fortunately, PGI hospital has also planned a trauma centre, which is under construction at present.

In May 2002, Academy of Traumatology (India) undertook a maiden study of trauma systems, one hundred and forty-five institutions across the country of all states in India were invited to participate in the survey. Fifty institutions participated in the survey. The overall data was fairly representative of urban and rural settings, private and public hospitals and facilities across all geographical regions of the country.

The following data emerged from the study:

Injury as public health problem

Road-traffic accidents are increasing at an alarming

annual rate of 3%. In 1997, 10.1% of all deaths in India are due to accidents and injuries. A vehicular accident is reported every 3 minutes and a death every 10 minutes on Indian roads. During 1998, nearly 80,000 lives were lost and 330,000 people were injured. Of these, 78% were men in age group of 20-44 years, causing significant impact on productivity. A trauma-related death occurs in India every 1.9 minutes. The majority of fatal road-traffic accident victims are pedestrians, two-wheeler riders and bicyclists. No credible data is available to ascertain the outcome of trauma victims; it is generally perceived that outcomes in patients with single system injury (e.g. musculoskeletal trauma) have improved. Unfortunately, the same cannot be said for poly-trauma. There is a high mortality rate amongst those with multi-system injuries, which can be attributed to the primitive state of trauma-care systems, lack of pre-hospital care and inadequate critical care. It is established that the mortality in serious injuries is six times worse in a developing country such as India compared to a developed country.

Despite trauma being a major public-health problem with high morbidity and mortality, the Ministry of Health does not have a designated unit to deal with issues related to trauma. There is no central government agency to integrate policy-making, planning, financing, drafting legislation or establishment of minimum standards for the performance of a trauma-care system. No reliable institutional arrangement exists to lead the development of such a system in any Indian state. In 26% of the systems surveyed, the overall responsibility for leading the system was undefined. The Centralized Ambulance Transport Service (CATS) of the Government of the State of New Delhi is the only noteworthy state initiative in this direction. This is restricted mainly to pre-hospital care. Only 28% of respondents identified the presence of a unified leadership coordinating various components and agencies. The existing systems for trauma care are elementary in nature, predominantly restricted to cities and semi-urban areas, without integration of region or statewide systems. No such systems exist in rural and remote areas to offer prompt life-saving treatment and safe transfer to an appropriate facility. Consequently fatal accident rate (expressed per kilometer of travel) in India is estimated to be seven-fold worse compared to most advanced states. In cities such as Mumbai, Pune, Bangalore, Hyderabad, Ahmedabad and Chennai, the trauma systems are at an embryonic stage, predominantly supported by non-government and private agencies.

No law exists to ensure prompt access to life-saving treatment for trauma victims. Statutory provisions to aid national, state, or interstate planning and implementation of trauma-care systems, regardless of jurisdictional boundaries, are yet to evolve. Issues such as the accreditation of trauma centers and critical care units, specialist licensing of health personnel and mandatory training of physicians lack national guidelines. The publication of ISCCM guidelines for ICUs is an important step in that direction. Legislative provisions for the minimum qualification of ambulance personnel, the type and quality of ambulance equipment and essential hospital capabilities are not in place. Available personnel and their skills often do not match the needs of the patients. The optimal number and type of pre-hospital personnel for ambulances is not defined. The state of preparedness to transport the critically injured person is almost non-existent. Many valuable lives are lost for want of ambulance and due to lack of skill to shift under care, at the earliest.

Saving Lives on the Move

Rittik Donde wrote in *Economic Times* about the ray of hope kindled by Roy and Tripathi, who believe that care begins on way to hospital.

For years, calling an ambulance in India has been a painful experience for those needing emergency care and their dear ones. An eternal wait would be followed by the visit of a rickety vehicle lacking much sophistication beyond a bed and siren. Apathetic drivers on the road would ignore the vehicle as they nudge ahead in traffic jams and the golden hour would often be lost before reaching the gates of the hospital. Death would be blamed on god and everything would be back to square one. And nobody did any thing about it. Until two years ago.

Then, two engineers without any knowledge of

automobiles gave up their engineering careers with German firm Dragger and started selling well-equipped ambulances, in which emergency treatment could be started as soon as the patient is taken aboard. It was a new concept and hard to sell initially. But with their relentless marketing, the duo have made hospitals see the value of treatment on the go and made their startup—Aeon Medical Services—a preferred name among health-care institutions in the country.

Ranjan Roy and Abani Tripathi, the entrepreneurs, say most ambulances in India are merely passenger transport vehicles and are inefficient in the task of handling the first hour after an emergency. "In most ambulances, there is only an oxygen mask and few other equipment which are not enough to start point of care treatment by emergency response units," Mr. Roy says. Aeon, on the other hand, a buys vehicles, imports equipment from Europe and builds integrated ambulances for intensive care, trauma and cardiac care applications. A patient being taken on one of these vehicles would be getting targeted, specialised emergency treatment even m the midst of a traffic bottleneck.

"Considering the traffic situation in a city like Mumbai or Delhi, ii a patient has to go from Borivli to Asian Heart Institute in Bandra, it takes at least one hour. We fit our ambulances with specialised medical equipment such as cardiac revivers and other such type of equipment as is mostly found in ambulances abroad. What this does is that it allows the emergency medical personnel to start the treatment immediately thus improving chances for survival for the patient," says Mr. Roy.

Companies such as Tata Motors, Eicher and Bajaj Tempo) do offer vehicles that can be converted into ambulances, but selling fully-appointed ambulances has ever attracted them as a business. That's where the two engineers found their opportunity. The medical fraternity was on the look for standardised vehicles matching the quality of those running in the advanced world. Tripathi and Roy used their European connection from Dragger and started sourcing equipment from Italy's Spencer. "But this was not the tough part. Since both us have biomedical background, we knew where to look for medical equipment, but knowledge about the auto industry was as good as anybody else in the country;' Mr. Roy says.

Aeon has already bagged many high-profile customers. Wockhardt group accounted for nearly Rs. 7.5 crore in its fiscal 2006-07 revenues. Aeon also services other clients like the Apollo Hospital in Calcutta and Satyam Groups EMRI in Andhra Pradesh. But the ride for Aeon was not always smooth for Tripathi and Roy. "Getting the right people was a big problem for us. For not only did we need people with the right skill set, we needed them to shift lock stock and barrel to Pitampur," says Mr. Roy. They recruited garage mechanics from Kolkata, Mumbai and North India and trained them.

Aeon was started with an investment of Rs. 2 crore including an equity investment of Rs. 8 lakh from the promoters, while the rest being in the form of loans from financial institutions and banks. The market for specialised ambulances and medical equipment is still nascent. Mr. Roy says that the market for basic life support vehicles is around 500 per year priced at Rs. 15 lakh per vehicle while that for advanced life support vehicles is also 500 vehicles per year but priced at Rs. 20 lakh per car. Bulk of the business for Aeon now comes not from hospitals but from emergency service providers like FMRI and Chikitsa.

Now Roy and Tripathi want to bring disaster management portfolio under Aeon's wings. We have now trained our guns on Mumbai's disaster management cell and other such government units across the country. The 7/11 blasts in Mumbai and tsunami in South India have made government realise how important point of care treatment is during such incidents, says Mr. Roy.

The concept of a dedicated trauma team is not accepted at all levels. At a majority of hospitals in the public system, the casualty medical officer is the only one to respond to a demand for major resuscitation. This paradox is striking, resulting in the most seriously injured patients frequently being dealt with by the most junior and inexperienced staff. There are no plans for dynamic and flexible responses to the optimal management of trauma patients. The lack of precise and predetermined role allocation during peak periods of activity stresses the fragile current systems and workforce.

Lack of skilled and highly skilled manpower

The state medical and nursing councils control the educational and licensing requirements for physicians and nurses. However, formal education and specialty training (in emergency medicine, trauma surgery and critical care) are not mandatory for personnel involved in trauma care and available only at select private institutions. The standardized education in trauma life-support skills is made available through the efforts of Academy of Traumatology (India) under the 'National Trauma Management Course' (NTMC) with accreditation from the International Association for Surgery of Trauma and Surgical Intensive Care (IATSIC). Currently this training is available mainly in larger centers and is intended for doctors only. The issues of educational standards, certification and continuing education and evaluation requirements for doctors involved in trauma care are yet to be addressed. The National Board of Examinations has recently begun registering courses in trauma care, though in a very limited manner. There are no minimum stipulated educational standards for paramedic and ambulance personnel. Paramedic training programmes are offered in major institutions but there is no accreditation, review or provision for periodic update of skills and knowledge.

Gross inadequacy in Pre-hospital Care exists

Pre-hospital care is virtually non-existent in most rural and semi-urban areas in India, and implementation of the 'golden hour' concept is still an unachieved goal. The concept of a coordinating agency and a designated authority is restricted mainly to cities where trauma systems are operational in some form. Quite often there is an overlapping of private and public facilities and ambulance services in an urban geographical area. Gross discrepancy is seen in pre-hospital services between urban and rural settings, as well as between paying and non-paying patients. In the absence of guidelines and trained paramedical staff, decisions about evacuation of the victim and the choice of the destination hospital are made on an individual-case basis. These choices are often made at the behest of patients or their kin. Formal licensing to run an ambulance service is not mandatory.

Ambulance services are run by a multitude of organizations including government, police, fire brigades, hospitals and private agencies. Of the facilities surveyed, 12% reported a total absence of any ambulance service. Air ambulance services are not widely available and only 4% of the surveyed systems have even minimal access to air transportation, run by private agencies.

The absence of minimal educational and training standards for paramedics brings in unskilled labour to handle the most delicate of tasks. Many private hospitals in large cities offer efficient pre-hospital care, but this covers too small an area and too small a segment of the population. The care is unaffordable for most patients. No national or regional guidelines exist for triage, patient-delivery decisions, pre-hospital treatment plans and transfer protocols. Policies, procedures and regulations governing medical directions are in place only in some city systems. There are recent attempts to provide one-time formal training in pre-hospital care to the ambulance personnel in various parts of the country. Currently, only 4% of the ambulance personnel have any certified formal training. The number of paramedics in the ambulances varies considerably. One-third of ambulances serve only as transport vehicles with no paramedic staff. Only 28% of the ambulances have two or more paramedics. Only 50% of ambulance services have minimal skills and resources for providing airway support and appropriate splintage. The majority of ambulances have the means for intravenous infusion (74%) and blood-pressure measurement (62%). Despite technological advances, communication in trauma systems in India remains rudimentary and inefficient. Only 14% of the systems have a dedicated central telephone number for incident reporting. Some 30% of the trauma systems, mainly in cities, are equipped with wireless communication. Only 4% of systems have a comprehensive network operational between hospitals and ambulances.

Lack of Preparedness

India is a disaster-prone country with frequent floods, cyclones, landslides, earthquakes violent protests, civil disturbances, communal and caste clashes. Train accidents and industrial mishaps are not uncommon. Government plans are in place, in general, to deal with disasters. However, regular drills to test preparedness are not carried out. Only 26% of the systems in the survey reported a well-documented disaster management plan. The rest of the systems have plans under development, or no plans. This deficiency has resulted in excessive numbers of deaths in natural disasters. In 1999, there was an increase of 20.8% in fatalities due to such disasters compared to the previous year. This figure for 2001 is likely to rise even further as a result of a killer earthquake in Gujarat, causing over 12,000 deaths. Many more disasters have occurred since then.

Facilities that offer treatment for trauma victims, report 10% to 30% of their beds occupied by people injured in road accidents. Most government hospitals offer free care, but the quality of that care differs from one centre to another. Most medical college hospitals provide a reasonable level of care; these hospitals are able to fulfil the role of tertiary trauma centers but critical care continues to remain the weak link in such settings for a variety of reasons. Private and corporate hospitals, located mostly in large cities, are equipped with modern diagnostic and imaging facilities, good operating environments and intensive-care units. Some of them also run dedicated trauma services. However, there are no norms to govern their standards and their relations with the public trauma system. District hospitals often lack trained staff, adequate infrastructure for management of poly-trauma and supply of consumables. Small hospitals and clinics mushrooming across India are simply unable to cope with poly-trauma. Such small clinics struggle to manage severely injured patients, resulting in substandard care and high mortality. Only 54% of the hospitals have set protocols for triage. In 30% of the hospitals, the casualty medical officers are the only physicians available to provide resuscitation. Their level of training and experience in providing life support is not uniform. The concept and practice of forming dedicated trauma-response teams is yet to percolate beyond tertiary-care hospitals. In acute and elective management of trauma patients, only 36% of the facilities follow NTMC, or locally developed clinical protocols.

There are no dedicated trauma surgeons in India. Orthopaedic surgeons lead the trauma response in 50% of facilities. In the remainder, the responsibility is not clearly defined. Clinical decisions are often delayed, in the absence of clear perceptions of clinical responsibility amongst specialists, putting patients with multi-system injury at a greater risk. Nearly half of the systems surveyed have no protocol for inter-hospital transfers. Linkages between rural and urban facilities do not exist in most regions. The availability of specialist care (for e.g. spinal trauma, burns, head injuries, childhood injuries, etc.) is restricted to major cities and teaching hospitals. Transfer to such a specialty centre in an emergency is often difficult and time-consuming, resulting in delay in decision-making and management and also unaffordable expenditure.

Rehabilitation, though an integral element of any trauma-care system, is a neglected area. It is restricted to physiotherapy centers. Although 76% of the facilities offer physiotherapy services, only a third offer occupational rehabilitation and psychological counseling. The surveyed hospitals failed to demonstrate strong links and transfer agreements between acute facilities and rehabilitation units. The disabled is left alone to fend for herself.

The information systems in most places are manual and rudimentary. There is no central trauma registry in any state. Most hospitals have reliable data on trauma admissions, but only 40% have data on the clinical outcome of the trauma patients. This has a negative impact on development and implementation of an effective public policy on trauma care.

In the wake of the gross disparity between accessibility and affordability of trauma care; quality assurance is a major casualty. In the absence of a lead agency and with a poor information system, evaluation and research on trauma systems is a difficult proposition. Monitoring of the performance of the system and its individual components, and any quality-improvement programme, is far away. Very little work has been done to evaluate the working of trauma systems in India. CATS, New Delhi and CMC Hospital, Vellore have assessed some components of their systems.

What lies in store in the future?

The future appears both daunting and challenging. It is estimated that from its present position of the ninth leading cause of deaths in India, trauma will move up to third position by 2020. It is also estimated that in the developing countries over 6 million will die and 60 million will be injured, or disabled, in the next 10 years. India will have a large share in this, with an estimated economic loss of around 2% of GDP. To meet this challenge several efforts are required: resource creation, education, legislation, upgrading pre-hospital and hospital based care, public awareness and a change in the attitude of the policy-makers. The public health institutions will also benefit from adopting WHO Essential Trauma Care guidelines for trauma care, which is aimed at low cost improvements to the trauma care.

Although the overall picture in trauma care is not as dismal as it used to be three decades ago, 'trauma care for all' continues to remain a distant dream in India. Despite significant overall progress in many other fields, trauma systems in India continue to remain at a formative stage for various reasons. A concerted effort from all the parties involved, as well as the society, is the need of the hour.

A case study of a big hospital in Mumbai

In a study, carried out in Lokmanya Tilak Municipal General (LTMG) Hospital in Mumbai, between 1 August 2001 and 31 May 2002, 1074 severely injured patients were included. This study is likely to assist error reduction in 3 important ways. The first is through identification of specific categories of errors that may be targeted. The most commonly identified groups related to airway and hemorrhage control, the ABCs of acute severe trauma management. Several other major error categories were also relatively specific to trauma: inappropriate management of an unstable patient, missed or delayed diagnoses, management of feeding tubes, and over-resuscitation with fluids. The second way this study may help is through considering the type and underlying psychological cause, which may provide insights into the most useful error-reduction strategies. For example, execution errors are addressed through technical training, and ensuring that those performing the tasks are technically competent and appropriately credentialed. Input errors require clinicians to be aware of potential problems and appropriately use and interpret diagnostic tests. The majority of error-associated deaths, however, were intention errors affecting treatment. Indeed, some errors that seemed at first to be execution errors, such as failure to achieve orotracheal intubation leading to anoxic brain injury, may be more appropriately viewed as intention errors, in that one should always be ready to perform a surgical airway in the event of a challenging intubation. Intention errors are greatly reduced by protocols and algorithms that simplify or serve as reminders for particularly complex or time-critical management decisions. The third way in which this study supports error reduction is by demonstrating the likely effectiveness of such evidence-based institutional protocols. In their comparison of major error categories and institutional policies, they instituted new policies that related directly to 4 of the 14 error categories. All 4 policies had emerged after recognition that errors were occurring and that a policy was needed to address them. In all 4, error-associated deaths were less frequent after institution of the policy. It is important to realize that deaths, while the most serious outcome, are just the tip of the iceberg of morbidity associated with errors, and for every prevented death there are probably many patients for whom nonfatal single or multiple organ failure is averted.

Survival analysis was completed for 98.3% of the patients. The majority of the patients were men (84%) and the average age was 31 years. 90.4% were blunt injuries, with road traffic crashes (39.2%) being the most common cause. The predicted mortality was 10.89% and the observed mortality was 21.26%. The average probability of survival (Ps) was 89.14. The M and Z statistics were 0.84 and -14.1593, respectively. The injured in this study were found to be older, the injuries more severe and with poorer outcomes, than in other studies. Sixty-four patients (0.14% admissions, 2.47% deaths) had recognized errors in care that contributed to their death. Important error patterns included: failure to successfully intubate, secure or protect an airway (16%), delayed operative or angiographic control of acute abdominal/pelvic hemorrhage (16%), delayed intervention for ongoing intra-thoracic hemorrhage (9%), inadequate DVT or gastrointestinal prophylaxis (9%), lengthy initial operative procedures rather than damage control surgery in unstable patients (8%), over-resuscitation with fluids (5%), and complications of feeding tubes (5%). Resulting data-directed institutional and regional trauma system policy changes have demonstrably reduced the incidence of associated error-related deaths. This review has identified error patterns that are likely common in all trauma systems, and for which policy interventions can be effectively targeted.

Various aspects of errors include:

1. Error Impact, which in this study was death.
2. Error Type, classified as many others have done as errors in diagnosis, treatment, prevention, or other (equipment failures; communication failures; and errors in transfer).
3. Error Domain, for which they were most interested in the phase of trauma management when it occurred, and for which the classifications were: initial assessment and resuscitation (including prehospital); secondary survey and tests (e.g., CT); inter-hospital transfers; initial interventions (e.g., OR, Angio); ICU; general ward; and rehabilitation.
4. Error Cause, which refers to the psychological cause, that is, it relates to what was probably going on in the mind of the person who erred. Reason has contributed much to this understanding, and they used an internal processing classification, that included: Input error: the input data are incorrectly perceived; therefore, an incorrect intention is formed and the wrong action is performed. Intention error: the input data are correctly perceived, but an incorrect intention is formed, and the wrong action is performed. Execution error: the input data are correctly perceived and the correct intention is formed, but the wrong action is performed; that is, the action is not what was intended.

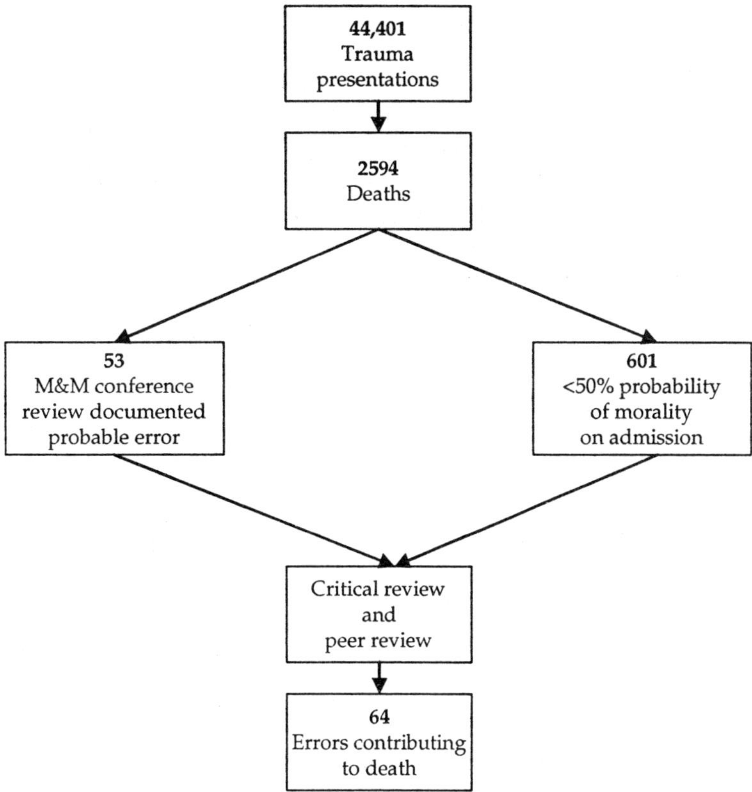

Source: Ann Surg, 2006.

The occurrence of errors relative to each policy's implementation was then plotted to give an indication of whether or not such policies had been effective in reducing error occurrence. Observations were categorized into whether or not a new policy was implemented during the study period.

The major clinical groupings of errors included hemorrhage control (28%), airway management (16%), inappropriate management of unstable patients (14%), complications of procedures (12%), inadequate prophylaxis (11%), missed or delayed diagnoses (11%), over-resuscitation with fluids (5%), and other poor management decisions (3%).

Delayed control of abdominal or pelvic hemorrhage using operative or angiographic methods was usually due to delays in the emergency department (ED) assessment of a patient in shock, and occasionally involved the performance of other non-urgent tests or procedures. Delayed control of intra-thoracic hemorrhage was most often a delay in the diagnosis of massive hemo-thorax with inadequate evacuation of blood from the chest, or inadequate recognition of the volume that had already been evacuated. Half of all fatal airway errors involved unsuccessful attempts at endotracheal intubations and failure to adequately gain or regain control using simple maneuvers or a surgical airway. The other airway errors were failure to adequately protect the airway from aspiration during subsequent phases of care. In the operating room, damage-control principles dictate that control of hemorrhage and control of contamination should be prioritized, deferring prolonged surgical interventions and reconstruction until correction of hypothermia, acidosis, and coagulopathy is accomplished in the ICU. They found 5 cases in which these principles were not followed, and the patient subsequently progressed to death due to exsanguination or multiorgan failure. They found 7 cases in which a missed injury or delayed diagnosis led to death. In 4 cases, there was a positive test result that failed to be acted on (a head CT showing subdural hemorrhage, a pericardial ultrasound showing a tamponade, a positive blood culture, and hyperkalemia on blood chemistry). Over-resuscitation is a consequence of aggressive fluid management in the face of hypotension, often due to primary pump failure. The pulmonary consequences of over-resuscitation were fatal in 3 patients.

By phase of trauma management, 34% of errors occurred in the ED (20% during initial assessment and resuscitation, 14% during the secondary survey and initial diagnostic tests), 8% during stabilization and interhospital transport, 11% during initial interventions (surgery and/or angiography), 37% during the intensive care unit stay, and 9% during the general or rehabilitation ward inpatient stay.

Errors of treatment predominated; however, diagnostic errors were particularly evident in the secondary survey and ICU phases, and errors of prophylaxis were most evident after the initial management was completed, in the ICU and post-ICU phases. While half of all errors were intention errors and occurred throughout the hospital stay, input errors and execution errors were particularly prominent in the ICU phase of care, and to a lesser extent, the initial assessment and resuscitation phase.

They have demonstrated that, even in mature trauma systems, errors still occasionally lead to patients' deaths. Among 44,401 admissions and 2594 deaths over 9 years, 2.47% of deaths at the institution were contributed to by errors. This is among the lowest reported preventable death rate in trauma patients. Despite increasing numbers and increasing complexity of cases at the institution, the findings compare favourably with the 23% pedestrian and bicycle fatalities regarded as potentially preventable 18 years ago. As others have suggested, a 2% to 3% error-related death rate may be an absolute baseline in complex trauma systems.

Error reduction cannot be solely attributed to the implementation of policies or protocols, however. Changes in staffing, training, equipment, supervision, and any number of other reasons are likely to also affect error occurrence. Of course, the effect of looking repeatedly for recurrent problems or errors may itself contribute to a reduction in errors through a Hawthorne-type effect of enhanced awareness. Yet by examining the types of errors that occur with some frequency as to constitute a repetitive pattern, we are forced to consider what protocol and policy options might affect real improvement. We have recently recognized overly aggressive resuscitation as a problem causing 3 deaths in the past 3 years. To minimize the risk of over-resuscitation, in 2005 a new protocol was instituted that required early invasive central venous monitoring in the ED, and clear guidelines to limiting fluids, beginning inotropic agents, and obtaining rapid control of bleeding. Challenges emerging from this study that are yet to be addressed include reducing deaths associated with delays to the operating room or angiography for abdominopelvic hemorrhage, employing surgical or other airway maneuvers when faced with a challenging airway, and ensuring damage control principles are followed when necessary.

A glimpse of the Western World

In the Western World, trauma is the leading cause of death for individuals under 45 years of age, and it remains the fourth leading cause of death for all ages combined. In 1994, 8,687 people died following accidents in Canada. Approximately four times as many patients suffer severe disability related to accidents each year.

Prehospital care for trauma patients is provided by emergency medical personnel using either Basic Life Support (BLS) or Advanced Life Support (ALS) techniques. BLS (or "scoop and run") consists of non-invasive interventions such as wound dressing, immobilization, fracture splinting, oxygen administration, and non-invasive cardiopulmonary resuscitation. ALS encompasses all of these BLS techniques in addition to invasive procedures, including intubation, initiation of IV access with fluid replacement, administration of medications, and in rare cases application of pneumatic antishock garments (PASG). The rationale for the use of on-site ALS in trauma is that these interventions will reduce the rate of physiologic and hemodynamic deterioration, thus stabilizing the patient before arrival at the hospital. It is expected that this will result in increased chances of survival. The paradox is that on-site ALS increases the amount of time that is spent on the scene and hence increases the delay to definitive in-hospital care. To date, the controversy between the "scoop and run" *versus* "stay and stabilize" approach to pre-hospital trauma care remains unresolved and has been the subject of a limited number of studies, most of which were based on small numbers of selected patients. Studies supporting ALS have failed to show an association between on-site ALS and increased survival among patients with major trauma. Studies supporting BLS have shown higher survival rates for patients treated using the "scoop and run" approach compared to those treated using on-site ALS. The validity of these studies is often compromised due to the lack of control for confounding variables and appropriate comparison groups.

A 1992 study by Schmidt *et al.* compared trauma patients with equivalent Injury Severity Scores (ISS) transported by helicopter in Germany to patients transported by helicopter in the United States. In Germany, patients received treatment by a paramedic and a trauma surgeon and in the United States by a paramedic and a nurse. They found that the German patients received significantly more advanced interventions, including IV fluids, endotracheal intubations, and thoracic decompressions, than the American group. This led to a decrease in early mortality and improved outcome compared to patients in the Major Trauma Outcome Study (MTOS).

Similarly, the effectiveness of on-site intubations in improving outcome of severely injured patients has not been adequately evaluated. The rationale for on-scene intubations is that this intervention will maintain airway patency and oxygenation. As with IV placement, the argument against intubations is that it causes significant delays to definitive in-hospital care. Unlike IV placement, however, there is some agreement that in certain severely injured and unconscious patients, intubations should be initiated at the scene or en route to the hospital.

The unresolved controversy regarding the on-site management of trauma patients is reflected in the regional variation of pre-hospital patient management protocols. This variation is observed profoundly in Canada, where the type of on-site care available to trauma patients ranges from BLS provided by emergency medical technicians (EMTs) to physician-provided ALS. The type of pre-hospital care available to trauma patients is determined by regional policies that are dictated by local political, cultural, and economic factors as well as the influential opinion of local experts.

The objectives of the study were three-fold:

- To compare the effectiveness of three different pre-hospital trauma care systems—one with only EMTs providing BLS and adhering to the "scoop and run" approach), one with paramedics available to provide on-site ALS (PMD-ALS), and the third with physicians available to provide on-site ALS (MD-ALS)-in reducing trauma-related mortality.

- To evaluate and compare the effectiveness of three different types of on-site management (EMT-BLS, PMD-ALS, and MD-ALS) in reducing trauma-related mortality.
- To evaluate and compare the effectiveness of two different types of on-site care (ALS and BLS) in reducing trauma-related mortality.

The results of the study show that the use of on-site ALS, in general, does not provide any benefits in reducing mortality in patients with major trauma. This result is generalizable to patients injured in urban centers served by highly organized trauma care systems with access to a level I trauma center. The data from this study show that when physicians provide on-site ALS to trauma patients, the risk of mortality is significantly increased when compared to both EMT-provided BLS and paramedic-provided ALS. On-site ALS provided by paramedics was not associated with a reduction in mortality when compared to EMTs.

The results of this study are compatible with others in the literature that support the "scoop and run" approach for the pre-hospital management of trauma patients in an urban setting. The lack of effectiveness of ALS in general has often been attributed to the increased time required to perform ALS procedures at the scene. However, there is now a considerable evidence to suggest that certain ALS procedures, such as IV fluid replacement, may be harmful for patients with major trauma. The increased risk of mortality associated with MD-ALS is probably due to the lack of standardized protocols and lack of specific training. The results of this study, in combination with the already existing evidence in the current literature, fail to support the use of ALS in the pre-hospital management of urban trauma patients. These conclusions may or may not apply to rural trauma patients. Resources should be allocated for the establishment of trauma care systems and networks that ensure rapid transport of major trauma patients to highly specialized trauma hospitals. In these systems, emphasis should be placed on minimizing on-scene time and establishing patient transfer corridors to decrease time to definitive in-hospital care and maximize efficiency of the hospital care.

SOURCES

Government of Delhi, Evaluation Unit, Planning Department, Report of Evaluation Study on CATS 2001.

Government of India, Ministry of Health and Family Welfare, National Health Policy, 2002.

Joshipura, M.K., Total Trauma Care: International Perspective, Hospital Today, 1996; 11:43-4.

Joshipura, M.K., Mock, C., Goosen, J., Peden, M., Essential Trauma Care: strengthening trauma systems round the world, Injury 2004; 35:841-5.

Mock, C.N., Jurkovich, G.J., nii-Amon-Kotei D., Arreola-Risa C., Maier, R.V., Trauma mortality patterns in three nations at different economic levels: Implications for global trauma system development, J. Trauma 1998; 44:804-14.

National Crime Records Bureau, New Delhi, Accidental Deaths and Suicide in India, 1999.

Sethi, A.K., Tyagi, A., Trauma Untamed as yet. Trauma Care 2001;11:89-90.

Suresh, D.S., Trauma Systems in India—the CMC, Vellore Experience, Asian Archives of Anaesthesiology and Resuscitation, 2002; XLXII:21-3.

Wegman, Fred, Road Accidents: Worldwide a problem that can be tackled successfully!, AIPCR Publication No. 13.01.B, 1996.

WHO, South East Asia Regional Office, SCN Department, New Delhi - Disability, Violence—Injury, Prevention and Rehabilitation. *Newsletter*, 2001, Vol. 2, No. 1.

CHAPTER

10

Complementary and Alternative Medicine (CAM)

India's Healthcare Strength

Various systems of Indian medicines view the mind and body as unified, and approach healing as an internal process. Of late we have started talking of holistic medicine, recognizing the complementary role of the alternative systems of medicine. For example, in addition to using anti-inflammatory drugs to ease muscle pain, they also use Yoga, massage, chiropractic, and/or osteopathic manipulation. Alternative approaches are generally thought of as being used instead of conventional methods. For example, this might mean seeing a homeopath or naturopath or Ayurvedic doctor instead of your regular doctor. India received over 2 lakhs of health tourists from abroad in the year 2006, most of them went to Kerala in search of CAM. They were not disappointed.

Some reasons people consider CAM

- Belief that Western medicine is not holistic.
- A perspective that the cause of a problem may lie in life experiences, not diseases.

- Concern about the safety of modern medications and their much publicized side effects.
- Seeing CAM as less invasive and want to try it prior to seeing a medical doctor.
- Objections to what they see as "instant fix-it" or "pill-popping" attitudes.
- Lack of trust in doctors, or fear of medical errors.
- Religious beliefs that preclude drugs or surgery.
- Desire for a sense of spirit, missing in Western approaches.
- Exploring practices that have been popular in traditional India, to treat chronic ailments.
- Feeling that Western medicine is too mechanical, dogmatic, or compartmentalized.

There are some important characteristics of the therapeutic modalities offered by these medical traditions.

1. Foremost characteristic is safety

This is because the individual botanicals, minerals and the compound formulae have been established there through an empirical process lasting several hundred to several thousand years. Because of that process many of those treatments have outstanding record of safety and effectiveness. In addition, some of the botanicals used in Ayurveda—for example, peppers—are among the first plants to be cultivated by man and have been in use for several thousand years.

2. Broad action on the macro-organism

In fact terms adaptogen and the most recent one bioprotectant were developed on the basis of the mechanisms of action of several plants derived from Ayurveda materia medica. For example, curcuminoids or derivatives of Curcuma longa (turmeric) are being recognized now as versatile phenolic anti-oxidants, providing two-pronged anti-oxidant activity: prevention of free radical formation and intervention to neutralize existing free radicals. This action of curcuminoids exemplifies a new mechanism characteristic of the therapeutical ingredients called "bioprotectants".

3. Attention to the digestive processes

The other recognized feature of Ayurveda and related arts like Tibetan medicine is its emphasis on proper functioning of the digestive tract, specifically digestion and absorption, or bioavailability, of food, nutrients, and (when necessary) drugs.

Primary care for the digestive tract is approached in Ayurveda by providing a digestive formula to correct the suspected nutritional problem. Secondary care is provided by supplementing various formula with a digestion-enhancing component. Importantly the nutrient for the "digestive process" is understood in Ayurveda not only as food that we eat, but also air that we breathe and significantly the "food" that feeds our mental and emotional processes.

Medical education in Indian Systems of Medicine and Homoeopathy has been a cause of concern. After enactment of Indian Medicines Central Council Act, 1970 and Homoeopathy Central Council Act, 1973, five-and-a-half years Under-Graduate course and three years Post-Graduate course were introduced, provisions for adequate clinical exposure and internship made. The number of Indian Systems of Medicine and Homoeopathy colleges have increased phenomenally to 404. The Central Councils have implemented various educational regulations to ensure minimum standards of education. Depite this, there has been a mushroom growth of sub-standard colleges causing erosion to the standards of education and harm to medical training and practice. Liberal permission by the State Government, loopholes in the existing Acts and weakness in the enforcement of standards of education have contributed to this state of affairs.

Intellectual Property Rights (IPR) of ISM

Our wealth of knowledge on formulations and medicinal uses of plants available in ancient texts and treatises have been attracting foreign interest and a large number of such medicinal uses have been patented by them claiming as innovations though these are already available in the public domain and therefore can not be patented. This has happened as such knowledge is not available in easily accessible form and in the language generally used by the patent examiners overseas. This has harmed our national interest as the process for retrieval and contesting patents is very costly and time consuming which we can ill-afford. Protection of India's traditional medicinal knowledge would be undertaken through a progressive creation of a Digital Library for each system and eventually for uncodified knowledge leading to innovation and good health outcomes.

Relevant International fora would be addressed about the need for fair and equitable sharing of benefits to the custodians of the knowledge and a system of compensating the originators of such knowledge introduced. TRIPs has provided the signatory countries the freedom to choose intellectual property protection of plant varieties either under a patent regime or a *sui generis* system or a combination thereof. A *sui generic* system will be set-up to provide grassroots innovators of plant-based knowledge an incentive to disclose knowledge.

Naturopathic Medicine sees physical and mental health as arising from a healing power in the body that establishes, maintains, and restores health. Naturopathic practice may encompass hydrotherapy, botanical medicine, dietary and nutritional considerations, and counseling and lifestyle modifications learning to relax the mind and body will ease many symptoms. Examples of mind body healing include: Relaxation techniques or deep breathing, Yoga, Hypnosis, Biofeedback, Chiropractic, Osteopathy, and Massage, etc.

Traditional Chinese Medicine (TCM), is based on the flow of vital energy throughout the body. In a healthy state, the yin and yang (negative and positive energies) are balanced, while a disease state results from an imbalance. Thus, the use of herbs, nutrition, meditation, acupuncture, and exercise are intended to restore balance and return the body, mind, emotions and spirit to health.

Energetic therapies are used to describe practices like Reiki, external Qi Gong, therapeutic touch, and bioenergetics that involve non-local interactions viz., interactions in which there is no physical contact between the practitioner and the patient. All of them involve non-tactile, non-contact interactions between practitioner and patient, in which the practitioner uses information garnered from other senses to assess and treat the patient's condition.

Ayurvedic System

Ayurveda is the oldest medical system, where the focus is on energy and balance rather than symptoms that seeks to restore wholeness in the mind-body-spirit system. Each person has a particular combination of physical, mental and emotional characteristics known as Vata, Pitta, and Kapha. Physical and mental health is achieved by balancing diet, exercise, sleep, and sexual activity. Some of the tools of Ayurveda include a variety of stress management techniques, meditation, aromatherapy, yoga, and massage. The four pillars of Ayurvedic health maintenance are: (1) detoxification, (2) palliation, (3) rejuvenation, and (4) spiritual hygiene.

Ayurveda's concepts and Studies

All ayurvedic studies conducted on herbal and holistic medicine in ancient India, followed from the fountainhead of the two principle ayurvedic schools. The School of Physicians (Atreya) and the School of Surgeons (Dhanvantari) epitomized the eight main areas of ayurvedic studies and specialization during ancient times.

Kayachikitsa or internal medicine

This natural alternative medicine recognizes that the body of a person is the product of the constant psychosomatic interactions. The imbalances in the three doshas of vata-pitta-kapha occur sometimes by the mind and sometimes by the body's dhatu (tissues) and mala (toxin deposits). Hence, the kayachikitsa branch of this system of herbal and holistic medicine, delves deep into ascertaining the root cause of the illness.

The section of Nidana Sthana of Charaka Samhita deals with etiology, pathogenesis and diagnosis of an illness. Six stages of the development of disease are enumerated as aggravation, accumulation, overflow, relocation, build up in a new site and manifestation into a recognizable disease. One of the significant methods of treatment under kayachikitsa is panchakarma. This is a method of reversing the disease path from its manifestation stage back into its site of original development through special forms of emesis, purgation and enema, etc. Another unique aspect of kayachikitsa is rejuvenation called kaya kalpa.

Shalya Tantra or surgery

It is a significant branch of ayurveda. The name of the sage-physician Susruta is synonymous with surgery. From his treatise Susruta Samhita we come to know that thousand of years ago sophisticated methods of surgery were practiced in India.

The original text of Susruta discusses in detail about an exhaustive range of surgical methods including about how to deal with various types of tumors, internal and external injuries, fracture of bones, complications during pregnancy and delivery, and obstruction in intestinal loop. Susruta was the first surgeon to develop cosmetic surgery. His surgical treatment for trichiasis can be to some of the modern operative techniques used for this eye disease. The long foreign rule in India and lack of promotion stalled the progress of ayurvedic surgery in the middle of the second millennium.

Shalakya Tantra or Eye and ENT

The name of this branch was called Shalakya due to excessive use of 'Shalaka', which means a rod or probe. Though all the three main classics of ayurveda deals on this subject, Susruta Samhita describes more deeply about this branch. Susruta discussed about 72 diseases of the eye. He has stipulated drug therapy for various types of conjunctivitis and glaucoma along with surgical procedures of the removal of cataract, pterygium, diseases of ear, nose and throat besides cosmetic surgery for traumatized nose and ear (rhinoplasty and auraplasty).

Agada tantra or Toxicology

This branch of ayurveda described various methods of cleaning the poisons out of the body as well as recommends antidotes for particular poisons. It deals with a wide range of natural toxins originating from wild lives (animals, birds, insects, etc.), plants/herbs (belladonna, aconite, etc.), vegetables, minerals (leads, mercury, arsenal, etc.) and artificial poisons prepared from poisonous drugs. This branch also deals with air and water pollution, which are basically the causes of various dangerous epidemics.

Kaumarabhritya

This branch deals comprehensively about prenatal, postnatal baby care and gynecology. With the view to achieve its ultimate aim of creating a healthy and disease free society ayurveda strives to make the baby from the time of its conception upto the time of its growth into an adult. Kaumarabhritya has recognized that the mental and physical state of the mother has direct links with the health of the child. It has recommended particular diet, regimen, nutrition and conduct for women during and after delivery. Apart from that Kaumarabhritya deals with various disorders concerning children's health such as gastrointestinal diseases, teething disorder, rickets other than midwifery.

Vajkarana

This branch of science explains the art of producing healthy progeny for the creation of a better society. Hence, deals with various diseases like infertility and conditions relating to weak shukra dhatu or the vital reproductive fluids of the body. Apart from prescribing a lot of effective formulations to provide nutrition to enhance the quality of vital body fluids it specifically emphasized to lead a highly disciplined life. This branch of ayurveda highlighted that celibacy is essential for good health. It helps increase the will power, intellect and memory in addition to a healthy body. The shukra dhatu has a direct link with ojas or the immunity of the body. Hence, vajikaran prescribed the therapeutic use of various aphrodisiacs and tonic preparations for enhancing the vigor and reproductive capabilities of men that also strengthens other body tissues like muscles, fats, bones and blood.

Bhuta Vidya

This branch of ayurveda specifically deals with the diseases of mind or psychic conditions, which can be caused by super natural forces. Different experts have explained the word bhuta differently. Some experts say that bhuta means ghosts and similar bad spirits who cause abnormal psychological conditions. Others say bhuta represents microscopic organisms such as virus, bacteria that are not visible to naked eye. Ayurveda also believes in the past karma as a causative factor of certain diseases. Bhuta Vidya deals with the causes, which are directly not visible and have no direct explanation in terms of tridosha.

Rasayana

The rasayana therapy increases the life force (ojas) and immunity of a person and thus there is a regeneration of cells and tissues in the body. Rasayana is a therapeutic process to defer old age. The sages of ancient times led long, disease-free, and vigorous lives with the help of rasayanas. Lord Indra is supposed to have given the knowledge of these panaceas to the sages. Literally, rasayana means the augmentation of rasa, the vital fluid produced by the digestion of food. It is the rasa flowing in the body which sustains life. Rasayana in ayurveda is, the method of treatment through which the rasa is maintained in the body.

The three medicine categories are known in ayurveda as rasayana, vajikarana, and aushadhis, respectively. These categories are complementary to each other. Rasayanas prepared from the herbs and medicinal plants of amalaki, haritiki, triphala, bhringaraja, ashwagandha, punarnava, chitraka and many other herbal medicines have been used from time immemorial and have been instrumental in giving long, disease-free, and vigorous lives to their users.

Jewels or ratnas include precious and semiprecious stones, which are used as drugs because of their therapeutic properties. Major jewels or maharatnas include: diamond—hiraka; ruby—manikya; pearl—mukta; topaz—pushparaga; sapphire—neelam; emerald—tarksha; cat's eye—vaidurya; zircon—gomedak; and caulk—vidruma. Uparatnas or minor jewels like sun-stone—suryakant, moonstone—chandrakanta, and crystal—sphatik were in use. Rasayana is held as the culmination of ayurvedic wisdom.

According to World Health Organization report, over 80% of the world population relies on plant-based traditional medicine for their primary healthcare needs.

Milestones in the Development of Ayurveda

- Divine origin from Lord Brahma—Dates back to origin of human race
- Health, Diseases and Medicinal Plants in Rig-veda and Atharv-veda—5000 BC
- Origin of Attreya and Dhanwantari School of Ayurveda—1000 BC
- Documentation of Charaka Samhita—600 BC
- Documentation of Sushruta Samhita—500 BC
- Advent of Muslim Rulers and start of the Decline of Ayurveda—1100 to 1800
- Resurrection of the system of Medicine under the rule of Peshwas—1800 AD
- Ayurvedic medicine opened in Government Sanskrit College, Calcutta—1827
- Discontinuation of classes in Government Sanskrit College by British—1833
- Dr. Komar Commission; investigation in indigenous system of medicine—1917
- Indian National Congress Convention at Nagpur recommended acceptance of Ayurvedic system of medicine as India's National Healthcare System—1920
- Mahatma Gandhi inaugurated Ayurvedic and Unani Tibbia College Delhi—1921
- Malviya established Ayurveda college in B.H.U., Varanasi—1927
- Drugs and Cosmetics Act for Ayurvedic/Siddha/ Unani Medicines—1940
- Bhore Committee or Health Survey and Development Committee recognized past services of indigenous medicines—1943
- Chopra Committee recommended systems of old and modern systems of medicines to evolve a common system of medicine—1946
- Pharmaceutical Enquiry Committee headed by Dr. Bhatia, for intensive research in indigenous drugs of Ayurveda—1953

- Dave Committee for uniform standards of Ayurveda education—955
- Establishment of Institute of Post-Graduate Training and Research in Gujarat Ayurvedic University, Jamnagar, Gujarat—1956 to 1957
- Udupa Committee set-up. It recommended that there is a need for integrated system of medicine and a training course in Siddha and Ayurveda— 1958
- Establishment of Post-Graduate Institute of Ayurveda at Banaras Hindu University, Varanasi, Uttar Pradesh—1963 to 1964
- Drugs and Cosmetics Act, 1940 for Indian systems of medicines/drugs—1964
- Central Board of Siddha and Ayurvedic Education—1964 to 1965
- Apex Research Body for Indian medicine and Homoeopathy, 'Central Council for Research in Indian Medicine and Homoeopathy (CCRIMH)'—1969
- Pharmacopoeia Laboratory for Indian medicine, Ghaziabad, U.P.—1970
- Constitution of Central Council of Indian Medicine (CCIM) under an Act—1970
- National Institute of Ayurveda, Jaipur, Rajasthan—1972 to 1973
- Publication of Ayurvedic formulary containing 444 preparations—1976
- Central Council of Research in Ayurveda and Siddha (CCRAS)—1978
- Amended Drugs and Cosmetics Act regulating import/export of Indian Systems of Medicine—1982
- Setting up of Indian Medicine Pharmaceutical Corporation Ltd. in Mohan, Almora Distt., Uttaranchal—1983
- Silver Jubilee function of Jawaharlal Nehru Ayurvedic Medicinal Plants Garden, Pune. Inaugurated by Shri R. Venkataraman, Vice-president of India—1986
- Second World Conference on Yoga and Ayurveda held at Banaras Hindu University, Varanasi, Uttar Pradesh—1986

- Jawaharlal Nehru Anusandhan Bhawan, Institutional Area, Janakpuri, New Delhi by Hon'ble Vice-President of India, Dr. Shankar Dayal Sharma—1988
- National Academy of Ayurveda (Rashtriya Ayurveda Vidyapeeth)—1989
- Creation of separate Department of Indian Systems of Medicine and Homoeopathy in Ministry of Health and Family Welfare, Government of India—1995
- Introduction of Extra mural Research Programme for accredited organizations with central assistance—1996
- Implementation of Central Scheme in 33 organizations for development of agro-techniques of important medicinal plants—1997
- Maiden participation of Ayurveda alongwith other systems in India International Trade Fair—1998
- Implementation of Central Scheme in 32 laboratories for developing pharmacopoeial standards of Medicinal Plants/ISM Formualations—1998
- Establishment of specialty clinic of Ayurveda in Central Government Hospital (Safdarjung Hospital), New Delhi—1998
- Implementation of IEC (Information, Education and Communication) Scheme for NGOs for propagation and popularization of Ayurveda—1998 to 1999
- Participation in Mystique India—1997 to 1999
- Introduction of Vanaspati Van Scheme for cultivation of Medicinal Plants—1999
- Inauguration of Ayurveda conference at Newyork, USA by Hon'ble Prime Minister of India Sh. Atal Bihari Vajpayee—2000
- Gazette Notification for constitution of Medicinal Plant Board under the Deptt. of Indian Systems of Medicine and Homoeopathy—2000
- Publication of 2nd volume of Ayurvedic Pharmacopoeia—2000
- Introduction of Ayurvedic Medicines in RCH Programme—2000

- Constitution of Advisory group for research in Ayurveda—2000
- Policy Decision on mainstreaming of Ayurveda in RCH programme as per National Population Policy—2000
- Implementation of Central Scheme of assistance for strengthening of State Drug Testing Laboratories and Pharmacies—2000 to 2001
- Publication of 3rd volume of Ayurvedic Pharmacopoeia—2001
- Publication of English edition of 2nd volume of Formulary of India—2001
- Maiden participation of ISM tableau on Republic Day—2001
- Exhibition and presentation of Ayurveda during World Health Assembly—2001
- Presentation on evidence based support by Deptt. of ISM&H before House of Lords, U.K. against Sir Walton Committee's Report on status and nomenclature of Ayurveda among Complementary CAM—2001
- "Made in India" exhibition organized by CII in South Africa—2001

Medical Tourism and Export of Ayurvedic Practitioners

The interest in our systems overseas for gentler and plant-based treatment has been growing rapidly. More than that certain therapies are becoming extremely popular and tourists/visitors come to India for therapies like Panchkarma and Yoga. Medical tourism not only popularizes our system but offers good avenue for foreign exchange earning. Little has been done to create a chain of Panchkarma Centres and establish centres of excellence for yoga therapy, meditation and teaching.

Financing Indian System/Ayurveda

ISM shares only 2-4% of the National Health Budget. This should be raised to 10% of the total health plan at the Central level and further growth should be designed to climb at the rate of 5% in every FiveYear Plan. For the first five years of the New Policy, Central Government will directly provide or earmark budgets for consolidation of infrastructure, purchase of drugs and support for opening speciality clinics and ISM services.

Herbal medicine

Over the last two decades there has been a steady increase in the demand for herbal drugs. However, the demand for good quality medicinal plants and herbs have not been met. The prices of several plants have increased sharply, making them unaffordable and some species of medicinal plants are also reported to be endangered because of increasing pressure on forests.

The Planning Commission had constituted a Task Force on the Conservation, Cultivation, Sustainable Use and Legal Protection of Medicinal Plants. The Task Force recommended: establishment of medicinal plants conservation areas (MPCA), covering all ecosystems, forest types and sub-types; ex-situ conservation of rare, endangered medicinal plants may be tried out in established gardens managed by the Departments of Agriculture, Horticulture or Forests; gene banks created by the Department of Biotechnology should store the germplasm of all medicinal plants; establishment of 'Vanaspati vans' in degraded forest areas; forest areas rich in medicinal plants should be identified, management plans formulated and sustainable harvesting encouraged under the Joint Forest Management System; technically qualified NGOs must be encouraged to take up the task of improving awareness and increasing availability of plant stock and involved in the promotion of agro-techniques for cultivation of medicinal plants; screening/testing/clinical evaluation of herbal products to be taken up and completed; drug testing laboratories for ISM&H products should be established with qualified staff; establishment of a Traditional Knowledge Digital Library so that information on medicinal plants and their use in the country could be accessed readily; and establishment of a Medicinal Plant Board for integrated development of the medicinal plants.

Herbal supplements may be popular, but are they for you? That depends on the herb, your current health and your medical history. Herbal supplements have active ingredients that can affect how your body functions, just as over-the-counter and prescription drugs do. Herbal supplements may be particularly risky for certain individuals and their labels are often vague, confusing and of little help when it comes to making a selection. If you're considering herbal supplements, educate yourself about any products you intend to use before purchasing them, and talk to your doctor about any herbal supplements you're considering taking.

How do you choose an herbal supplement?

The limited amount of regulation makes choosing an herbal supplement of the highest quality a difficult prospect. In order to choose the best herbal supplement brands:

- Look for standardized herbal supplements. The U.S. Pharmacopoeia's "USP Dietary Supplement Verified" seal on a supplement indicates the supplement has met certain manufacturing standards. These standards include testing the product for uniformity, cleanliness and freedom from environmental contaminants such as lead, mercury or drugs. Other groups that certify herbal supplements include ConsumerLab.com, Good Housekeeping and NSF International. Although each group takes a slightly different approach, the goal of each is to certify that herbal supplements meet a certain standard. Don't assume that all herbal products on the market are safe. Even the groups that test herbal supplements aren't obligated to report products that fail to live up to their standards.
- Buy only single-herb products. And choose products that clearly show how much of the herb each dose contains. Some products are mixtures of several herbs with unknown proportions of each.
- Beware of claims that sound too good to be true. If a claim sounds outrageous to you, trust your instinct. No one herbal supplement can possibly address a wide spectrum of health concerns.
- Be extremely cautious about herbal supplements

manufactured outside the United States. Many European herbs are highly regulated and standardized. But toxic ingredients and prescription drugs have been found in some herbal supplements manufactured in other countries.

Who shouldn't use herbal supplements?

- You're taking prescription or over-the-counter (OTC) medications. Some herbs can cause serious side effects when mixed with prescription and OTC drugs such as aspirin, blood thinners or blood pressure medications. Talk to your doctor about possible interactions.
- A proven medical treatment is available for your medical condition. A traditional medication with an established record for safety and effectiveness will generally be less likely to result in adverse side effects.
- You're pregnant or breast-feeding. As a general rule, don't take any medications—prescription, OTC or herbal—when you're pregnant or breast-feeding unless your doctor approves. Medications that may be safe for you as an adult may be harmful to your fetus or your breast-feeding infant.
- You're having surgery. Many herbal supplements can affect the success of surgery. Some may decrease the effectiveness of anesthetics or cause dangerous complications such as bleeding or high blood pressure. Tell your doctor about any herbs you're taking or considering taking as soon as you know you need surgery.
- You're younger than 18 or older than 65. Older adults may metabolize medications differently. And few herbal supplements have been tested on children or have established safe doses for children.

Homoeopathic Medicine ("like cures like")

"It was developed in the early 20th century. It does not treat a "disease" by name (such as depression) but rather by symptoms (including things that affect symptoms, such as sounds, smells, tastes, moods, energy, time of day or temperature when symptoms are worse, etc.). Micro-quantities of specific substances are used to cure symptoms, which would actually be caused by larger doses of the same substance? Conventional drugs are usually prescribed in individual capacities to act upon specific parts of the body, so it follows that several different drugs might be prescribed to treat the various symptoms of one individual. Homeopathic medicine offers an alternative. Instead of giving one medicine for a person's headache, another for his constipation, another for his irritability and yet another to counteract the effects of one or more the medicines, the homoeopathic physician prescribes a single medicine at a time that will stimulate the person's immune and defense capacity and bring about an overall improvement in that person's health. The procedure by which the homoeopath finds the precise individual substance is the very science and arts of homoeopathy.

The treatment was discovered some 200 years ago by a German doctor, Friedrich Samuel Hahnemann, who found when he took a dose of quinine. It made him feverish, gave him the symptoms he would have expected to get if he had contracted malaria, then very common. It is the very same principle that was discovered at around the same time in Britain by Dr. Edward Jenner, who proved true the old wives' tale about cowpox protecting against smallpox. He went on to develop the vaccine that made his name in history and which eradicated the disease world-wide. Hahnemann pursued the principle in different directions and found that if the strength of a homoeopathic remedy were diluted, its effect was improved. Homeopathic medicine is a natural pharmaceutical system that utilises microdoses of substances from the plant, mineral and animal kingdom to arouse a person's natural healing substances from the plant, mineral and animal kingdoms to arouse a person's natural healing response. Homeopathy is a sophisticated method of individualising small doses of medicine in order to initiate that healing response.

Unlike conventional drugs, which act primarily by having direct effect upon physiological process related to a person's symptoms' homoeopathic medicines are, thought to work by stimulating the person's immune system, which raises his or her overall level of health thereby enabling him or her to re-establish health and prevent disease.

As people develop greater understanding and respect for the body's immune system, homoeopathy will gain popularity as a primary pharmacological means to stimulate immune response. Those convenient medical therapies that primarily treat and suppress symptoms will be accepted for their valuable role in healthcare, but not necessarily as a first course of treatment. Homoeopaths have found clinical experience that their medicines often replace conventional drugs and eliminate the need for heroic procedures. Ideally, homeopaths are taking the best of the natural science to create a kind of care that will be commonplace in future.

Even a skeptical Edelman agrees that Homoeopathy is an unorthodox but no longer crazy way to perform immunotherapy. By homoeopathy any ailment, acute or chronic, local or general can be treated except diseases where surgery is unavoidable. Even in cases of enlarged tonsils, kidney stones, warts, piles, homeopathy has received accolades. Moreover good homoeopathic prescribing has made many operations unnecessary.

Are doctors opposed to CAM?

Most doctors aren't opposed to complementary and alternative medicine. It's true that some doctors may not want to discuss complementary and alternative medicine therapies, but as many as half the doctors in the United States refer people to complementary and alternative practitioners. Your doctor may, in fact, be willing to discuss these options with you. Conventional doctors have good reason to be skeptical when it comes to complementary and alternative medicine. Some alternative medicine practitioners make exaggerated claims about curing diseases, and some ask you to forgo treatment from your conventional doctor to use their unproven therapies. Some forms of alternative medicine can even hurt you. Complementary and alternative medicine may give you additional treatment options, but while some of those options can help you, others can hurt you. When considering complementary and alternative medicine, steer a middle course between uncritical acceptance and outright rejection. Be open-minded yet skeptical at the same time.

A growing number of doctors are working to better understand herbal therapies so that they can help you make informed decisions about your healthcare. If your doctor isn't comfortable discussing herbal supplements with you, ask for a referral to a specialist who is knowledgeable in that field.

Whether CAM has scientific basis?

Many people claim that CAM has no scientific basis and it has failed to evolve on the modern Indian scene due to lack of scientific research. It is well known that physicians with qualification in systems like Ayurveda and homoeopathy trust and practice modern medicine more often. A Professor from a US university's department of pharmacology said that homoeopathy has barely changed since the start of the 19th Century and was "more like religion than science". He suggested it would be better if courses in aromatherapy, acupuncture, herbal medicine, reflexology, magneto therapy, naturopathy and traditional Chinese medicine and others were taught as part of a cultural history rather than alternative systems of medicine. Let Ayurveda and other systems of CAM invest in research and submit itself for scrutiny to scientific world to emerge as reliable systems of cure.

The Internet offers an ideal way to discover the latest in complementary and alternative medicine. Web sites can be updated at any time to keep up with new products, therapies and advances in the field. But beware—the Internet is also one of the greatest sources of misinformation. According to a study in the Sept. 17, 2003, issue of the "Journal of the American Medical Association," of 433 complementary and alternative medicine Web sites examined, most made misleading or unproven health claims about the herbal remedies they sold.

- *Check out the site sponsor.* Web sites created by major medical centers, national organizations, universities and government agencies are the most credible.
- *Determine the site's objective.* Is the sponsor trying to educate you or just sell you something? Stay away from sites that don't clearly distinguish between scientific evidence and advertisements.
- *Find out if the information is current.* Look for a date. Older material may not include recent findings, such as newly discovered side effects or advances in the field.
- *Red flag words.* The advertisements or promotional materials usually include words such as "satisfaction guaranteed," "miracle cure" or "new discovery." If the product were in fact a cure, it would be widely reported in the media and your doctor would recommend it.
- *Pseudomedical jargon.* Though terms such as "purify," "detoxify" and "energize" may sound impressive and may even have an element of truth, they're generally used to cover up a lack of scientific proof. Watch out for these words.
- *Cure-alls.* The manufacturer claims that the product can treat a wide range of symptoms, or cure or prevent a number of diseases. No single product can do all this.
- *Anecdotal evidence.* Testimonials are no substitute for solid scientific documentation.
- *False accusations.* The manufacturer of the product accuses the government or a medical profession of suppressing important information about the product's benefits.
- *Understand scientific studies.* If you read about studies in journal articles, assess the quality of the research. Look for words such as "double-blind," "controlled" and "randomized."
- *Clinical studies.* These involve studies on human beings—not animals. They generally come after studies that demonstrate the safety and effectiveness of the treatment in animals and in

the lab. Studies done solely in test tubes and petri dishes can't prove benefit to humans.

- *Randomized, controlled trials.* Participants in these trials usually are divided into groups. One group receives the treatment under investigation. Another group may be a control group—participants receive standard treatment, no treatment or an inactive substance called a placebo. Participants are assigned to these groups on a random basis. This helps ensure that the groups will be similar.
- *Double-blind studies.* In these studies, neither the researchers nor the human subjects know who will receive the active treatment and who will receive the placebo.

Look for peer-reviewed journals—those that only publish articles reviewed by an independent panel of medical experts.

CHAPTER

11

Futuristic Approach

Healthcare's Face will Undergo a Sea Change

Healthcare, which is dollar 35 billion industry at present, is expected to reach dollar 75 billions in the next five years. According to a CII estimate the healthcare sector in the next 10 years can account for over seven percent of the GDP and provide employment to nine million people. Apart from making healthcare available to the masses at affordable prices, the sector will employ more people directly than power, railways and telecom put together. The CII national committee on healthcare, had proposed that every industrial unit should adopt 50 km of area around it for providing primary health services. They can team up with the government for this purpose and make use of the primary health centers in every area. "If each of the 10,000 units take the responsibility for an area of 50 km around it, that will give a big boost to healthcare in the country", says Dr. Trehan. If there is a realization among the Indian industry that helping the poor can lead to better health and productivity, many problems of healthcare can be addressed. Modernization of the healthcare systems and greater collaboration with the healthcare industry to provide innovative drugs, modern medical equipment, better healthcare services, as well as to expand healthcare insurance are the primary goals. Induction of information technology for facilitation and applying new discoveries like stem cell implant for treatment of incurable diseases can go a long way in ameliorating the healthcare for Indian masses.

With 1.5 beds per thousand population, India is at par with some of the least developed countries of the world. An addition of even a single bed per thousand population will require 1.1 million beds and an expenditure of US dollar 80 billions. Where is the money? "The healthcare strategies framed by WHO would not work in a country like India and therefore we have to have a policy of our own", said Dr. Devi Prasad Shetty, Chairman, Narayana Hrudayalaya, Bangalore.

Emerging trends in healthcare

1. Private sector takes the lead; 80-85% delivery of out-patients services.
2. Increasing accessibility of health insurance.
3. standardization and accreditation of healthcare.
4. well informed Indian patient and demand from foreigners.
5. Manpower development and reversal of brain drain.
6. Technology centered approach.
7. PPP approach for universal care.
8. The hype of medical tourism.
9. Medicities galore; need for over 1 lakh of beds addition.
10. Massive investment to the tune of $100 billions in health infrastructure.

Need for universal medical insurance cover

One of the main products of the health insurance will be the health insurance for the people for groups of people from the lower socio-economic strata. In fact, these are the people or groups of people who need the insurance most. It is expected that the government and the civil society will ensure health insurance for all in the futuristic plan. As a pilot experiment,

Dr. Shetty is in the process of offering health insurance coverage to the farmers of Karnataka. In the Phase-I they are going to cover 10 percent of the State's population, that is roughly about 50 lakh farmers. Each farmer-member is expected to contribute Rs. 5 to Rs. 10 a month and he/she will be insured for all types of operations starting from appendices to heart surgery. These procedures will be totally free and other than this free service they will also get medical treatment at a concessional rate. The prediction is that within the next 5 or 10 years most of the government hospitals will become sick since their way of running this organization involves 90 percent of budgetary allocation being given for salaries. There is very little money left for upgrading the facilities or creating a comparative environment.

The insurable population in India has been assessed at 250 million and at an average of Rs. 1000 per person the premium amount per year would be Rs. 25000 crores and is expected to treble in ten years. While the insurance product will dutifully reflect the demands of this colossal market and related technological developments in medicine, it should be required to extend beyond hospitalization and cover domiciliary treatment too. The insurance regulatory authority has announced priority in licensing to companies set-up with health insurance as key business and has emphasized the need for developing new products on fair terms to those at risk among the poor and in rural areas. In order to be socially relevant and commercially viable the scheme must aim at a proper mix of health hazards and cover many broad social classes and income groups. This is possible in poor locations or communities only if a group view is taken and on that basis a population-based risk is assessed and community rated premiums determined covering families for all common illnesses and based on epidemiologically determined risk. In order that exclusions co-payments deductibles, etc. remain minimum and relevant to our social situation, some well judged government merit subsidy can be incorporated into anti-poverty family welfare or primary education or welfare pension schemes meant for old age. Innovative community-based new products can be developed by using the scattered experience of such products for instance in SEWA, so that a minimum core cover can be developed as a model for innovative insurance by panchayats with reinsurance backup by companies and government bearing part of promotional costs. The bulk of the formal sector may be covered by an expanded mandatory insurance with affordable cover and convenient modes of premium payment.

Clinics likely to face regulatory checks

Doctors may have to meet stringent regularly provision before being given license to run clinics. The Centre is planning to create a regulatory body in set-up minimum Standards for different kind of healthcare providers. The proposal has already received the prime minister's approval and likely to be announced in December as part the medium-term health policy of the government.

The provisions of the new legislation would be applicable for all clinical establishments including diagnostic centres's and private testing labs.

Today, a doctor can open a clinic whenever and wherever he wants to. The practice would become a hinge of past with the government's decision to regulate private clinics. Private sector provides for over 68% of total hospitals in the country, 37% of hospital beds and over 80% of other healthcare provisions.

There are stringent measures being considered by the government to regulate private healthcare facilities. Standards would be set for physical space, human resources, infrastructure and clinical standards according to the facility. Different roles would be laid for 30-bed, 50-bed, 100-bed and single- and multiple-speciality hospitals. Also, all private hospitals would have to attend to emergencies without considering the financial capability of the patient, an official in health ministry said. (Guha and Narayan)

> "The private healthcare system has remained by and large fragmented and uncontrolled. There are evidences of serious quality deficiencies in many healthcare practices."

Medicare cities model of healthcare

Medical cities may be the next ideal step towards building India's healthcare and medical expertise, but the numbers are still insufficient. Even under the current, growing corporate set-up, a Technopak report points out that almost 90 percent of the private healthcare is being serviced by an unorganized sector. The need is to take India's current ratio of 1.5 beds per 1000 people to the world average of four beds per 1000. It would also entail starting smaller medicities in tier-three cities. What is the concept of a medical or health city? A cluster of hospitals, a holistic healthcare centre, a large hospital sprawled across acres of land? Certainly. But it doesn't end here. In simpler terms, the difference between a hospital and a medical city is as vast as the difference between a corner shop and a mega store. What you won't find at the shop, you will be certain to get at the store. In what could be the beginning of a medical renaissance, medical cities could change the way medical education and research and development is conducted in India, taking it from public to private to corporate. A medical city translates into an institution that has the resources and excellence to take clinical treatment out of operation theatres to classrooms and laboratories.

"It is an institution of the caliber to train people from the level of a medical school right to the highest level of medical education. But this needs to be done through the highest level of faculty, which is not only into practicing medicine but equally involved in teaching and research", said Dr. Naresh Trehan

"The whole idea of a medicity is to provide the highest quality of healthcare at a reasonable cost", said Mr. Shivender Mohan Singh of Fortis group and president, Indian Healthcare Federation.

"One medicity can offer the best care for a wide range of specialities and services at the same time," observed Analjit Singh, Chairman, Max Healthcare.

"By creating quality infrastructure we are certain of getting quality output . . . though we are into medical education, it is also not a charity initiative" said Shivinder M. Singh, managing director, Fortis Healthcare. Recently, Aditya Birla Memorial Hospital started near Pune and Dr. Pratap C. Reddy swung the doors open to the Apollo Health City in Hyderabad, and at the same time Shivinder M. Singh began work on two Fortis Medicities, one in Gurgaon and another in Lucknow, with the promise of eight more in the pipeline. Industry watchers are doubtful that healthcare costs will decrease. Others say, "The medical cities might even translate into higher costs of healthcare for the consumer." Dr. Rana Mehta, at Technopak, agrees. "Since the investment will be by corporates alone, costs might not come down at all." Apollo's Prasad admits that at the Health City, cost of healthcare remains parallel to the cost at any other Apollo hospital. Medical cities are marked by mammoth investment and long gestation periods. The gestation period can squeeze a lot of money out of the investor without offering much in return. While well-off Indian people and foreign medical tourists can take treatment at corporate hospitals, the masses can get the benefit from the public hospitals (then less crowded).

PGI and other institutions of excellence

Institutions like the Post-graduate institute of medical education and research Chandigarh (PGI), All India Institute of Medical Sciences in Delhi, Christian Medical College in Vellore and Maulana Azad Medical College in Delhi have been pockets of excellence in teaching and research in the country. Until 2005, India had only 229 medical colleges of which 106 were established through the private route with Manipal Hospital in Bangalore towering above the rest for its excellence in research, especially stem cell research. But despite these institutions, with only 25000 medical graduates each year, the Indian ratio of doctors to population stands small at 0.6 doctors per 1000 people, the world average being 1.8 per 1,000. This translates into an immediate need of another 12-13 lakh doctors, a gap so vast it will take decades to fill. A glimmer of hope now flickers in plans of medical India's corporate world and within bricks of foundation that have been laid to mark medical city projects. For a huge country like India with healthcare the current buzz, it is hardly surprising that medical and health cities seem to be surfacing on the horizon.

NABH

National Accreditation Board for Hospitals and Healthcare Providers (NABH) is a constituent board of Quality Council of India, set-up with cooperation of Ministry of Health and Family Welfare, Government of India and the health industry, to establish and operate accreditation programme for healthcare organizations. The board is structured to cater to much desired needs of the consumers and to set benchmarks for progress of health industry. The board while being supported by all stakeholders including industry, consumers, government, has full functional autonomy in its operation. Max hospital in Delhi was given accreditation by the board in 2007.

NABH Accredited Hospitals

B.M. Birla Heart Research Centre, Kolkata

MIMS Hospital, Calicut

Max Super-Speciality Hospital, New Delhi

Max Devki Devi Heart and Vascular

Institute, New Delhi

Kerala Institute of Medical Sciences, Thiruvananthapuram

Joint Commissione International (JCI)

Joint Commission launched its international accreditation program in 1999 but has accredited more than 15,000 healthcare organizations in US. Its accreditation is a nationwide seal of approval that indicates a hospital meets high performance standards. The World Health Organization (WHO) designated the Joint Commission on Accreditation of Healthcare Organizations and Joint Commission International as its Collaborating Centre on Patient Safety in 2005. Over 60 hospitals being accredited by JCI world-wide including, India.

JCI Accredited Hospitals

Indraprastha Apollo Hospital, New Delhi
Apollo Hospital, Chennai
Apollo Hospital, Hyderabad
Wockhardt Hospital, Mumbai
Shroff Eye Hospital, Mumbai
Fortis, Mohali
Grewal Eye Institute, Chandigarh

Emerging burden of disease in India

Murry and Lopez have provided a possible scenario of the burden of disease (BOD) for India in the year 2020. The key concept entails not only mortality but disability viewed in terms of healthy years of life lost. A careful analysis of the Global Burden of Disease (GBD) study focusing on age-specific morbidity during 2000 in ten most common diseases (excluding injuries) shows that sixty percent of morbidity is due to infectious diseases and common tropical diseases, a quarter due to life-style disorders and 13% due to potentially preventable peri-natal conditions. In this forecast, BOD is expected to dramatically decrease in respect of diarrhoeal diseases and respiratory infections and less dramatically for maternal conditions. TB is expected to plateau by 2000, and HIV infections are expected to rise significantly up to 2010. We have already the distinction of elimination or control acceptable to public health standards of small pox and guinea worm diseases. It has now been proposed to eliminate or control the following diseases within limits acceptable to public health practice. Further it is hoped that the following landmarks will be created in controlling diseases:

- Polio Yaws and leprosy by 2005 which seems distinctly feasible though the removal of social stigma and reconstructive surgery and other rehabilitation arrangements in regard to leprosy would remain inadequate for a decade or more.
- Kalaazar and Filalriasis by 2010 which also seems feasible due to its localized prevalence and the possibility of greater community-based work.

- Blindness prevalence to 0.5% by 2010 sees less feasible due to a graying population. At present the programme is massively supported by foreign aid as there are many other legitimate demands on domestic health budgets.
- AIDS reaching zero growth by 2007 appears to be problematic.

Surge of Silvers

The proportion of people above 65 will increase and as a result the burden of non-communicable diseases will rise. Finally, cardiovascular diseases resulting from the risk associated with smoking, urban stress and improper diet are expected to increase dramatically. Under the same BOD methodology another view is available from a four-state analysis done in 1996, these four states—AP, Karnataka, W. Bengal and Punjab—represent different stages in the Indian health transition. The analysis reveals that the poorer and more populated states. West Bengal, will still face a large incidence of communicable diseases. More prosperous states, such as Punjab will witness sharply increasing incidence of non-communicable diseases especially, in urban areas. It also highlights the policy dilemma of how to balance between the articulate middle upper class demand for more access to technologically advanced and subsidized clinical services and the more pressing needs of the poor for coverage of basic disease control interventions. This conflict over deployment of public resources will only get exacerbated in future. What matters most in such estimates are not societal averages with respect to health but sound data illumining specifically the health conditions of the disadvantaged in local areas. It also incorporates the long tradition of health sector analysis looking at unequal access, income poverty and unjustly distributed resources as the trigger to meet health needs of the poor. That tradition has been totally replaced by the currently dominant school of international thought about health which is concerned primarily with efficiency of systems measured by cost effectiveness criteria. The essential ingredients of good healthcare are: (i) universal access, and access to an adequate level, and access without excessive burden, (ii) fair distribution of financial costs for access and fair distribution of burden in rationing care and capacity and a constant search for improvement to a more just system, (iii) training providers for competence empathy and accountability, pursuit of quality care ad cost effective use of the results of relevant research. (Srinivasan, R.).

Without being too defensive or critical about its past failures, the rural health structure should be strengthened and funded and managed efficiently in all States.

The Bhore Committee (1946) lies in the dust bin?

The Bhore Committee (1946) was the first policy statement on healthcare in independent India. Free India accepted the onerous load of free services to all not withstanding a fast increasing population. The Committee curiously took no account of indigenous systems, which people were actually using nor surprisingly paid any attention to the public duties of the private sector in medicine. It took the Alma Ata declaration and the report of the joint ICSSR/ICMR report to call for a comprehensive approach to healthcare. National Health Policy, 1983 (NHP-83) was critical of the western model of healthcare. It suggested a holistic decentralized and low cost system working through a network of trained doctors, para-professionals and volunteers devoted to community needs and providing self-reliance. Progress in implementing an NHP has been patchy, due to unfocussed strategies and under estimation of costs. Moreover, health planning in India had always had a centralized and remained top down and largely technocratic and managerial backed by no social imagination. There was no attempt to downstage responsibility for care to levels below doctors or a non-doctor-based healthcare linked to genuine community responsibility for local health planning and implementation, like spraying insecticides or mother's education in managing diarrhoea in children or making use of ISMH traditions for preventive services. Some segments will remain always more vulnerable—such as women (due to patriarchy and traditions of intra-family denial), aged (whose percentage will increase dramatically with improved healthcare), children (whose survival but not always development will increase with immunization) and the disabled (constituting a tenth of the population).

Unfinished burden of diseases

Apart from the above, there remains a vast unfinished burden in preventing, controlling or eliminating other major communicable diseases and in bringing down the risk of deaths in maternal and peri-natal conditions. Endemic diseases arising from infection or lack of nutrition continue to account for almost two-thirds of mortality and morbidity in India. Indeed eleven out of thirteen diseases recommended by the Bhore Committee were infectious diseases and at least three of them may well continue to be with us for the next two decades Barring Leprosy which is almost on the path to total control, the other key communicable diseases will be TB, Malaria and Aids—to which diarrhoea in children and complicated and high risk maternity should be added in view of their pervasive incidence and avoidable mortality among the poorer and under served sectors.

Non-communicable diseases

Three major such diseases viz., cancer cardiovascular diseases and renal conditions and mental health conditions have of late shown worrisome trends. Cures for cancer are still elusive in spite of palliatives and expensive and long drawn chemo- or radio-therapy which often inflict catastrophic costs. In the case of CVD and renal conditions known and tried procedures are available for relief. There is evidence of greater prevalence of cancer even among young adults due to the stress of modern living. In India cancer is a leading cause of death with about 1.5 to 2 million cases at any time to which 7 lakh new cases are added every year with 3 lakh deaths. Over 15 lakh patients require facilities for diagnosis and treatment. Studies by WHO show that by 2026 with the expected increase in life expectancy, cancer burden in India will increase to about 14. lac cases. CVD cases and Diabetes cases are also increasing with an 8 to 11% prevalence of the latter due to fast lifestyles and lack of exercise. Traumas and accidents leading to injuries are offshoots of the same competitive living conditions and urban traffic conditions. Data show one death every minute due to accidents or more than 1800 deaths every day in Delhi alone about 150 cases are reported every day from accidents on the road and for every death 8 living patients are added to hospitals due to injuries. There is finally the emerging aftermath of insurgencies and militant violence leading to mental illnesses of various types. It is estimated that 10 to 20 persons out of 1000 population suffer from severe mental illness and 3 to 5 times more have emotional disorder. While there are some facilities for diagnosis and treatment exist in major cities there is no access whatever in rural areas. It is acknowledged that the only way of handling mental health problems is through including it into the primary healthcare arrangements implying trained screening and counseling at primary levels for early detection.

The burden of non-communicable diseases will be met more and more by private sector specialized hospitals which spring up in urban centers. Facilities in prestigious public centers will also be under strain and they should be redesigned to take advantage of community-based approach of awareness, early detection and referral system (model developed successfully in the Regional Cancer Center, Kerala). For the less affluent sections prolonged high tech cure will be unaffordable. Therefore public funds should go to promote a routine of proper screening, health education and self care, and timely investigations to see that interventions are started in stages I and II. Indeed the target could be stepped up progressively to 10% by 2025. It also suggests that Central funding should constitute 25% of total public expenditure in health against the present 15%. Tamil Nadu is an instance where a review showed that out of 1400 PHCs 94% functioned in their own buildings and had electricity. 98% of ANMs and 95% of pharmacists were in position. On an average every PHC treated about 100 patients 224 out of the 250 open—24-hour PHCs had ambulances. What this illustrates is that every State must look for imaginative uses to which existing structures can be put to fuller use such as making 24-hours services open or trauma facilities in PHCs on highway locations, etc.

Maternal and child health (MCH) services can give us

a window of opportunity to dramatically bring down alarming maternal mortality currently one of the highest in the world. From NFHS I data, it was estimated at 424 per lakh births it has risen to 540 per lakh births in NFHS II, but the WHO estimate puts it higher at 570. There can be a systematic campaign over five years to increase institutional deliveries as near as possible to the Tamil Nadu level, also taking into account assisted, home deliveries by trained staff with doctors at call. For the interim TBAs should be relied on through a mass awareness campaign involving Gram Panchayats too. Over a period of time there is no reason why ANMs entitled benefits of children to help in their growth and not remain as welfare measure. Using the infrastructures fully and with community participation and extensive social mobilization many tasks in nutrition are feasible and can be in position to make impact by 2010. Associated with this is the issue of infant and child mortality, (70 out of 1000 dying in the first year and 98 before vide years) and low birth weight (22% UW at birth and 47% EJW at below 3 years) most mortality occurs from diarrhoea and the stagnation in IMR in the last few years is bound to have a negative effect on population stabilization goals. There is every reason to hope that the NPP 2000 target of 30 per thousand live births by 2010 will be met barring a few pockets of inaccessible and resource lean areas with stubborn persistence of poverty and dominantly composed of weaker sections.

Maharashtra Vision 2020

This project would address the infant mortality rate which is as high as 56 and 33 per 1000 in rural and urban areas of Maharashtra respectively, mainly concentrated in the tribal belts of Gadchiroli, Dhule and Chandrapur. "In the first meeting of the body, suggestions were made by the members that the infant mortality rate should come down to 14 per 1000 population, as is the case with Kerala," says Yesudian. To which Duggal adds, "The public health system which has done reasonably well with services like immunisation and family planning, has failed in provision of curative care in rural areas. It is this lack of access which results in high IMR and hence we need to strengthen the PHCs." For Maharashtra another critical area to be addressed is nutrition, as data shows that despite having the highest per capita income in the country Maharashtra's population suffers high levels of malnutrition. National Family Health Survey data shows that 40 percent of women in reproductive age group have a body mass index of less than the threshold of 18.5 kg per meter square. "According to the WHO if in any population more than 35 percent is under a BMI of 18.5 then it is a catastrophic situation," says Duggal. Similarly, data on children shows that 50 percent of children under 3 years of age are under-weight. Expert also suggest more money to spent in healthcare, as the existing level of public spending in Maharashtra on healthcare is one of the lowest in the country with just 0.6 percent of state GDP being spent by the government; in 1985-86 to 1989-90 period it had peaked to one percent and thereafter a declining trend has set in. Punjab requires several things. Firstly, it requires a proper health management information system which is the backbone for immediate access to information on different health indicators such as birth rate, death rate, neo-natal, peri-natal, infant and child mortality rates, method-wise contraceptive prevalence rate, disease patterns, etc. at the district level. New information technology can play a vital role in this regard.

Public health in Punjab

Punjab should focus on promoting more effective utilization of public health infrastructure. It is a major concern that despite the availability of a vast public health infrastructure, the overall share of public sector in outdoor and indoor treatment (16 and 18 percent in rural and urban areas respectively for outdoor health services and 29 and 26 percent in rural and urban areas respectively for indoor health services) is much lower than expected. Most health institutions, particularly the rural ones, continue to focus excessively on immunisation and family planning activities, ignoring the curative aspects. Health policy should give due care to the curative aspects along with the preventive aspects. Some of the suggestions for improving curative services pertain to easy, queue-less accessibility, service-availability for longer duration (if 24 hours is not feasible), clean premises (enabling people to visit government health facilities like a private health facility), provision of medicines, diagnostic services under one roof on no-profit no-loss basis with appropriate subsidies for economically weaker sections. The policy should ensure regulation of both the public and private sector. At present, the state government is not even aware about the exact number of private clinics/hospitals/ nursing homes and practitioners working in the state. While mandatory registration, service monitoring, fees regulation, and rating are must for private health sector facilities, rationalisation of postings, strict guidelines for deputations, and priority settings in rural postings are must for public sector. Further, rising costs of treatment, in both the public and private sector, warrant a viable health insurance policy. Health policy should make efforts to provide diagnostic equipments at all referral hospitals from Primary Health Centres (PHCs) onwards. In order to meet the financial limitations, such services may be outsourced to the private sector at government approved rates. This will promote public-private partnership, smash the nexus between doctors at public health facilities and owners of diagnostic centres, and would result in stoppage of certain malpractices akin to fee-splitting, uncalled for diagnosis, referral, etc.

Challenge of lifestyle

The disease patterns have changed over the years. The growing incidence of life-style diseases such as cardio-vascular diseases, diabetes, gastroenteritis, urology, and newly emerging diseases such as HIV/AIDS, dengue, and bird flu are posing new challenges for the state. The policy should examine the feasibility of setting up special clinics at the district hospitals to deal with some of these problems. Anaemia still continues to be rampant in the State with 37 percent of women and 80 percent of children being anaemic. The health policy may consider starting suitable nutritional awareness programme, initially at the school and Anganwadi level. Rising number of suicides in the state signify need for more mental health specialists. Punjab's health policy should take into account the district-wise future healthcare requirements considering rising population, inward migration, urbanization and industrialization. It needs to spell out area-wise prevalence of tropical and other diseases, ensure optimal utilization of health manpower and resources; enhance availability of primary healthcare/para-medical staff; set out strategies to cope with rising pressure on tertiary healthcare institutions; and bring about awareness for a better quality of healthcare comprising environment and occupational health, adequate availability of drinking water, hygienic living conditions, nutritious food, removal of drug addiction and other health hazards.

Recent statement by some leaders of the ruling party about promotion of medical tourism in the state is heartening provided they improve the hardware as well as software in the healthcare sector for the benefit of its own subjects first.

Longevity and wellness Scenario

Longevity estimates by 2025 could be around 70 years, perhaps, without any distinction between men and women. Optimistic forecast would envisage success in polio, yaws, leprosy, kalaazar, filaria and blindness. As regards TB it is possible to arrest further growth in absolute numbers by 2010 and thereafter to bring it to less than a million within internationally accepted limits by 2025. In regard to Malaria, the incidence can be reduced by a third or even up to half within a decade. In that case, one can expect near freedom from Malaria from most of the countries by 2025. As regards AIDS, it looks unlikely that infection can be leveled of by 2007. The prognosis in regard to the future shape of HIV/ AIDS is uncertain. However, it can be a feasible aim to reduce maternal mortality from the present 400 to 100 per lakh population by 2010 and achieve world standards by 2025. As regards child health and nutrition, it is possible to reach IMR/30 per thousand live births by 2010 in most parts of the country though in some areas, it may take a few years more. What is important is the chance of two-thirds decline in moderate malnutrition and abolition of serious malnutrition completely by 2015. In the case of Cancer, it is feasible to set-up an integrated system for proper screening, early detection, self-care and timely investigation and referral. As regards the private sector in medicine, it should be possible in the course of this decade to settle the public role of private medical practice—independent or institutional. For this purpose, more experiments are to be done for promoting public-private partnerships, focusing on the issue of how to erect on the basis of shared public health outcomes as the key basis for the partnership. A sensible mixture of external regulation and professional self-regulation can be devised in the consultation with the profession to ensure competence, quality and accountability.

Shape of the private healthcare to come

What role should be assigned to it? How far and how closely should it be regulated? Over the last several decades, independent private medical practice has become widespread but has remained stubbornly urban with polyclinics, nursing homes and hospitals proliferating often through doctor entrepreneurs. At our level tertiary hospitals in major cities are in many cases run by business houses and use corporate business strategies and hi-tech specialization to create demand and attract those with effective demand or the critically vulnerable at increasing costs. Standards in some of them are truly world class and some doctors who work there are outstanding leaders in their areas. But given the commodification of medical care as part of a business plan it has not been possible to regulate the quality, accountability and fairness in healthcare. The criteria for evaluation would be accreditation, transparency in fees, medical audit, accountable record-keeping, credible grievance procedures, etc. Acute care has become the key priority and continues to attract manpower and investment into related specialty education and facilities for technological improvement. Common treatments, diagnostic procedures and family medicine are replaced and priced out of the reach of most citizens in urban areas. On the top of it public health spending accounts for only 25% of expenditure and the rest all being met as out of pocket expenditure.

Perceptions of plural systems

People intuitively develop capacity to make choices for being treated under the western or indigenous systems of medicines, keep a balance between good habits traditionally developed for healthy living and modern lifestyles, decide on where to go for chronic and acute care and how to apportion intra-family utilization of healthcare resources. The professional is generally bound by his discipline and its inherent logic of causation and effect and tends to discount even what work as successful practice. Some movement is occurring among eminent allopathic doctors trying, for instance, to rework Ayurveda theory in a modern idiom starting from respectful reverse analysis for actual successful contemporary practice of Ayurveda and provide a theoretical frame linking it to contemporary needs. There is evidence from public health campaigns in Tamil Nadu where every seventh person spontaneously expressed a preference for Sidha Medicine.

Homeopathy for chronic ailment is widely accepted. The herbal base for Ayurvda medicine widely practiced in the Himalayan belt has down world attention a huge export market remains to be tapped according to the knowledgeable trade sources but the danger of bio-privacy remains and legal enablements should be put in place soon that would fully expand on our rights under the WTO agreements. Appropriate regulation is needed to protect people from fraud and other dangers but the larger question is how to make the perceptions of the professionals and planners regarding indigenous system of medicine less ambivalent. The separate department for ISM&H should be able to bring about functional integration of ISM and western medicine in service delivery at PHC levels by 2005 whereby it will usher in an uniquely Indian system of care.

Information technology in healthcare

University of Florida (UF) and IBM (NYSE: IBM) have introduced new, groundbreaking technology that provides a "roadmap" for extending the functionality of all kinds of devices—wireless or wired, near or far. Using the power of standards in the embedded-device and IT domains, open communities and alliances, this technology will enable automatically recognized devices to send the information they register to authorized third parties, such as specialized healthcare providers. This information, in turn, can help enterprises in many industries understand their customers' needs in real-time—once or on an ongoing basis—and help them in specially tailored, continually evolving ways. In the Healthcare Industry, the positive implications for the infirmed and elderly are substantial.

Telemedicine has brought one of the paradigm shifts in the healthcare industry. Dr. Devi Shetty has treated over 3700 patients at remote areas through this technology. In the business of treating diseases when somebody is unwell, there is 99 percent possibility that the person does not require an operation. If an operation is not necessary then you can examine and diagnose a patient from a remote area. Telemedicine today has given the capacity to the ordinary doctors to do extraordinary things. Dr. Shetty and colleagues run modern coronary care units in the remote locations with the help of a satellite connection provided by ISRO. Currently they are in the process of setting up 27 coronary care units with telemedicine projects at the 27 district headquarters hospitals of Karnataka. Their entire service for telemedicine facility all over the world is free.

Some objectives for which E-Medicine has originated

1. To make high quality healthcare available to traditionally under privileged population. In India, there is a large rural-based population separated by large distances which need access to regular quality medical care. E-medicine can enhance citizen's equality in the availability of various medical services and clinical healthcare, despite these economic and geographic barriers.
2. Save the time wasted by both providers and patients in traveling from one geographic location to another to avail services on time. Think of a patient who requires immediate specialist consultancy, and there is no specialist available to cater to him. This is where e-medicine could be utilized for effective healthcare delivery.
3. Reduce costs of medical care—The ever-rising cost of healthcare is becoming a prime concern. The

incidental expenses related to patient care, i.e. the cost associated with factors other than the actual medial care such as travel, accommodation for relatives, food etc. also contribute substantially to the overall cost of treatment. In a country where health insurance is yet to catch up, all these are borne by patients, in many cases by selling property and livestock. If hospitals can reduce these costs associated with treatment, it would go a long way in reducing the burden of care on the patient. E-medicine seems to be the answer. APOLLO (Hyderabad) and ASIA HEART FOUNDATION (Bangalore) are emerging as key players. Madras Medical College is the first government medical college to have E-Medicine installed in INDIA. PGI hospital at chandigarh has fairly well developed system of tele-medicine. Organizations such as ISRO, have taken innovative approach to facilitate healthcare delivery by launching an exclusive health satellite. It provides almost 100% uptime, making it the best medium for a country such as India with diversity in terrain.

Stem cells; the life cells

Stem cells are the building blocks of our blood and immune systems. They form the white cells (white blood

corpuscles) that fight infection, red cells (red blood corpuscles) that carry oxygen and platelets that promote healing. Stem cells are present in our bone marrow and they generate new cells throughout our lives. Other than bone marrow, the blood in the umbilical cord also has stem cells. The umbilical cord stem cells have a number of important advantages compared to the bone marrow stem cells viz. umbilical cord blood stem cells are easier to gather than stem cells from the bone marrow. They have the unique ability to regenerate/reproduce into over 200 types of tissues. Above all, such stem cells, collected from the umbilical cord of your child, can be frozen and kept in a bank, which can be used later. God forbid, if something untoward happens to your child you won't have to turn heaven and hell to find a matching donor.

Stem cells are already in use to cure ailments like acute leukaemia, chronic leukaemia, myelodysplastic syndromes, stem cell disorders, myeloproliferative disorders, lymphoproliferative disorders, phagocyte disorders, inherited disorders like Osteoporosis, B-Thalassemia, inherited metabolic disorders, inherited erythrocyte abnormalities like Beta Thalassemia and Sickle cell disease, and other malignancies like multiple myeloma, plasma cell leukaemia, renal cell carcinoma and retinoblastoma.

Trials are on for treatment of cardiac diseases, diabetes, Multiple Sclerosis, muscular dystrophy, Parkinson's disease, spinal cord injury and stroke. Scientists are hopeful of stem cell applications in Alzheimer's disease, Lupus and rheumatoid arthritis in future.

LifeCell

It is India's first private stem cell bank, where you can store the umbilical cord of your child for a fee, for future use. LifeCell, in collaboration with CRYO-CELL International, USA facilitates the cryogenic Preservation of stem cells at its unique facility in Chennai. LifeCell has set-up a 21,000 sq. ft. laboratory at the cost of Rs. 14 crore on the outskirts of Chennai city. The storage of stem cells is done at—196 Centigrade under liquid nitrogen. LifeCell has offices in Ahmedabad, Bangalore, Chennai, Coimbatore, Delhi, Gurgaon, Hyderabad, Kochi, Kolkata, Mumbai, Surat,

Chandigarh, Pune, Jaipur, Noida, Calicut, Trivandrum and Dubai and plans to set-up more offices within and outside the country. LifeCell has only a private stem cell bank currently, but now for the first time in the country, they are planning to have a public stem cell bank also.

What is a public stem cell bank?

"In our private stem cell bank, customers store their umbilical cord stem cells for their future use by paying us an amount. But if they do not want to store it for their own future use, they can donate the stem cells to the public bank. We can also collect stem cells from various hospitals and store them for the public to use," V.R. Chandramouli, CEO of LifeCell, explained. In the case of a public bank, they have to do more tests on HLAs (Human Leukocyte Antigens) or proteins, like the tests done for blood groups in blood banks. In the case of umbilical cord protein matching, all the six proteins need not match; even a 4:6 matching is possible unlike the bone marrow matching. The probability of umbilical cord stem cell matching with anyone in the world is larger than that of a bone marrow stem cell matching. Out of the 6,800 cases of stem cell transplants that were done last year to cure various malignant and non-malignant diseases, more than 300 cases were done from the stem cells collected from umbilical cords.

"We are talking about what goes waste after each birth. With 25 million births happening in India, it is an opportunity for India. In the process, the entire world will be benefited. LifeCell gets paid only for the analytical and storage services. All other benefits will go to the trust. Many multinational companies in the US run such trusts but they also use the umbilical cord stem cells for R&D because a lot of research is going on right now on stem cells. Today, one stem cell costs about $25,000 (more than Rs. 11 lakh)," Chandramouli said. Of the 25 million births that take place every year in India, LifeCell is looking at a figure of 200,000-250,000 collections every year. "We are talking about the entire world. There should not be any exploitation. There should also be affordability," said Chandramouli. The government should come out with proper guidelines before allowing private companies to start public stem cell banks that will cater mainly to those who are rich.

Sources

Visaria, L., Innovations in Tamil Nadu Seminar 489, May 2000.

Ramachandran, V.A., Perspective on reforms Seminar 489, May 2000.

Keohave, R. and Nye, J., Globalization Foreign Policy Spring 2000.

Menon, Meera, Corporatization of Health, *The Hindu*, Folio on Health, 2000.

Mishra, V.S., Health Implications of Ageing, *MFC Bulletin*, 266/267.

Gulati, L. and Irudaya, Rajan, The added years, *EPW*, Oct. 30, 1999.

Bose, Ashish, Demographic Transition, Seminar 488, April 2000.

Cassell, Eric, "The Sorcerer's Broom", Hastings Center Report, Nov.-Dec. 1993.

Gwatkin, D. and Others, The burden of disease and Global poor, *HDN World Bank*, 2000.

Bhat, R., Private Healthcare in India, *IHPP*, 1995.

Naylor, D.A., Fine Balance, HDNetwork, World Bank, 1999.

World Bank (A), India: Policy and Financing Strategies for PHC Services, World Bank, May 1995.

World Bank (B), India: New Directions in health sector development, Feb. 1997.

Gwatkin D.R. [A], Bulletin of WHO, Vol. 78/1, 2000.

World Bank (C), Quality of Growth, Thomas, V. *et al.*, WBk, 2000.

Krishanan, T.N., Disinvesting in Health, ed. Mohan Rao, OUP, 2000.

Jha, P. *et al.*, Avoidable Mortality in India (Mimeo 2000).

Sen, Amartya, Bulletin of WHO, Vol. 78/2, 2000.

Bhat, Mari, Fertility trends, NFHS 1, EPW, 14 April, 2000.

Gopalan, EPW, 7 April, 2001.

APPENDIX I

NATIONAL HEALTH POLICY—2002

I. INTRODUCTORY

1.1 A National Health Policy was last formulated in 1983, and since then there have been marked changes in the determinant factors relating to the health sector. Some of the policy initiatives outlined in the NHP-1983 have yielded results, while, in several other areas, the outcome has not been as expected.

1.2 The NHP-1983 gave a general exposition of the policies which required recommendation in the circumstances then prevailing in the health sector. The noteworthy initiatives under that policy were:

(i) A phased, time-bound programme for setting up a well-dispersed network of comprehensive primary healthcare services, linked with extension and health education, designed in the context of the ground reality that elementary health problems can be resolved by the people themselves;

(ii) Intermediation through 'Health volunteers' having appropriate knowledge, simple skills and requisite technologies;

(iii) Establishment of a well-worked out referral system to ensure that patient load at the higher levels of the hierarchy is not needlessly burdened by those who can be treated at the decentralized level;

(iv) An integrated net-work of evenly spread speciality and super-speciality services; encouragement of such facilities through private investments for patients who can pay, so that the draw on the Government's facilities is limited to those entitled to free use.

1.3 Government initiatives in the pubic health sector have recorded some noteworthy successes over time. Smallpox and Guinea Worm Disease have been eradicated from the country; Polio is on the verge of being eradicated; Leprosy, Kala Azar, and Filariasis can be expected to be eliminated in the foreseeable future. There has been a substantial drop in the Total Fertility Rate and Infant Mortality Rate. The success of the initiatives taken in the public health field are reflected in the progressive improvement of many demographic/epidemiological/ infrastructural indicators over time.

Achievements Through The Years—1951-2000

Indicator	*1951*	*1981*	*2000*
Demographic Changes			
Life Expectancy	36.7	54	64.6(RGI)
Crude Birth Rate	40.8	33.9(SRS)	26.1(99 SRS)
Crude Death Rate	25	12.5(SRS)	8.7(99 SRS)
IMR	146	110	70 (99 SRS)
Epidemiological Shifts			
Malaria (cases in million)	75	2.7	2.2
Leprosy cases per 10,000 population	38.1	57.3	3.74
Small Pox (no. of cases)	>44,887	Eradicated	
Guineaworm (no. of cases)		>39,792	Eradicated
Polio		29709	265
Infrastructure			
SC/PHC/CHC	725	57,363	1,63,181 (99-RHS)
Dispensaries and Hospitals (all)	9209	23,555	43,322 95–96-CBHI)
Beds (Pvt. and Public)	117,198	569,495	8,70,161 95-96-CBHI)
Doctors (Allopathy)	61,800	2,68,700	5,03,900 (98-99-MCI)
Nursing Personnel	18,054	1,43,887	7,37,000 (99-INC)

1.4 While noting that the public health initiatives over the years have contributed significantly to the improvement of these health indicators, it is to be acknowledged that public health indicators/disease-burden statistics are the outcome of several complementary initiatives under the wider umbrella of the developmental sector, covering Rural Development, Agriculture, Food Production, Sanitation, Drinking Water Supply, Education, etc. Despite the impressive public health gains as revealed in the statistics in, there is no gainsaying the fact that the morbidity and mortality levels in the country are still unacceptably high. These unsatisfactory health indices are, in turn, an indication of the limited success of the public health system in meeting the preventive and curative requirements of the general population.

1.5 Out of the communicable diseases which have persisted over time, the incidence of Malaria staged a resurgence in the 1980s before stabilising at a fairly high prevalence level during the 1990s. Over the years, an increasing level of insecticide-resistance has developed in the malarial vectors in many parts of the country, while the incidence of the more deadly P-Falciparum Malaria has risen to about 50 percent in the country as a whole. In respect of TB, the public health scenario has not shown any significant decline in the pool of infection amongst the community, and there has been a distressing trend in the increase of drug resistance to the type of infection prevailing in the country. A new and extremely virulent communicable disease—HIV/AIDS—has emerged on the health scene since the declaration of the NHP-1983. As there is no existing therapeutic cure or vaccine for this infection, the disease constitutes a serious threat, not merely to public health but to economic development in the country. The common water-borne infections—Gastroenteritis, Cholera, and some forms of Hepatitis—continue to contribute to a high level of morbidity in the population, even though the mortality rate may have been somewhat moderated.

1.6 The period after the announcement of NHP-83 has also seen an increase in mortality through 'life-style' diseases—diabetes, cancer and cardiovascular diseases. The increase in life expectancy has increased the requirement for geriatric care. Similarly, the increasing burden of trauma cases is also a significant public health problem.

1.7 Another area of grave concern in the public health domain is the persistent incidence of macro and micro- nutrient deficiencies, especially among women and children. In the vulnerable sub-category of women and the girl child, this has the multiplier effect through the birth of low birth weight babies and serious ramifications of the consequential mental and physical retarded growth.

1.8 NHP-1983, in a spirit of optimistic empathy for the health needs of the people, particularly the poor and under-privileged, had hoped to provide 'Health for All by the year 2000 AD', through the universal provision of comprehensive primary healthcare services. In retrospect, it is observed that the financial resources and public health administrative capacity which it was possible to marshal, was far short of that necessary to achieve such an ambitious and holistic goal. Against this backdrop, it is felt that it would be appropriate to pitch NHP-2002 at a level consistent with our realistic expectations about financial resources, and about the likely increase in Public Health administrative capacity. The recommendations of NHP-2002 will, therefore, attempt to maximize the broad-based availability of health services to the citizenry of the country on the basis of realistic considerations of capacity. The changed circumstances relating to the health sector of the country since 1983 have generated a situation in which it is now necessary to review the field, and to formulate a new policy framework as the National Health Policy-2002. NHP-2002 will attempt to set out a new policy framework for the accelerated achievement of Public health goals in the socio-economic circumstances currently prevailing in the country.

2. CURRENT SCENARIO

2.1 FINANCIAL RESOURCES

2.1.1 The public health investment in the country over the years has been comparatively low, and as a percentage of GDP has declined from 1.3 percent in 1990 to 0.9 percent in 1999. The aggregate expenditure in the Health sector is 5.2 percent of the GDP. Out of this, about 17 percent of the aggregate expenditure is public health spending, the balance being out-of-pocket expenditure. The central budgetary allocation for health over this period, as a percentage of the total Central Budget, had been stagnant at 1.3 percent (now 0.9% of GDP), while that in the States has declined from 7.0 percent to 5.5 percent. The current annual per capita public health expenditure in the country is no more than Rs. 200. Given these statistics, it is no surprise that the reach and quality of public health services has been below the desirable standard. Under the constitutional structure, public health is the responsibility of the States. In this framework, it has been the expectation that the principal contribution for the funding of public health services will be from the resources of the States, with some supplementary input from Central resources. In this backdrop, the contribution of Central resources to the overall public health funding has been limited to about 15 percent. The fiscal resources of the State Governments are known to be very inelastic. This is reflected in the declining percentage of State resources allocated to the health sector out of the State Budget. If the decentralized public health services in the country are to improve significantly, there is a need for the injection of substantial resources into the health sector from the Central Government Budget. This approach is a necessity—despite the formal Constitutional provision in regard to public health,—if the State public health services, which are a major component of the initiatives in the social sector, are not to become entirely moribund. The NHP-2002 has been formulated taking into consideration these ground realities in regard to the availability of resources.

2.2 EQUITY

2.2.1 In the period when centralized planning was accepted as a key instrument of development in the country, the attainment of an equitable regional distribution was considered one of its major objectives. Despite this conscious focus in the development process, the statistics given in Box-II clearly indicate that the attainment of health indices has been very uneven across the rural-urban divide.

Also, the statistics bring out the wide differences between the attainments of health goals in the better-performing States as compared to the low-performing States. It is clear that national averages of health indices hide wide

Differentials in Health Status Among States

Sector	*Population BPL (%)*	*IMR/ per 1000 Live Births (1999-SRS)*	*<5 Mortality per 1000 (NFHS-II)*	*Weight per Age-% of Children Under 3 years (<-2SD)*	*MMR/ Lakh (Annual Report 2000)*	*Leprosy cases per 10000 population*	*Malaria +ve Cases in year 2000 (in thousands)*
India	26.1	70	94.9	47	408	3.7	2200
Rural	27.09	75	103.7	49.6	-	-	-
Urban	23.62	44	63.1	38.4	-	-	-
Better Performing States							
Kerala	12.72	14	18.8	27	87	0.9	5.1
Maharashtra	25.02	48	58.1	50	135	3.1	138
TN	21.12	52	63.3	37	79	4.1	56
Low Performing States							
Orissa	47.15	97	104.4	54	498	7.05	483
Bihar	42.60	63	105.1	54	707	11.83	132
Rajasthan	15.28	81	114.9	51	607	0.8	53
UP	31.15	84	122.5	52	707	4.3	99
MP	37.43	90	137.6	55	498	3.83	528

disparities in public health facilities and health standards in different parts of the country. Given a situation in which national averages in respect of most indices are themselves at unacceptably low levels, the wide inter-State disparity implies that, for vulnerable sections of society in several States, access to public health services is nominal and health standards are grossly inadequate. Despite a thrust in the NHP-1983 for making good the unmet needs of public health services by establishing more public health institutions at a decentralized level, a large gap in facilities still persists. Applying current norms to the population projected for the year 2000, it is estimated that the shortfall in the number of SCs/PHCs/CHCs is of the order of 16 percent. However, this shortage is as high as 58 percent when disaggregated for CHCs only. The NHP-2002 will need to address itself to making good these deficiencies so as to narrow the gap between the various States, as also the gap across the rural-urban divide.

2.2.2 Access to, and benefits from, the public health system have been very uneven between the better-endowed and the more vulnerable sections of society. This is particularly true for women, children and the socially disadvantaged sections of society. The statistics given in highlight the handicap suffered in the health sector on account of socio-economic inequity.

Differentials in Health Status Among Socio-Economic Groups

Indicator	*Infant Mortality/ 1000*	*Under 5 Mortality/ 1000*	*% Children Underweight*
India	<u>70</u>	<u>94.9</u>	<u>47</u>
Social Inequity			
Scheduled Castes	83	119.3	53.5
Scheduled Tribes	84.2	126.6	55.9
Other Disadvantaged	76	103.1	47.3
Others	61.8	82.6	41.1

2.2.3 It is a principal objective of NHP-2002 to evolve a policy structure which reduces these inequities and allows the disadvantaged sections of society a fairer access to public health services.

2.3 DELIVERY OF NATIONAL PUBLIC HEALTH PROGRAMMES

2.3.1 It is self-evident that in a country as large as India, which has a wide variety of socio-economic settings, national health programmes have to be designed with enough flexibility to permit the State public health administrations to craft their own programme package according to their needs. Also, the implementation of the national health programme can only be carried out through the State Governments' decentralized public health machinery. Since, for various reasons, the responsibility of the Central Government in funding additional public health services will continue over a period of time, the role of the Central Government in designing broad-based public health initiatives will inevitably continue. Moreover, it has been observed that the technical and managerial expertise for designing large-span public health programmes exists with the Central Government in a considerable degree; this expertise can be gainfully utilized in designing national health programmes for implementation in varying socio-economic settings in the States. With this background, the NHP-2002 attempts to define the role of the Central Government and the State Governments in the public health sector of the country.

2.3.2.1 Over the last decade or so, the Government has relied upon a 'vertical' implementational structure for the major disease control programmes. Through this, the system has been able to make a substantial dent in reducing the burden of specific diseases. However, such an organizational structure, which requires independent manpower for each disease programme, is extremely expensive and difficult to sustain. Over a long time-range, 'vertical' structures may only be affordable for those diseases which offer a reasonable possibility of elimination or eradication in a foreseeable time-span.

2.3.2.2 It is a widespread perception that, over the last decade and a half, the rural health staff has become a vertical structure exclusively for the implementation of family welfare activities. As a result, for those public health programmes where there is no separate vertical structure, there is no identifiable service delivery system at all. The Policy will address this distortion in the public health system.

2.4 THE STATE OF PUBLIC HEALTH INFRASTRUCTURE

2.4.1 The delineation of NHP-2002 would be required to be based on an objective assessment of the quality and efficiency of the existing public health machinery in the field. It would detract from the quality of the exercise if, while framing a new policy, it were not acknowledged that the existing public health infrastructure is far from satisfactory. For the outdoor medical facilities in existence, funding is generally insufficient; the presence of medical and para-medical personnel is often much less than that required by prescribed norms; the availability of consumables is frequently negligible; the equipment in many public hospitals is often obsolescent and unusable; and, the buildings are in a dilapidated state. In the indoor treatment facilities, again, the equipment is often obsolescent; the availability of essential drugs is minimal; the capacity of the facilities is grossly inadequate, which leads to over-crowding, and consequentially to a steep deterioration in the quality of the services. As a result of such inadequate public health facilities, it has been estimated that less than 20 percent of the population, which seek OPD services, and less than 45 percent of that which seek indoor treatment, avail of such services in public hospitals. This is despite the fact that most of these patients do not have the means to make out-of-pocket payments for private health services except at the cost of other essential expenditure for items such as basic nutrition.

2.5 EXTENDING PUBLIC HEALTH SERVICES

2.5.1 While there is a general shortage of medical personnel in the country, this shortfall is disproportionately impacted on the less-developed and rural areas. No incentive system attempted so far, has induced private medical personnel to go to such areas; and, even in the public health sector, the effort to deploy medical personnel in such under-served areas, has usually been a losing battle. In such a situation, the possibility needs to be examined of entrusting some limited public health functions to nurses, paramedics and other personnel from the extended health sector after imparting adequate training to them.

2.5.2 India has a vast reservoir of practitioners in the Indian Systems of Medicine and Homoeopathy, who have undergone formal training in their own disciplines. The possibility of using such practitioners in the implementation of State/Central Government public health programmes, in order to increase the reach of basic healthcare in the country, is addressed in the NHP-2002.

2.6 ROLE OF LOCAL SELF-GOVERNMENT INSTITUTIONS

2.6.1 Some States have adopted a policy of devolving programmes and funds in the health sector through different levels of the Panchayati Raj Institutions. Generally, the experience has been an encouraging one. The adoption of such an organisational structure has enabled need-based allocation of resources and closer supervision through the elected representatives. The Policy examines the need for a wider adoption of this mode of delivery of health services, in rural as well as urban areas, in other parts of the country.

2.7 NORMS FOR HEALTHCARE PERSONNEL

2.7.1 It is observed that the deployment of doctors and nurses, in both public and private institutions, is *ad-hoc* and significantly short of the requirement for minimal standards of patient care. This policy will make a specific recommendation in regard to this deficiency.

2.8 EDUCATION OF HEALTHCARE PROFESSIONALS

2.8.1 Medical and Dental Colleges are not evenly spread across various parts of the country. Apart from the uneven geographical distribution of medical institutions, the quality of education is highly uneven and in several instances even sub-standard. It is a common perception that the syllabus is excessively theoretical, making it difficult for the fresh graduate to effectively meet even the primary healthcare needs of the population. There is a general reluctance on the part of graduate doctors to serve in areas distant from their native place. NHP-2002 will suggest policy initiatives to rectify the resultant disparities.

2.8.2.1 Certain medical disciplines, such as molecular biology and gene-manipulation, have become relevant in the period after the formulation of the previous National Health Policy. The components of medical research in recent years have changed radically. In the foreseeable future such research will rely increasingly on the new disciplines. It is observed that the current under-graduate medical syllabus does not cover such emerging subjects. The Policy will make appropriate recommendations in respect of such deficiencies.

2.8.2.2 Also, certain speciality disciplines—Anesthesiology, Radiology and Forensic Medicine—are currently very scarce, resulting in critical deficiencies in the package of available public health services. This Policy will recommend some measures to alleviate such critical shortages.

2.9 NEED FOR SPECIALISTS IN 'PUBLIC HEALTH' AND 'FAMILY MEDICINE

2.9.1 In any developing country with inadequate availability of health services, the requirement of expertise in the areas of 'public health' and 'family medicine' is markedly more than the expertise required for other clinical specialities. In India, the situation is that public health expertise is non-existent in the private health sector, and far short of requirement in the public health sector. Also, the current curriculum in the graduate/post-graduate courses is outdated and unrelated to contemporary community needs. In respect of 'family medicine', it needs to be noted that the more talented medical graduates generally seek specialization in clinical disciplines, while the remaining go into general practice. While the availability of post-graduate educational facilities is 50 percent of the total number of qualifying graduates each year, and can be considered adequate, the distribution of the disciplines in the post-graduate training facilities is overwhelmingly in favour of clinical specializations. NHP-2002 examines the possible means for ensuring adequate availability of personnel with specialization in the 'public health' and 'family medicine' disciplines, to discharge the public health responsibilities in the country.

2.10 NURSING PERSONNEL

2.10.1 The ratio of nursing personnel in the country *vis-*

à-vis doctors/beds is very low according to professionally accepted norms. There is also an acute shortage of nurses trained in super-speciality disciplines for deployment in tertiary care facilities. NHP-2002 addresses these problems.

2.11 USE OF GENERIC DRUGS AND VACCINES

2.11.1 India enjoys a relatively low-cost healthcare system because of the widespread availability of indigenously manufactured generic drugs and vaccines. There is an apprehension that globalization will lead to an increase in the costs of drugs, thereby leading to rising trends in overall health costs. This Policy recommends measures to ensure the future Health Security of the country.

2.12 URBAN HEALTH

2.12.1.1 In most urban areas, public health services are very meagre. To the extent that such services exist, there is no uniform organizational structure. The urban population in the country is presently as high as 30 percent and is likely to go up to around 33 percent by 2010. The bulk of the increase is likely to take place through migration, resulting in slums without any infrastructure support. Even the meagre public health services which are available do not percolate to such unplanned habitations, forcing people to avail of private healthcare through out-of-pocket expenditure.

2.12.1.2 The rising vehicle density in large urban agglomerations has also led to an increased number of serious accidents requiring treatment in well-equipped trauma centres. NHP-2002 will address itself to the need for providing this unserved urban population a minimum standard of broad-based healthcare facilities.

2.13 MENTAL HEALTH

2.13.1 Mental health disorders are actually much more prevalent than is apparent on the surface. While such disorders do not contribute significantly to mortality, they have a serious bearing on the quality of life of the affected persons and their families. Sometimes, based on religious faith, mental disorders are treated as spiritual affliction. This has led to the establishment of unlicensed mental institutions as an adjunct to religious institutions where reliance is placed on faith cure. Serious conditions of mental disorder require hospitalization and treatment under trained supervision. Mental health institutions are woefully deficient in physical infrastructure and trained manpower. NHP-2002 will address itself to these deficiencies in the public health sector.

2.14 INFORMATION, EDUCATION AND COMMUNICATION

2.14.1 A substantial component of primary healthcare consists of initiatives for disseminating to the citizenry, public health-related information. IEC initiatives are adopted not only for disseminating curative guidelines (for the TB, Malaria, Leprosy, Cataract Blindness Programmes), but also as part of the effort to bring about a behavioural change to prevent HIV/AIDS and other life-style diseases. Public health programmes, particularly, need high visibility at the decentralized level in order to have an impact. This task is difficult as 35 percent of our country's population is illiterate. The present IEC strategy is too fragmented, relies too heavily on the mass media and does not address the needs of this segment of the population. It is often felt that the effectiveness of IEC programmes is difficult to judge; and consequently it is often asserted that accountability, in regard to the productive use of such funds, is doubtful. The Policy, while projecting an IEC strategy, will fully address the inherent problems encountered in any IEC programme designed for improving awareness and bringing about a behavioural change in the general population.

2.14.2 It is widely accepted that school and college students are the most impressionable targets for imparting information relating to the basic principles of preventive healthcare. The policy will attempt to target this group to improve the general level of awareness in regard to 'health-promoting' behaviour.

2.15 HEALTH RESEARCH

2.15.1 Over the years, health research activity in the country has been very limited. In the Government sector, such research has been confined to the research institutions under the Indian Council of Medical Research, and other institutions funded by the States/Central Government. Research in the private sector has assumed some significance only in the last decade. In our country, where the aggregate annual health expenditure is of the order of Rs. 80,000 crores, the expenditure in 1998-99 on research, both public and private sectors, was only of the order of Rs. 1150 crores. It would be reasonable to infer that with such low research expenditure, it is virtually impossible to make any dramatic break-through within the country, by way of new molecules and vaccines; also, without a minimal back-up of applied and operational research, it would be difficult to assess whether the health expenditure in the country is being incurred through optimal applications and appropriate public health strategies. Medical Research in the country needs to be focused on therapeutic drugs/vaccines for tropical diseases, which are normally neglected by international pharmaceutical companies on account of their limited profitability potential. The thrust will need to be in the newly-emerging frontier areas of research based on genetics, genome-based drug and vaccine development, molecular biology, etc. NHP-2002 will address these inadequacies and spell out a minimal quantum of expenditure for the coming decade, looking to the national needs and the capacity of the research institutions to absorb the funds.

2.16 ROLE OF THE PRIVATE SECTOR

2.16.1 Considering the economic restructuring under way in the country, and over the globe, in the last decade, the changing role of the private sector in providing healthcare will also have to be addressed in this Policy. Currently, the contribution of private healthcare is principally through independent practitioners. Also, the private sector contributes significantly to secondary-level care and some tertiary care. It is a widespread perception that private health services are very uneven in quality, sometimes even sub-standard. Private health services are also perceived to be financially exploitative, and the observance of professional ethics is noted only as an exception. With the increasing role of private healthcare, the implementation of statutory regulation, and the monitoring of minimum standards of diagnostic centres/medical institutions becomes imperative. The Policy will address the issues regarding the establishment of a comprehensive information system, and based on that the establishment of a regulatory mechanism to ensure the maintaining of adequate standards by diagnostic centres/medical institutions, as well as the proper conduct of clinical practice and delivery of medical services.

2.16.2 Currently, non-Governmental service providers are treating a large number of patients at the primary level for major diseases. However, the treatment regimens followed are diverse and not scientifically optimal, leading to an increase in the incidence of drug resistance. This policy will address itself to recommending arrangements which will eliminate the risks arising from inappropriate treatment.

2.16.3 The increasing spread of information technology raises the possibility of its adoption in the health sector. NHP-2002 will examine this possibility.

2.17 THE ROLE OF CIVIL SOCIETY

2.17.1 Historically, it has been the practice to implement major national disease control programmes through the public health machinery of the State/Central Governments. It has become increasingly apparent that certain components of such programmes cannot be efficiently implemented merely through government functionaries. A considerable change in the mode of implementation has come about in the last two decades, with the increasing involvement of NGOs and other institutions of civil society. It is to be recognized that widespread debate on various public health issues has, in fact, been initiated and sustained by NGOs and other members of the civil society. Also, an increasing contribution is being made by such institutions in the delivery of different components of public health services. Certain disease control programmes require close inter-action with the beneficiaries for regular administration of drugs; periodic carrying out of pathological tests; dissemination of information regarding disease control and other general health information. NHP-2002 will address such issues and suggest policy instruments for the implementation of public health programmes through individuals and institutions of civil society.

2.18 NATIONAL DISEASE SURVEILLANCE NETWORK

2.18.1 The technical network available in the country for disease surveillance is extremely rudimentary and to the extent that the system exists, it extends only up to the district level. Disease statistics are not flowing through an integrated network from the decentralized public health facilities to the State/Central Government Health Administration. Such an arrangement only provides belated information, which, at best, serves a limited statistical purpose. The absence of an efficient disease surveillance network is a major handicap in providing a prompt and cost-effective healthcare system. The efficient disease surveillance network set-up for Polio and HIV/AIDS has demonstrated the enormous value of such a public health instrument. Real-time information on focal outbreaks of common communicable diseases—Malaria, GE, Cholera and JE—and the seasonal trends of diseases, would enable timely intervention, resulting in the containment of the thrust of epidemics. In order to be able to use an integrated disease surveillance network for operational purposes, real-time information is necessary at all levels of the health administration. The Policy would address itself to this major systemic shortcoming in the administration.

2.19 HEALTH STATISTICS

2.19.1 The absence of a systematic and scientific health statistics data-base is a major deficiency in the current scenario. The health statistics collected are not the product of a rigorous methodology. Statistics available from different parts of the country, in respect of major diseases, are often not obtained in a manner which make aggregation possible or meaningful.

2.19.2.1 Further, the absence of proper and systematic documentation of the various financial resources used in the health sector is another lacuna in the existing health information scenario. This makes it difficult to understand trends and levels of health spending by private and public providers of healthcare in the country, and, consequently, to address related policy issues and to formulate future investment policies.

2.19.2.2 NHP-2002 will address itself to the programme

for putting in place a modern and scientific health statistics database as well as a system of national health accounts.

2.20 WOMEN'S HEALTH

2.20.1 Social, cultural and economic factors continue to inhibit women from gaining adequate access even to the existing public health facilities. This handicap does not merely affect women as individuals; it also has an adverse impact on the health, general well-being and development of the entire family, particularly children. This policy recognises the catalytic role of empowered women in improving the overall health standards of the community.

2.21 MEDICAL ETHICS

2.21.1 Professional medical ethics in the health sector is an area which has not received much attention. Professional practices are perceived to be grossly commercial and the medical profession has lost its elevated position as a provider of basic services to fellow human beings. In the past, medical research has been conducted within the ethical guidelines notified by the Indian Council of Medical Research. The first document containing these guidelines was released in 1960, and was comprehensively revised in 2001. With the rapid developments in the approach to medical research, a periodic revision will no doubt be more frequently required in future. Also, the new frontier areas of research—involving gene manipulation, organ/human cloning and stem cell research—impinge on visceral issues relating to the sanctity of human life and the moral dilemma of human intervention in the designing of life forms. Besides this, in the emerging areas of research, there is the uncharted risk of creating new life forms, which may irreversibly damage the environment as it exists today. NHP—2002 recognises that this moral and religious dilemma, which was not relevant even two years ago, now pervades mainstream health sector issues.

2.22 ENFORCEMENT OF QUALITY STANDARDS FOR FOOD AND DRUGS

2.22.1 There is an increasing expectation and need of the citizenry for efficient enforcement of reasonable quality standards for food and drugs. Recognizing this, the Policy will make an appropriate policy recommendation on this issue.

2.23 REGULATION OF STANDARDS IN PARA MEDICAL DISCIPLINES

2.23.1 It has been observed that a large number of training institutions have mushroomed, particularly in the private sector, for para medical personnel with various skills—Lab Technicians, Radio Diagnosis Technicians, Physiotherapists, etc. Currently, there is no regulation/ monitoring, either of the curriculae of these institutions, or of the performance of the practitioners in these disciplines. This Policy will make recommendations to ensure the standardization of such training and the monitoring of actual performance.

2.24 ENVIRONMENTAL AND OCCUPATIONAL HEALTH

2.24.1 The ambient environmental conditions are a significant determinant of the health risks to which a community is exposed. Unsafe drinking water, unhygienic sanitation and air pollution significantly contribute to the burden of disease, particularly in urban settings. The initiatives in respect of these environmental factors are conventionally undertaken by the participants, whether private or public, in the other development sectors. In this backdrop, the Policy initiatives, and the efficient implementation of the linked programmes in the health sector, would succeed only to the extent that they are complemented by appropriate policies and programmes in the other environment-related sectors.

2.24.2 Work conditions in several sectors of employment in the country are sub-standard. As a result, workers engaged in such employment become particularly vulnerable to occupation-linked ailments. The long-term risk of chronic morbidity is particularly marked in the case of child labour. NHP-2002 will address the risk faced by this particularly vulnerable section of society.

2.25 PROVIDING MEDICAL FACILITIES TO USERS FROM OVERSEAS

2.25.1 The secondary and tertiary facilities available in the country are of good quality and cost-effective compared to international medical facilities. This is true not only of facilities in the allopathic disciplines, but also of those belonging to the alternative systems of medicine, particularly Ayurveda. The Policy will assess the possibilities of encouraging the development of paid treatment-packages for patients from overseas.

2.26 *THE IMPACT OF GLOBALIZATION ON THE HEALTH SECTOR*

2.26.1 There are some apprehensions about the possible adverse impact of economic globalisation on the health sector. Pharmaceutical drugs and other health services have always been available in the country at extremely inexpensive prices. India has established a reputation around the globe for the innovative development of original process patents for the manufacture of a wide-range of drugs and vaccines within the ambit of the existing patent laws. With the adoption of Trade Related Intellectual Property Rights (TRIPs), and the subsequent alignment of domestic patent laws consistent with the commitments under TRIPs, there will be a significant shift in the scope of the parameters regulating the manufacture of new drugs/vaccines. Global experience has shown that the introduction of a TRIPs—consistent patent regime for drugs in a developing country results in an across-the-board increase in the cost of drugs and medical services. NHP-2002 will address itself to the future imperatives of health security in the country, in the post-TRIPS era.

2.27 *INTER-SECTORAL CONTRIBUTION TO HEALTH*

2.27.1 It is well recognized that the overall well-being of the citizenry depends on the synergistic functioning of the various sectors in the socio-economy. The health status of the citizenry would, *inter alia*, be dependent on adequate nutrition, safe drinking water, basic sanitation, a clean environment and primary education, especially for the girl child. The policies and the mode of functioning in these independent areas would necessarily overlap each other to contribute to the health status of the community. From the policy perspective, it is therefore imperative that the independent policies of each of these inter-connected sectors, be in tandem, and that the interface between the policies of the two connected sectors, be smooth.

2.27.2 Sectoral policy documents are meant to serve as a guide to action for institutions and individual participants operating in that sector. Consistent with this role, NHP-2002 limits itself to making recommendations for the participants operating within the health sector. The policy aspects relating to inter-connected sectors, which, while crucial, fall outside the domain of the health sector, will not be covered by specific recommendations in this Policy document. Needless to say, the future attainment of the various goals set out in this policy assumes a reasonable complementary performance in these inter-connected sectors.

2.28 POPULATION GROWTH AND HEALTH STANDARDS

2.28.1 Efforts made over the years for improving health standards have been partially neutralized by the rapid growth of the population. It is well recognized that population stabilization measures and general health initiatives, when effectively synchronized, synergistically maximize the socio-economic well-being of the people. Government has separately announced the 'National Population Policy-2000'. The principal common features covered under the National Population Policy-2000 and NHP-2002, relate to the prevention and control of communicable diseases; giving priority to the containment of HIV/AIDS infection; the universal immunization of children against all major preventable diseases; addressing the unmet needs for basic and reproductive health services, and supplementation of infrastructure. The synchronized implementation of these two Policies—National Population Policy-2000 and National Health Policy-2002—will be the very cornerstone of any national structural plan to improve the health standards in the country.

2.29 ALTERNATIVE SYSTEMS OF MEDICINE

2.29.1 Under the overarching umbrella of the national health framework, the alternative systems of medicine—Ayurveda, Unani, Siddha and Homoeopathy—have a substantial role. Because of inherent advantages, such as diversity, modest cost, low level of technological input and the growing popularity of natural plant-based products, these systems are attractive, particularly in the underserved, remote and tribal areas. The alternative systems will draw upon the substantial untapped potential of India as one of the eight important global centers for plant diversity in medicinal and aromatic plants. The Policy focuses on building up credibility for the alternative systems, by encouraging evidence-based research to determine their efficacy, safety and dosage, and also encourages certification and quality-marking of products to enable a wider popular acceptance of these systems of medicine. The Policy also envisages the consolidation of documentary knowledge contained in these systems to protect it against attack from foreign commercial entities by way of malafide action under patent laws in other countries. The main components of NHP-2002 apply equally to the alternative systems of medicines. However, the Policy features specific to the alternative systems of medicine will be presented as a separate document.

3. OBJECTIVES

3.1 The main objective of this policy is to achieve an acceptable standard of good health amongst the general population of the country. The approach would be to increase access to the decentralized public health system by establishing new infrastructure in deficient areas, and by upgrading the infrastructure in the existing institutions. Overriding importance would be given to ensuring a more equitable access to health services across the social and geographical expanse of the country. Emphasis will be given to increasing the aggregate public health investment through a substantially increased contribution by the Central Government. It is expected that this initiative will strengthen the capacity of the public health administration at the State level to render effective service delivery. The contribution of the private sector in providing health services would be much enhanced, particularly for the population group which can afford to pay for services. Primacy will be given to preventive and first-line curative initiatives at the primary health level through increased sectoral share of allocation. Emphasis will be laid on rational use of drugs within the allopathic system. Increased access to tried and tested systems of traditional medicine will be ensured. Within these broad objectives, NHP-2002 will endeavour to achieve the time-bound goals mentioned below.

Goals to be Achieved by 2000-2015

Goal	Year
Eradicate Polio and Yaws	2005
Eliminate Leprosy	2005
Eliminate Kala Azar	2010
Eliminate Lymphatic Filariasis	2015
Achieve Zero level growth of HIV/AIDS	2007
Reduce Mortality by 50% on account of TB, Malaria and Other Vector and Water Borne diseases	2010
Reduce Prevalence of Blindness to 0.5%	2010
Reduce IMR to 30/1000 and MMR to 100/Lakh	2010
Increase utilization of public health facilities from current Level of <20 to >75%	2010
Establish an integrated system of surveillance, National Health Accounts and Health Statistics.	2005
Increase health expenditure by Government as a % of GDP from the existing 0.9% to 2.0%	2010
Increase share of Central grants to constitute at least 25% of total health spending	2010
Increase State Sector Health spending from 5.5% to 7% of the budget	2005
Further increase to 8%	2010

4. POLICY PRESCRIPTIONS

4.1 FINANCIAL RESOURCES

4.1.1 The paucity of public health investment is a stark reality. Given the extremely difficult fiscal position of the State Governments, the Central Government will have to play a key role in augmenting public health investments. Taking into account the gap in healthcare facilities, it is planned, under the policy to increase health sector expenditure to 6 percent of GDP, with 2 percent of GDP being contributed as public health investment, by the year 2010. The State Governments would also need to increase the commitment to the health sector. In the first phase, by 2005, they would be expected to increase the commitment of their resources to 7 percent of the Budget; and, in the second phase, by 2010, to increase it to 8 percent of the Budget. With the stepping up of the public health investment, the Central Government's contribution would rise to 25 percent from the existing 15 percent by 2010. The provisioning of higher public health investments will also be contingent upon the increase in the absorptive capacity of the public health administration so as to utilize the funds gainfully.

4.2 EQUITY

4.2.1 To meet the objective of reducing various types of inequities and imbalances-inter-regional; across the rural-urban divide; and between economic classes—the most cost-effective method would be to increase the sectoral outlay in the primary health sector. Such outlets afford access to a vast number of individuals, and also facilitate preventive and early stage curative initiative, which are cost effective. In recognition of this public health principle, NHP-2002 sets out an increased allocation of 55 percent of the total public health investment for the primary health sector; the secondary and tertiary health sectors being targeted for 35 percent and 10 percent respectively. The Policy projects that the increased aggregate outlays for the primary health sector will be utilized for strengthening existing facilities and opening additional public health service outlets, consistent with the norms for such facilities.

4.3 DELIVERY OF NATIONAL PUBLIC HEALTH PROGRAMMES

4.3.1.1 This policy envisages a key role for the Central Government in designing national programmes with the active participation of the State Governments. Also, the Policy ensures the provisioning of financial resources, in addition to technical support, monitoring and evaluation at the national level by the Centre. However, to optimize the utilization of the public health infrastructure at the primary level, NHP-2002 envisages the gradual convergence of all health programmes under a single field administration. Vertical programmes for control of major diseases like TB, Malaria, HIV/AIDS, as also the RCH and Universal Immunization Programmes, would need to be continued till moderate levels of prevalence are reached. The integration of the programmes will bring about a desirable optimisation of outcomes through a convergence of all public health inputs. The Policy also envisages that programme implementation be effected through autonomous bodies at State and district levels. The interventions of State Health Departments may be limited to the overall monitoring of the achievement of programme targets and other technical aspects. The relative distancing of the programme implementation from the State Health Departments will give the project team greater operational flexibility. Also, the presence of State Government officials, social activists, private health professionals and MLAs/MPs on the management boards of the autonomous bodies will facilitate well-informed decision-making.

4.3.1.2 The Policy also highlights the need for developing the capacity within the State Public Health administration for scientific designing of public health projects, suited to the local situation.

4.3.2 The Policy envisages that apart from the exclusive staff in a vertical structure for the disease control programmes, all rural health staff should be available for the entire gamut of public health activities at the decentralized level, irrespective of whether these activities relate to national programmes or other public health initiatives. It would be for the Head of the District Health administration to allocate the time of the rural health staff between the various programmes, depending on the local need. NHP-2002 recognizes that to implement such a change, not only would the public health administrators be required to change their mindset, but the rural health staff would need to be trained and reoriented.

4.4 THE STATE OF PUBLIC HEALTH INFRASTRUCTURE

4.4.1.1 As has been highlighted in the earlier part of the Policy, the decentralized Public health service outlets have become practically dysfunctional over large parts of the country. On account of resource constraints, the supply of drugs by the State Governments is grossly inadequate. The patients at the decentralized level have little use for diagnostic services, which in any case would still require them to purchase therapeutic drugs privately. In a situation in which the patient is not getting any therapeutic drugs, there is little incentive for the potential beneficiaries to seek the advice of the medical professionals in the public health system. This results in there being no demand for medical services, so medical professionals and paramedics often absent themselves from their place of duty. It is also observed that the functioning of the public health service outlets in some States like the four Southern States—Kerala, Andhra Pradesh, Tamil Nadu and Karnataka—is relatively better, because some quantum of drugs is distributed through the primary health system network, and the patients have a stake in approaching the Public Health facilities. In this backdrop, the Policy envisages kick-starting the revival of the Primary Health System by providing some essential drugs under Central Government funding through the decentralized health system. It is expected that the provisioning of essential drugs at the public health service centres will create a demand for other professional services from the local population, which, in turn, will boost the general revival of activities in these service centres. In sum, this initiative under NHP-2002 is launched in the belief that the creation of a beneficiary interest in the public health system, will ensure a more effective supervision of the public health personnel through community monitoring, than has been achieved through the regular administrative line of control.

4.4.1.2 This Policy recognizes the need for more frequent in-service training of public health medical personnel, at the level of medical officers as well as paramedics. Such training would help to update the personnel on recent advancements in science, and would also equip them for their new assignments, when they are moved from one discipline of public health administration to another.

4.4.1.3 Global experience has shown that the quality of public health services, as reflected in the attainment of improved public health indices, is closely linked to the quantum and quality of investment through public funding in the primary health sector. It gives statistics which clearly show that standards of health are more a function of the accurate targeting of expenditure on the decentralised primary sector (as observed in China and Sri Lanka), than a function of the aggregate health expenditure.

Public Health Spending in Select Countries

Indicator	*% Population with income of <$1 day*	*Infant Mortality Rate/1000*	*% Health Expenditure to GDP*	*% Public Expenditure on Health to Total Health Expenditure*
India	44.2	70	5.2	17.3
China	18.5	31	2.7	24.9
Sri Lanka	6.6	16	3	45.4
UK	-	6	5.8	96.9
USA	-	7	13.7	44.1

Therefore the Policy, while committing additional aggregate financial resources, places great reliance on the strengthening of the primary health structure for the attaining of improved public health outcomes on an equitable basis. Further, it also recognizes the practical need for levying reasonable user-charges for certain secondary and tertiary public healthcare services, for those who can afford to pay.

4.5 EXTENDING PUBLIC HEALTH SERVICES

4.5.1.1 This policy envisages that, in the context of the availability and spread of allopathic graduates in their jurisdiction, State Governments would consider the need for expanding the pool of medical practitioners to include a cadre of licentiates of medical practice, as also practitioners of Indian Systems of Medicine and Homoeopathy. Simple services/procedures can be provided by such practitioners even outside their disciplines, as part of the basic primary health services in under-served areas. Also, NHP-2002 envisages that the scope of the use of paramedical manpower of allopathic disciplines, in a prescribed functional area adjunct to their current functions, would also be examined for meeting simple public health requirements. This would be on the lines of the services rendered by nurse practitioners in several developed countries. These extended areas of functioning of different categories of medical manpower can be permitted, after adequate training, and subject to the monitoring of their performance through professional councils.

4.5.1.2 NHP-2002 also recognizes the need for States to simplify the recruitment procedures and rules for contract employment in order to provide trained medical manpower in under-served areas. State Governments could also rigorously enforce a mandatory two-year rural posting before the awarding of the graduate degree. This would not only make trained medical manpower available in the underserved areas, but would offer valuable clinical experience to the graduating doctors.

4.6 ROLE OF LOCAL SELF-GOVERNMENT INSTITUTIONS

4.6.1 NHP-2002 lays great emphasis upon the implementation of public health programmes through local self-government institutions. The structure of the national disease control programmes will have specific components for implementation through such entities. The Policy urges all State Governments to consider decentralizing the implementation of the programmes to such Institutions by 2005. In order to achieve this, financial incentives, over and above the resources normatively allocated for disease control programmes, will be provided by the Central Government.

4.7 NORMS FOR HEALTHCARE PERSONNEL

4.7.1 Minimal statutory norms for the deployment of

doctors and nurses in medical institutions need to be introduced urgently under the provisions of the Indian Medical Council Act and Indian Nursing Council Act, respectively. These norms can be progressively reviewed and made more stringent as the medical institutions improve their capacity for meeting better normative standards.

4.8 EDUCATION OF HEALTHCARE PROFESSIONALS

4.8.1.1 In order to ameliorate the problems being faced on account of the uneven spread of medical and dental colleges in various parts of the country, this policy envisages the setting up of a Medical Grants Commission for funding new Government Medical and Dental Colleges in different parts of the country. Also, it is envisaged that the Medical Grants Commission will fund the upgradation of the infrastructure of the existing Government Medical and Dental Colleges of the country, so as to ensure an improved standard of medical education.

4.8.1.2 To enable fresh graduates to contribute effectively to the providing of primary health services as the physician of first contact, this policy identifies a significant need to modify the existing curriculum. A need-based, skill-oriented syllabus, with a more significant component of practical training, would make fresh doctors useful immediately after graduation. The Policy also recommends a periodic skill-updating of working health professionals through a system of continuing medical education.

4.8.2 The Policy emphasises the need to expose medical students, through the undergraduate syllabus, to the emerging concerns for geriatric disorders, as also to the cutting edge disciplines of contemporary medical research. The policy also envisages that the creation of additional seats for post-graduate courses should reflect the need for more manpower in the deficient specialities.

4.9 NEED FOR SPECIALISTS IN 'PUBLIC HEALTH' AND 'FAMILY MEDICINE'

4.9.1 In order to alleviate the acute shortage of medical personnel with specialization in the disciplines of 'public health' and 'family medicine', the Policy envisages the progressive implementation of mandatory norms to raise the proportion of post-graduate seats in these discipline in medical training institutions, to reach a stage wherein ¼th of the seats are earmarked for these disciplines. It is envisaged that in the sanctioning of post-graduate seats in future, it shall be insisted upon that a certain reasonable number of seats be allocated to 'public health' and 'family medicine'. Since the 'public health' discipline has an interface with many other developmental sectors, specialization in Public health may be encouraged not only for medical doctors, but also for non-medical graduates from the allied fields of public health engineering, microbiology and other natural sciences.

4.10 NURSING PERSONNEL

4.10.1.1 In the interest of patient care, the policy emphasizes the need for an improvement in the ratio of nurses *vis-à-vis* doctors/beds. In order to discharge their responsibility as model providers of health services, the public health delivery centres need to make a beginning by increasing the number of nursing personnel. The Policy anticipates that with the increasing aspiration for improved healthcare amongst the citizens, private health facilities will also improve their ratio of nursing personnel *vis-à-vis* doctors/beds.

4.10.1.2 The Policy lays emphasis on improving the skill-level of nurses, and on increasing the ratio of degree-holding nurses *vis-à-vis* diploma-holding nurses. NHP-2002 recognizes a need for the Central Government to subsidize the setting up, and the running of, training facilities for nurses on a decentralized basis. Also, the Policy recognizes the need for establishing training courses for super-speciality nurses required for tertiary care institutions.

4.11 USE OF GENERIC DRUGS AND VACCINES

4.11.1.1 This Policy emphasizes the need for basing treatment regimens, in both the public and private domain, on a limited number of essential drugs of a generic nature. This is a pre-requisite for cost-effective public healthcare. In the public health system, this would be enforced by prohibiting the use of proprietary drugs, except in special circumstances. The list of essential drugs would no doubt have to be reviewed periodically. To encourage the use of only essential drugs in the private sector, the imposition of fiscal disincentives would be resorted to. The production and sale of irrational combinations of drugs would be prohibited through the drug standards statute.

4.11.1.2 The National Programme for Universal Immunization against Preventable Diseases requires to be assured of an uninterrupted supply of vaccines at an affordable price. To minimize the danger arising from the volatility of the global market, and thereby to ensure long-term national health security, NHP-2002 envisages that not less than 50% of the requirement of vaccines/sera be sourced from public sector institutions.

4.12 URBAN HEALTH

4.12.1.1 NHP-2002 envisages the setting up of an organised urban primary healthcare structure. Since the physical features of urban settings are different from those in rural areas, the policy envisages the adoption of appropriate population norms for the urban public health infrastructure. The structure conceived under NHP-2002 is a two-tiered one: the primary centre is seen as the first-tier, covering a population of one lakh, with a dispensary providing an OPD facility and essential drugs, to enable access to all the national health programmes; and a second-tier of the urban health organisation at the level of the Government general hospital, where reference is made from the primary centre. The Policy envisages that the funding for the urban primary health system will be jointly borne by the local self-government institutions and State and Central Governments.

4.12.1.2 The Policy also envisages the establishment of fully-equipped 'hub-spoke' trauma care networks in large urban agglomerations to reduce accident mortality.

4.13 MENTAL HEALTH

4.13.1.1. NHP-2002 envisages a network of decentralised mental health services for ameliorating the more common categories of disorders. The programme outline for such a disease would involve the diagnosis of common disorders, and the prescription of common therapeutic drugs, by general duty medical staff.

4.13.1.2 In regard to mental health institutions for in-door treatment of patients, the Policy envisages the upgrading of the physical infrastructure of such institutions at Central Government expense so as to secure the human rights of this vulnerable segment of society.

4.14 INFORMATION, EDUCATION AND COMMUNICATION

4.14.1 NHP-2002 envisages an IEC policy, which maximizes the dissemination of information to those population groups which cannot be effectively approached by using only the mass media. The focus would therefore be on the inter-personal communication of information and on folk and other traditional media to bring about behavioural change. The IEC programme would set specific targets for the association of PRIs/NGOs/Trusts in such activities. In several public health programmes, where behavioural change is an essential component, the success of the initiatives is crucially dependent on dispelling myths and misconceptions pertaining to religious and ethical issues. The community leaders, particularly religious leaders, are effective in imparting knowledge which facilitates such behavioural change. The programme will also have the component of an annual evaluation of the performance of the non-Governmental agencies to monitor the impact of the programmes on the targeted groups. The Central/State Government initiative will also focus on the development of modules for information dissemination in such population groups, who do not normally benefit from the more common media forms.

4.14.2 NHP-2002 envisages giving priority to school health programmes which aim at preventive-health education, providing regular health check-ups, and promotion of health-seeking behaviour among children. The school health programmes can gainfully adopt specially designed modules in order to disseminate information relating to 'health' and 'family life'. This is expected to be the most cost-effective intervention as it improves the level of awareness, not only of the extended family, but the future generation as well.

4.15 HEALTH RESEARCH

4.15.1 This Policy envisages an increase in Government-funded health research to a level of 1 percent of the total health spending by 2005; and thereafter, up to 2 percent by 2010. Domestic medical research would be focused on new therapeutic drugs and vaccines for tropical diseases, such as TB and Malaria, as also on the sub-types of HIV/AIDS prevalent in the country. Research programmes taken up by the Government in these priority areas would be conducted in a mission mode. Emphasis would also be laid on time-bound applied research for developing operational applications. This would ensure the cost-effective dissemination of existing/future therapeutic drugs/vaccines in the general population. Private entrepreneurship will be encouraged in the field of medical research for new molecules/vaccines, *inter alia*, through fiscal incentives.

4.16 ROLE OF THE PRIVATE SECTOR

4.16.1.1 In principle, this Policy welcomes the participation of the private sector in all areas of health activities—primary, secondary or tertiary. However, looking to past experience of the private sector, it can reasonably be expected that its contribution would be substantial in the urban primary sector and the tertiary sector, and moderate in the secondary sector. This Policy envisages the enactment of suitable legislation for regulating minimum infrastructure and quality standards in clinical establishments/medical institutions by 2003. Also, statutory guidelines for the conduct of clinical practice and delivery of medical services are targeted to be developed over the same period. With the acquiring of experience in the setting and enforcing of minimum quality standards, the Policy envisages graduation to a scheme of quality accreditation of clinical establishments/medical institutions, for the information of the citizenry. The regulatory/accreditation mechanisms will no doubt also cover public health institutions. The Policy also encourages the setting up of private insurance instruments for increasing the scope of the coverage of the secondary and tertiary sector under private health insurance packages.

4.16.1.2 In the context of the very large number of poor

in the country, it would be difficult to conceive of an exclusive Government mechanism to provide health services to this category. It has sometimes been felt that a social health insurance scheme, funded by the Government, and with service delivery through the private sector, would be the appropriate solution. The administrative and financial implications of such an initiative are still unknown. As a first step, this policy envisages the introduction of a pilot scheme in a limited number of representative districts, to determine the administrative features of such an arrangement, as also the requirement of resources for it. The results obtained from these pilot projects would provide material on which future public health policy can be based.

4.16.2 NHP-2002 envisages the co-option of the non-governmental practitioners in the national disease control programmes so as to ensure that standard treatment protocols are followed in their day-to-day practice.

4.16.3 This Policy recognizes the immense potential of information technology applications in the area of tele-medicine in the tertiary healthcare sector. The use of this technical aid will greatly enhance the capacity for the professionals to pool their clinical experience.

4.17 THE ROLE OF CIVIL SOCIETY

4.17.1 NHP-2002 recognizes the significant contribution made by NGOs and other institutions of the civil society in making available health services to the community. In order to utilize their high motivational skills on an increasing scale, this Policy envisages that the disease control programmes should earmark not less than 10% of the budget in respect of identified programme components, to be exclusively implemented through these institutions. The policy also emphasizes the need to simplify procedures for government-civil society interfacing in order to enhance the involvement of civil society in public health programmes. In principle, the state would encourage the handing over of public health service outlets at any level for management by NGOs and other institutions of civil society, on an 'as-is-where-is' basis, along with the normative funds earmarked for such institutions.

4.18 NATIONAL DISEASE SURVEILLANCE NETWORK

4.18.1 This Policy envisages the full operationalization of an integrated disease control network from the lowest rung of public health administration to the Central Government, by 2005. The programme for setting up this network will include components relating to the installation of data-base handling hardware; IT inter-connectivity between different tiers of the network; and in-house training for data collection and interpretation for undertaking timely and effective response. This public health surveillance network will also encompass information from private healthcare institutions and practitioners. It is expected that real-time information from outside the government system will greatly strengthen the capacity of the public health system to counter focal outbreaks of seasonal diseases.

4.19 HEALTH STATISTICS

4.19.1.1 The Policy envisages the completion of baseline estimates for the incidence of the common diseases—TB, Malaria, Blindness—by 2005. The Policy proposes that statistical methods be put in place to enable the periodic updating of these baseline estimates through representative sampling, under an appropriate statistical methodology. The policy also recognizes the need to establish, in a longer time-frame, baseline estimates for non-communicable diseases, like CVD, Cancer, Diabetes, and accidental injuries, and communicable diseases, like Hepatitis and JE. NHP-2002 envisages that, with access to such reliable data on the incidence of various diseases, the public health system would move closer to the objective of evidence-based policy-making.

4.19.1.2 Planning for the health sector requires a robust information system, *inter-alia,* covering data on service facilities available in the private sector. NHP-2002 emphasises the need for the early completion of an accurate data-base of this kind.

4.19.2 In an attempt at consolidating the data base and graduating from a mere estimation of the annual health expenditure, NHP-2002 emphasises the need to establish national health accounts, conforming to the 'source-to-users' matrix structure. Also, the policy envisages the estimation of health costs on a continuing basis. Improved and comprehensive information through national health accounts and accounting systems would pave the way for decision-makers to focus on relative priorities, keeping in view the limited financial resources in the health sector.

4.20 WOMEN'S HEALTH

4.20.1 NHP-2002 envisages the identification of specific programmes targeted at women's health. The Policy notes that women, along with other under-privileged groups, are significantly handicapped due to a disproportionately low access to healthcare. The various Policy recommendations of NHP-2002, in regard to the expansion of primary health sector infrastructure, will facilitate the increased access of women to basic healthcare. The Policy commits the highest priority of the Central Government to the funding of the identified programmes relating to woman's health. Also, the policy recognizes the need to review the staffing norms of the public health administration to meet the specific requirements of women in a more comprehensive manner.

4.21 MEDICAL ETHICS

4.21.1.1 NHP-2002 envisages that, in order to ensure that the common patient is not subjected to irrational or profit-driven medical regimens, a contemporary code of ethics be notified and rigorously implemented by the Medical Council of India.

4.21.1.2 By and large, medical research within the country in the frontier disciplines, such as gene-manipulation and stem cell research, is limited. However, the policy recognises that a vigilant watch will have to be kept so that the existing guidelines and statutory provisions are constantly reviewed and updated.

4.22 ENFORCEMENT OF QUALITY STANDARDS FOR FOOD AND DRUGS

4.22.1 NHP-2002 envisages that the food and drug administration will be progressively strengthened, in terms of both laboratory facilities and technical expertise. Also, the policy envisages that the standards of food items will be progressively tightened up at a pace which will permit domestic food handling/manufacturing facilities to undertake the necessary upgradation of technology so that they are not shut out of this production sector. The Policy envisages that ultimately food standards will be close, if not equivalent, to Codex specifications; and that drug standards will be at par with the most rigorous ones adopted elsewhere.

4.23 REGULATION OF STANDARDS IN PARAMEDICAL DISCIPLINES

4.23.1 NHP-2002 recognises the need for the establishment of statutory professional councils for paramedical disciplines to register practitioners, maintain standards of training, and monitor performance.

4.24 ENVIRONMENTAL AND OCCUPATIONAL HEALTH

4.24.1 This Policy envisages that the independently-stated policies and programmes of the environment-related sectors be smoothly interfaced with the policies and the programmes of the health sector, in order to reduce the health risk to the citizens and the consequential disease burden.

4.24.2 NHP-2002 envisages the periodic screening of the health conditions of the workers, particularly for high-risk health disorders associated with their occupation.

4.25 PROVIDING MEDICAL FACILITIES TO USERS FROM OVERSEAS

4.25.1 To capitalize on the comparative cost advantage enjoyed by domestic health facilities in the secondary and tertiary sectors, NHP-2002 strongly encourages the providing of such health services on a payment basis to service seekers from overseas. The providers of such services to patients from overseas will be encouraged by extending to their earnings in foreign exchange, all fiscal incentives, including the status of "deemed exports", which are available to other exporters of goods and services.

4.26 IMPACT OF GLOBALISATION ON THE HEALTH SECTOR

4.26.1 The Policy takes into account the serious apprehension, expressed by several health experts, of the possible threat to health security in the post-TRIPs era, as a result of a sharp increase in the prices of drugs and vaccines. To protect the citizens of the country from such a threat, this policy envisages a national patent regime for the future, which, while being consistent with TRIPs, avails of all opportunities to secure for the country, under its patent laws, affordable access to the latest medical and other therapeutic discoveries. The policy also sets out that the Government will bring to bear its full influence in all international fora—UN, WHO, WTO, etc.—to secure commitments on the part of the Nations of the Globe, to lighten the restrictive features of TRIPs in its application to the healthcare sector.

5. SUMMATION

5.1 The crafting of a National Health Policy is a rare occasion in public affairs when it would be legitimate, indeed valuable, to allow our dreams to mingle with our understanding of ground realities. Based purely on the clinical facts defining the current status of the health sector, we would have arrived at a certain policy formulation; but, buoyed by our dreams, we have ventured slightly beyond that in the shape of NHP-2002, which, in fact, defines a vision for the future.

5.2 The health needs of the country are enormous and the financial resources and managerial capacity available to meet them, even on the most optimistic projections, fall somewhat short. In this situation, NHP-2002 has had to make hard choices between various priorities and operational options. NHP-2002 does not claim to be a road-map for meeting all the health needs of the populace of the country. Further, it has to be recognized that such health needs are also dynamic, as threats in the area of public health keep changing over time. The Policy, while being holistic, undertakes the necessary risk of recommending differing emphasis on different policy components. Broadly speaking, NHP-2002 focuses on the need for enhanced funding and an organizational restructuring of the national public health initiatives in order to facilitate more equitable access to the health facilities. Also, the Policy is focused on those diseases which are principally contributing to the disease burden—TB, Malaria and Blindness from the category of historical diseases; and HIV/AIDS from the category of 'newly emerging diseases'. This is not to say that other items contributing to the disease burden of the country will be ignored; but only that the resources, as also the principal focus of the public health administration, will recognize certain relative priorities. It is unnecessary to labour the point that under the umbrella of the macro-policy prescriptions in this document, governments and private sector programme planners will have to design separate schemes, tailor-made to the health needs of women, children, geriatrics, tribals and other socio-economically under-served sections. An adequately robust disaster management plan has to be in place to effectively cope with situations arising from natural and man-made calamities.

5.3 One nagging imperative, which has influenced every aspect of this Policy, is the need to ensure that 'equity' in the health sector stands as an independent goal. In any future evaluation of its success or failure, NHP-2002 would wish to be measured against this equity norm, rather than any other aggregated financial norm for the health sector. Consistent with the primacy given to 'equity', a marked emphasis has been provided in the policy for expanding and improving the primary health facilities, including the new concept of the provisioning of essential drugs through Central funding. The Policy also commits the Central Government to an increased under-writing of the resources for meeting the minimum health needs of the people. Thus, the Policy attempts to provide guidance for prioritizing expenditure, thereby facilitating rational resource allocation.

5.4 This Policy broadly envisages a greater contribution from the Central Budget for the delivery of Public Health services at the State level. Adequate appropriations, steadily rising over the years, would need to be ensured. The possibility of ensuring this by imposing an earmarked health cess has been carefully examined. While it is recognized that the annual budget must accommodate the increasing resource needs of the social sectors, particularly in the health sector, this Policy does not specifically recommend an earmarked health cess, as that would have a tendency of reducing the space available to Parliament in making appropriations looking to the circumstances prevailing from time to time.

5.5 The Policy highlights the expected roles of different participating groups in the health sector. Further, it recognizes the fact that, despite all that may be guaranteed by the Central Government for assisting public health programmes, public health services would actually need to be delivered by the State administration, NGOs and other institutions of civil society. The attainment of improved health levels would be significantly dependent on population stabilisation, as also on complementary efforts from other areas of the social sectors—like improved drinking water supply, basic sanitation, minimum nutrition, etc.—to ensure that the exposure of the populace to health risks is minimized.

5.6 Any expectation of a significant improvement in the quality of health services, and the consequential improved health status of the citizenry, would depend not only on increased financial and material inputs, but also on a more empathetic and committed attitude in the service providers, whether in the private or public sectors. In some measure, this optimistic policy document is based on the understanding that the citizenry is increasingly demanding more by way of quality in health services, and the health delivery system, particularly in the public sector, is being pressed to respond. In this backdrop, it needs to be recognized that any policy in the social sector is critically dependent on the service providers treating their responsibility not as a commercial activity, but as a service, albeit a paid one. In the area of public health, an improved standard of governance is a prerequisite for the success of any health policy.

NATIONAL HEALTH POLICY: 1983

Introduction

1. The Constitution of India envisages the establishment of a new social order based on equality, freedom, justice and the dignity of the individual. It aims at the elimination of poverty, ignorance and ill-health and directs the State to regard the raising of the level of nutrition and the standard of living of its people and the improvement of public health as among its

primary duties, securing the health and strength of workers, men and women, specially ensuring that children are given opportunities and facilities to develop in a healthy manner.

1.2 Since the inception of the planning process in the country, the successive Five Year Plans have been providing the framework within which the States may develop their health services infrastructure, facilities for medical education, research, etc. Similar guidance has sought to be provided through the discussions and conclusions arrived at in the Joint Conferences of the Central Councils of Health and Family. Welfare and the National Development Council. Besides, Central legislation has been enacted to regulate standards of medical education, prevention of food adulteration, maintenance of standards in the manufacture and sale of certified drugs, etc.

1.3 While the broad approaches contained in the successive Plan documents and discussion in the forums referred to in para 1.2 may have generally served the needs of the situation in the past, it is felt that an integrated, comprehensive approach towards the future development of medical education, research and health services requires to be established to serve the actual health needs and priorities of the country. It is in this context that the need has been felt to evolve a National Health Policy.

Our heritage

2. India has a rich, centuries-old heritage of medical and health sciences. The philosophy of Ayurveda and the surgical skills enunciated by Charaka and Shusharuta bear testimony to our ancient tradition in the scientific healthcare of our people. The approach of our ancient medical systems was of a holistic nature, which took into account all aspects of human health and disease. Over the centuries, with the intrusion of foreign influences and mingling of cultures, various systems of medicine evolved and have continued to be practised widely. However, the allopathic system of medicine has, in a relatively short period of time, made a major impact on the entire approach to healthcare and pattern of development of the health services infrastructure in the country.

Progress achieved

3. During the last three decades and more, since the attainment of Independence, considerable progress has been achieved in the promotion of the health status of our people. Smallpox has been eliminated; plague is no longer a problem; mortality from cholera and related diseases has decreased and malaria brought under control to a considerable extent. The mortality rate per thousand of population has been reduced from 27.4 to 14.8 and the life expectancy at birth has increased from 32.7 to over 52. A fairly extensive network of dispensaries, hospitals and institutions providing specialised curative care has developed and a large stock of medical and health personnel, of various levels, has become available. Significant indigenous capacity has been established for the production of drugs and pharmaceuticals, vaccines, sera, hospital equipments, etc.

The existing picture

4. In spite of such impressive progress, the demographic and health picture of the country still constitutes a cause for serious and urgent concern. The high rate of population growth continues to have an adverse effect on the health of our people and the quality of their lives. The mortality rates for women and children are still dis- tressingly high; almost one third of the total deaths occur among children below the age of 5 years; infant mortality is around 129 per thousand live births. Efforts at raising the nutritional levels of our people have still to bear fruit and the extent and severity of malnutrition continues to be exceptionally high. Communicable and non-communicable diseases have still to be brought under effective control and eradicated. Blindness, Leprosy and T.B. continue to have a high incidence. Only 31% of the rural population has access to potable water supply and 0.5% enjoys basic sanitation.

4.1. High incidence of diarrhoeal diseases and other preventive and infectious diseases, specially amongst infants and children, lack of safe drinking water and poor environmental sanitation, poverty and ignorance are among the major contributory causes of the high incidence of disease and mortality.

4.2. The existing situation has been largely engendered by the almost wholesale adoption of health manpower development policies and the establishment of curative centres based on the Western models, which are inappropriate and irrelevant to the real needs of our people and the socio-economic conditions obtaining in the country. The hospital-based disease, and cure-oriented approach towards the establishment of medical services has provided benefits to the upper crusts, of society, specially those residing in the urban areas. The proliferation of this approach has been at the cost of providing comprehensive primary healthcare services to the entire population, whether residing in the urban or the rural areas. Furthermore, the continued high emphasis on the curative approach has led to the neglect of the preventive, promotive, public health and rehabilitative aspects of healthcare. The existing approach, instead of improving awareness and building up self-reliance, has tended to enhance dependency and weaken the community's capacity to cope with its problems. The prevailing policies in regard to the education and training of medical and health personnel, at various levels, has resulted in the development of a cultural gap between the people and the personnel providing care. The various health programmes have, by and large, failed to involve individuals and families in establishing a self-reliant community. Also, over the years, the planning process has become largely oblivious of the fact that the ultimate goal of achieving a satisfactory health status for all our people cannot be secured without involving the community in the identification of their health needs and priorities as well as in the implementation and management of the various health and related programmes.

Need for evolving a health policy—the revised 20-Point Programme

5. India is committed to attaining the goal of "Health for All by the Year 2000 A.D." through the universal provision of comprehensive primary healthcare services. The attainment of this goal requires a thorough overhaul of the existing approaches to the education and training of medical and health personnel and the reorganisation of the health services

infrastructure. Furthermore, considering the large variety of inputs into health, it is necessary to secure the complete integration of all plans for health and human development with the overall national socio-economic development process, specially in the more closely health related sectors, e.g. drugs and pharmaceuticals, agriculture and food production, rural development, education and social welfare, housing, water supply and sanitation, prevention of food adulteration, maintenance of prescribed standards in the manufacture and sale of drugs and the conservation of the environment. In sum, the contours of the National Health Policy have to be evolved within a fully integrated planning framework which seeks to provide universal, comprehensive primary healthcare services, relevant to the actual needs and priorities of the community at a cost which the people can afford, ensuring that the planning and implementation of the various health programmes is through the organised involvement and participation of the community, adequately utilising the services being rendered by private voluntary organisations active in the Health sector.

5.1. It is also necessary to ensure that the pattern of development of the health services infrastructure in the future fully takes into account the revised 20-Point Programme. The said Programme attributes very high priority to the promotion of family planning as a people's programme, on a voluntary basis; substantial augmentation and provision of primary healthcare facilities on a universal basis; control of Leprosy, T.B. and Blindness; acceleration of welfare programmes for women and children; nutrition programmes for pregnant women, nursing mothers and children, especially in the tribal, hill and backward areas. The Programme also places high emphasis on the supply of drinking water to all problem villages, improvements in the housing and environments of the weaker sections of society; increased production of essential food items; integrated rural developments; spread of universal elementary education; expansion of the public distribution system, etc.

Population stabilisation

6. Irrespective of the changes, no matter how

fundamental, that may be brought about in the overall approach to healthcare and the restructuring of the health services, not much headway is likely to be achieved in improving the health status of the people unless success is achieved in securing the small family norm, through voluntary efforts, and moving towards the goal of population stabilisation. In view of the vital importance of securing the balanced growth of the population, it is necessary to enunciate, separately, a National Population Policy.

Medical and Health Education

7. It is also necessary to appreciate that the effective delivery of healthcare services would depend very largely on the nature of education, training and appropriate orientation towards community health of all categories of medical and health personnel and their capacity to function as an integrated team, each of its members performing given tasks within a coordinated action programme. It is, therefore, of crucial importance that the entire basis and approach towards medical and health education, at all levels, is reviewed in terms of national needs and priorities and the curricular and training programmes restructured to produce personnel of various grades of skill and competence, who are professionally equipped and socially motivated to effectively deal with day-to-day problems, within the existing constraints.

Towards this end, it is necessary to formulate, separately, a National Medical and Health Education Policy which: (i) sets out the changes required to be brought about in the curricular contents and training programme of medical and health personnel, at various levels of functioning; (ii) takes into account the need for establishing the extremely essential inter-relations between functionaries of various grades; (iii) provides guidelines for the production of health personnel on the basis of realistically assessed manpower requirements; (iv) seeks to resolve the existing sharp regional imbalances in their availability; and (v) ensures that personnel at all levels are socially motivated towards the rendering of community health services.

Need for providing primary healthcare with special emphasis on the preventive, promotive and rehabilitative aspects

8. Presently, despite the constraint of resources, there is disproportionate emphasis on the establishment of curative centres—dispensaries, hospitals, institutions for specialist treatment—the large majority of which are located in the urban areas of the country. The vast majority of those seeking medical relief have to travel long distance to the nearest curative centre, seeking relief for ailments which could have been readily and effectively handled at the community level. Also, for want of a well established referral system, those seeking curative care have the tendency to to visit various specialist centres, thus further contributing to congestions, duplication of efforts and consequential waste of resources. To put an end to the existing all-round unsatisfactory situation, it is urgently necessary to restructure the health services within the following broad approach:

(1) To provide, within a phased, time-bound programme a well dispersed network of comprehensive primary healthcare services, integrally linked with the extension and health education approach which takes into account the fact that a large majority of health functions can be effectively handled and resolved by the people themselves, with the organised support of volunteers, auxilliaries, para-medics and adequately trained multi-purpose workers of various grades of skill and competence, of both sexes. There are a large number of private, voluntary organisations active in the health field, all over the country. Their services and support would require to be utilised and intermeshed with the governmental efforts, in an integrated manner.

(2) To be effective, the establishment of the primary healthcare approach would involve large scale transter of knowledge, simple skill and technologies to Health Volunteers, selected by the communities and enjoying their confidence. The functioning of the front line workers, selected by the community would require to be related to definitive action plans for the translation of medical and health knowledge into practical action, involving the use of simple and inexpensive interventions which can be readily implemented by persons

who have undergone short periods of training. The quality of training of these health guides/workers would be of crucial importance to the success of this approach.

The success of the decentralised primary healthcare system would depend vitally on the organised building up of individual self-reliance and effective community participation; on the provision of organised, back-up support of the secondary and tertiary levels of the healthcare services, providing adequate logistical and technical assistance.

(4) The decentralisation of services would require the establishment of a well worked out referral system to provide adequate expertise at the various levels of the organisational set-up nearest to the community, depending upon the actual needs and problems of the area, and thus ensure against the continuation of the existing rush towards the curative centres in the urban areas. The effective establishment of the referral system would also ensure the optimal utilisation of expertise at the higher levels of the hierarchical structure. This approach would not only lead to the progressive improvement of comprehensive healthcare services at the primary level but also provide for timely attention being available to those in need of urgent specialist care, whether they live in the rural or the urban areas.

(5) To ensure that the approach to healthcare does not merely constitute a collection of disparate health interventions but consists of an integrated package of services seeking to tackle the entire range of poor health conditions, on a broad front, it is necessary to establish a nation-wide chain of sanitary-cum-epidemiological stations. The location and functioning of these stations may be between the primary and secondary levels of the hierarchical structure, depending upon the local situations and other relevant considerations. Each such station would require to have suitably trained staff equipped to identify, plan and provide preventive, promotive and mental healthcare services. It would be beneficial, depending upon the local situations, to establish such stations at the Primary Health Centres. The district health organisation should have, as an integral part of its set-up, a well organised epidemiological unit to coordinate and superintend the

functioning of the field stations. These stations would participate in the integrated action plans to eradicate and control diseases, besides tackling specific local environmental health problems.

In the urban agglomerations, the municipal and local authorities should be equipped to perform similar functions, being supported with adequate resources and expertise, to effectively deal with the local preventable public health problems. The aforesaid approach should be implemented and extended through community participation and contributions, in whatever form possible, to achieve meaningful results within a time-bound programme.

(6) The location of curative centres should be related to the populations they serve, keeping in view the densities of population, distances, topography, transport connections. These centres should function within the recommended referral system, the gamut of the general specialities required to deal with the local disease patterns being provided as near to the community as possible, at the secondary level of the hierarchical organisation. The concept of domiciliary care and the field-camps approach should be utilised to the fullest extent, to reduce the pressures on these centres, specially in efforts relating to the control and eradication of Blindness, Tuberculosis, Leprosy, etc. To maximise the utilisation of available resources, new and additional curative centres should be established only in exceptional cases, the basic attempt being towards the upgradation of existing facilities, at selected locations, the guiding principle being to provide specialist services as near to the beneficiaries as may be possible, within a well-planned network. Expenditure should be reduced through the fullest possible use of cheap locally available building materials, resort to appropriate architectural designs and engineering concepts and by economical investment in the purchase of machineries and equipments, ensuring against avoidable duplication of such acquisitions. It is also necessary to devise effective mechanisms for the repair, maintenance and proper upkeep of all bio-medical equipments to secure their maximum utilisation.

(7) With a view to reducing governmental expenditure and fully utilising untapped resources, planned programmes may be devised, related to the local requirements and potentials, to encourage the establishment of practice by private medical professional, increased investment by non- governmental agencies in establishing curative centres and by offering organised logistical, financial and technical support to voluntary agencies active in the health field.

(8) While the major focus of attention in restructuring the existing governmental health organisations would relate to establishing comprehensive primary healthcare and public health services, within an integrated referral system, planned attention would also require to be devoted to the establishment of centres equipped to provide speciality and super-speciality services, through a well dispersed network of centres, to ensure that the present and future requirements of specialist treatment are adequately available within the country. To reduce governmental expenditures involved in the establishment of such centres, planned efforts should be made to encourage private investments in such fields so that the majority of such centres, within the governmental set-up, can provide adequate care and treatment to those entitled to free care, the affluent sectors being looked after by the paying clinics. Care would also require to be taken to ensure the appropriate dispersal of such centres, to remove the existing regional imbalances and to provide services within the reach of all, whether residing in the rural or the urban areas.

(9) Special, well-coordinated programmes should be launched to provide mental healthcare as well as medical care and the physical and social rehabilitation of those who are mentally retarded, deaf, dumb, blind, physically disabled, infirm and the aged. Also, suitably organised of various disabilities.

(10) In the establishment of the re-organised services, the first priority should be accorded to provide services to those residing in the tribal, hill and backward areas as well as to endemic disease affected populations and the vulnerable sections of the society.

(11) In the re-organised health services scheme, efforts should be made to ensure adequate mobility of personnel, at all levels of functioning.

(12) In the various approaches, set out in (1) to (11) above, organised efforts would require to be made to fully utilise and assist in the enlargement of the services being provided by private voluntary organisations active in the health field. In this context, planning encouragement and support would also require to be afforded to fresh voluntary efforts, specially those which seek to serve the needs of the rural areas and the urban slums.

Re-orientation of the existing health personnel

9. A dynamic process of changes and innovation is required to be brought about in the entire approach to health manpower development, ensuring the emergence of fully integrated bands of workers functioning within the "Health Team" approach.

Private practice by governmental functionaries

10. It is desirable for the States to take steps to phase out of system of private practice by medical personnel in government service, providing at the same time for payment of appropriate compensatory no-practising allowance. The States would require to carefully review the existing situation, with special reference to the availability and dispersal of private practitioners, and take timely decisions in regard to this vital issue.

Practitioners of indigenous and other systems of medicine and their role in healthcare

11. The country has a large stock of health manpower comprising of private practitioners in various systems, for example, Ayurveda, Homoeopathy, Yoga, Naturopathy, etc. This resource has not so for been adequately utilized. The practitioners of these various systems enjoy high local acceptance and respect and consequently exert considerable influence on health beliefs and practise. It is, therefore,

necessary to initiate organised measures to enable each of these various systems of medicine and healthcare to develop in accordance with its genius. Simultaneously, planned efforts should be made to dovetail the functioning of the practitioners of these various systems and integrate their service, at the appropriate levels, within specified areas of responsibility and functioning, in the over-all healthcare delivery system, specially in regard to the preventive, primitive and public health objectives. Well considered steps would also require to be launched to move towards a meaningful phased integration of the indigenous and the modern systems.

Appendix 2

GUIDELINES FOR VILLAGE HEALTH AND SANITATION COMMITTEES, SUB-CENTRES, PHCs AND CHCs MINISTRY OF HEALTH AND FAMILY WELFARE, GOVERNMENT OF INDIA

GUIDELINES REGARDING CONSTITUTION OF VILLAGE HEALTH AND SANITATION COMMITTEES AND UTILIZATION OF UNITED GRANTS TO THESE COMMITTEES

The detailed Implementation Framework of the National Rural Health Mission [NRHM] approved by the Union Cabinet in July, 2006 provides for the constitution and orientation of all community leaders on Village Sub-Centre, Primary Health Centre and Community Health Centre Committees. The NRHM implementation has been planned within the framework of Panchayati Raj Institutions [PRIs] at various levels. The Village Health and Sanitation Committee envisaged under NRHM is also within the overall umbrella of PRI.

1. Composition of the Village Health and Sanitation Committee

To enable the Village Health and Sanitation Committee to reflect the aspirations of the local community especially of the poor households and women, it has been suggested that:

- At least 50% members on the Village Health and Sanitation Committee should be women.
- Every hamlet within a revenue village must be given due representation on the Village Health and Sanitation Committee to ensure that the needs of the weaker sections especially Scheduled Castes, Scheduled Tribes, Other Backward Classes are fully reflected in the activities of the committee.
- A provision of at least 30% representation from the Non-governmental sector.
- Representation to women's self-help group, etc. on these committees, will enable the Committee to undertake women's health activities more effectively.
- Notwithstanding the above, the overall composition and nomenclature of the Village Health and Sanitation Committees is left to the State Governments as long as these committees were within the umbrella of PRIs.

2. Orientation and Training

Every Village Health and Sanitation Committee after being duly constituted by the State Governments needs to be oriented and trained to carry out the activities expected of them.

Village Health Fund

Every such committee duly constituted and oriented would be entitled to an annual untied grant of Rs. 10,000, which could be used for any of the following activities:

(i) As a revolving fund from which households could draw in times of need to be returned in instalments thereafter.

(ii) For any village level public health activity like cleanliness drive, sanitation drive, school health activities, ICDS, Anganwadi level activities, household surveys, etc.

(iii) In extraordinary case of a destitute women or very poor household, the Village Health and Sanitation Committee untied grants could even be used for healthcare need of the poor household.

(iv) The untied grant is a resource for community action at the local level and shall only be used for community activities that involve and benefit more than one household. Nutrition, Education and Sanitation, Environmental Protection, Public Health Measures shall be key areas where these funds could be utilized.

(v) Every village is free to contribute additional grant towards the Village Health and Sanitation Committee. In villages where the community contributes financial resources to the Village Health and Sanitation Committee untied grant of Rs. 10,000, additional incentive and financial assistance to the village could be explored. The intention of this untied grant is to enable local action and to ensure that Public Health activities at the village level receive priority attention.

3. Maintenance of Bank Account

The Village Health and Sanitation Committee fund shall be credited to a bank account, which will be operated with the joint signature of ASHA/Health Link Worker/Anganwadi Worker along with the President of the Village Health and Sanitation Committee/Pradhan of the Gram Panchayat. The account maintenance of this joint account shall be the responsibility of the Village Health and Sanitation Committee especially the ASHA/AWW [wherever no ASHA]. The Village Health and Sanitation Committee, the ASHA/AWW shall maintain a register of funds received and expenditure incurred. The register shall be available for public scrutiny and shall be inspected from time to time by the ANM/MPW/Gram Panchayat.

4. Accountability

- Every Village Health and Sanitation Committee needs to maintain updated Household Survey data to enable need based interventions.
- Maintain a register where complete details of activities undertaken, expenditure incurred, etc. will be maintained for public scrutiny. This should be periodically reviewed by the ANM/Sarpanch.
- The Block level Panchayat Samiti will review the functioning and progress of activities undertaken by the VHSC.
- The District Mission in its meeting also through its members/block facilitators supporting ASHA [wherever ASHA's are in position] elicit information on the functioning of the VHSC.
- A data base may be maintained on VHCSs by the DPMUs.

GUIDELINES FOR USE OF SUB-CENTER (SC) FUNDS UNDER NRHM

1. As part of the National Rural Health Mission, it is proposed to provide each sub-center with Rs. 10,000 as an untied fund to facilitate meeting urgent yet discrete activities that need relatively small sums of money.
2. The fund shall be kept in a joint bank account of the ANM and the Sarpanch.
3. Decisions on activities for which the funds are to be spent will be approved by the Village Health Committee (VHC) and be administered by the ANM. In areas where the sub-center is not co-terminus with the Gram Panchayat (GP) and the sub-center covers more than one GP, the VHC of the Gram Panchayat where the SC is located will approve the Action Plan. The funds can be used for any of the villages, which are covered by the sub-center.

4. Untied Funds will be used only for the common good and not for individual needs, except in the case of referral and transport in emergency situations.
5. Suggested areas where Untied Funds may be used include:
   - Minor modifications to sub-center curtains to ensure privacy, repair of taps, installation of bulbs, other minor repairs, which can be done at the local level.
   - *Ad hoc* payments for cleaning up sub-center, especially after childbirth.
   - Transport of emergencies to appropriate referral centers.
   - Transport of samples during epidemics.
   - Purchase of consumables such as bandages in sub-center.
   - Purchase of bleaching powder and disinfectants for use in common areas of the village.
   - Labour and supplies for environmental sanitation, such as clearing or larvicidal measures for stagnant water.
   - Payment/reward to ASHA for certain identified activities.
6. Untied funds shall not be used for any salaries, vehicle purchase, and recurring expenditures or to meet the expenses of the Gram Panchayat.

GUIDELINES FOR UTILIZATION OF UNTIED FUND AND ANNUAL MAINTENANCE GRANT FOR PRIMARY HEALTH CENTRES (PHCs)

Health sector reforms under the National Rural Health Mission (NRHM) aims to increase functional, administrative and financial resources and autonomy to the field units under which every PHC will get Rs. 25,000 p.a. as untied grant for local health action. Similarly every PHC will get an Annual Maintenance Grant of Rs. 50,000 for improvement and maintenance of physical infrastructure. Provision of water, toilets, their use and their maintenance has to be the priorities. In addition, every PHC is being strengthened with provision of three staff nurses as against one at present and provision of two doctors (one male, one female) and Ayush practitioner.

2. Necessity of untied fund has been felt mainly due to unavailability of funds for undertaking any innovative Centre-specific need-based activity, as the allotment of funds to the States has traditionally been of the nature of tied funds for implementing a particular activity/scheme and this hardly left any funds with the public health facilities. This centralized management and schematic in-flexibility in the use of funds allotted to the States, did not provide any scope for local initiative and flexibility for local action at block and down below level. Also it has been observed that most of the Primary Health Centres have not been maintained properly due to lack of steady fund, available locally for repair/refurbishing of infrastructure and basic facilities.

3. Since there would be substantial fund flow to the districts to be utilized for the Centres under NRHM/RCH-II and other programmes, the untied funds should not duplicate what is/can be taken up under other programmes. Each activity planned by the Centre should have clear rationale so that the impact of the untied fund can be distinctively assessed. A separate register be maintained in the PHC giving sources of funds clearly for various activities.

4. PHC untied fund shall be kept in the bank account of the concerned Rogi Kalyan Samitti (RKS)/Hospital Management Committee (HMC). PHC level Panchayat Committee/Rogi Kalyan Samiti will have the mandate to undertake and supervise the work to be undertaken from Annual Maintenance Grant. Both the funds will be spent and monitored by RKS.

5. Suggested areas where Untied Fund may be used include:

- Minor modifications to the Center—curtains to ensure privacy, repair of taps, installation of bulbs, other minor repairs, which can be done at the local level.

- Patient examination table, delivery table, DP apparatus, hemoglobin meter, copper-T insertion kit, instruments tray, baby tray, weighing scales for mothers and for newborn babies, plastic/ rubber sheets, dressing scissors, stethoscopes, buckets, attendance stool, mackintosh sheet.
- Provision of running water supply.
- Provision of electricity.
- *Ad hoc* payments for cleaning up the Center, especially after childbirth.
- Transport of emergencies to appropriate referral centers.
- Transport of samples during epidemics.
- Purchase of consumables such as bandages in the Center.
- Purchase of bleaching powder and disinfectants for use in common areas.
- Under the jurisdiction of the Centre.
- Labour and supplies for environmental sanitation, such as clearing.
- Larvicidal measures for stagnant water.
- Payment/reward to ASHA for certain identified activities.
- Repair/operationalising soak pits.

6. The following nature of expenditures should not be incurred out of the untied fund:

- Purchase of Office Stationery and equipments, training-related equipments, Vehicles, etc.
- Engagement of full time or part time staff and payment of honorarium/incentives/wages of any kind.
- Purchase of drugs, consumables and furniture.
- Payments towards inserting advertisements in any Newspaper/Journal/Magazine and IEC-related expenditure.
- Organizing "Swasthya Mela" or giving stalls in any Mela for ostensible purpose of awareness generation of health schemes/programmes.

- Payment of incentives to individuals/groups in cash/kind.
- Meeting any recurring non-plan expenditure.
- Taking up any individual-based activity except in the case of referral and transport in emergency situations.

7. The Centers are not required to take prior approval before implementing the schemes from the untied funds but shall have to send quarterly SOE and UC.

SUGGESTED GUIDELINES FOR IMPLEMENTATION OF INDIAN PUBLIC HEALTH STANDARDS (IPHSs) IN SUB-CENTRES (SCs), PRIMARY HEALTH CENTRES (PHCs) AND COMMUNITY HEALTH CENTRES (CHCs)

Although a large number of Sub-centres, Primary Health Centres and Community Health Centres have been established to provide comprehensive promotive, preventive and curative services to the rural people in the country, most of these institutions, at present are not able to function up to the level expected of them due to varied reasons. National Rural Health Mission (NRHM), launched by the Hon'ble Prime Minister on 12 April 2005, envisages to get these institutions raised to the level of optimum availability of infrastructure, manpower, logistics, etc. to improve the quality of services and the corresponding level of utilization. Through wide consultation with various stakeholders, Indian Public Health Standards (IPHS) for these centres have been framed. The key aim of the Standards is to underpin the delivery of quality services which are fair and responsive to clients' needs, which should be provided equitably and which deliver improvements in health and well-being of the population. Each PHC and CHC, as part of IPHS, is required to set-up a Rogi Kalyan Samity/Hospital Management Committee, which will bring in community control into the management of public hospitals with a purpose to provide sustainable quality care with accountability and people's participation along with total transparency.

To bring these centres to the level of Indian Public

Health Standards, is no doubt, a challenge for most of the States and also may require a detailed institution specific facility survey to find out the gaps. However, considering the dynamic process of setting up of the standards and the current manpower availability, there is a need to bring these centres to IPHS in a phased manner as the existing institutions are having different level of functional status. Some are at very rudimentary stage, some are just functioning minimally and the others with little more input could come up to the level of IPHS. Taking these points into consideration, a set of guidelines has been framed to enable the States/UTs to bring these centres gradually to the IPHS level.

National Rural Health Mission (NRHM) envisages a fully functional sub-centre in coordination with the village level functionaries such as Anganwadi workers, ASHA, and the Village Health and Sanitation Committee. Similarly, all the PHCs should function as 24-hour PHCs in a gradual manner. NRHM also envisages a functional 30-bedded rural hospital at the block level providing emergency obstetric care and neonatal care in the first instance as FRU and gradually strengthen further to provide other specialists services as per the details in the IPHS. The guidelines for achieving standards for IPHS centre-wise are as below:

Sub-centre:

- Conduct a facility survey and identify the gaps.
- Ensure that all the existing Sub-centres should be posted with one ANM immediately. The vacant post may be filled up on contractual basis. There should be an in-built plan to take care of vacancies arising out of retirements, long leave, and other emergency situation so that the services of ANM are available without any interruption.
- The appointment of second ANM as envisaged in the IPHS for each Sub-centre is to be made locally on contractual basis as per the demand, phase-wise. The most difficult areas such as hilly and tribal areas may be given priority.

- The services of a Male Health Worker (MPW-M) is also necessary at the Sub-centre. The states should take steps to fill up the post of these MPWs (M) in a phased manner. The training capacity in the State for these MPWs also need to be enhanced.
- Utilization of untied fund for strengthening the functioning of Sub-centres.
- All the existing Sub-centres buildings should be made environment friendly, disabled friendly, with a good source of water supply, electricity/ solar power/other alternative energy sources. This can be ensured with the help of Panchayat and related sectors.
- Utilization of Annual Maintenance Grant for strengthening of infrastructure and basic necessities of the Sub-centres.
- The States may declare the names and the number of existing Sub-centres that have been made functional as per the IPHS for the purpose of showing achievements under NRHM and information to the public.

Primary Health Centre (PHC)—24 Hours Service Delivery Centre with emphasis on Institutional Delivery

NRHM envisages that all the Primary Health Centres (20,000-30,000 population) should function as a 24×7 centre in a phased manner to improve the institutional deliveries conducted at these centres. The steps that may be needed are as follows:

- Conduct an institution specific facility survey and identify the gaps.
- In order to make the PHC 24×7 delivery of services, the services of Staff Nurses are essential. It must be ensured that there should be at least 4 Staff Nurses to perform rotation duties round the clock. In order to improve the institutional deliveries, appointment of at least three Staff Nurses may be recruited on contractual basis to fill the gaps. A labour room

with appropriate equipments and drugs with round the clock referral transport support either managed by the PHC or by the NGOs/CBOs for referring patients in case of emergency is essential. The States may take stock of the situation of the training capacity and the facilities available in the training institutions for turning over the required number of Staff Nurses.

- Appointment of two Medical Officers (MBBS) (preferably one lady MO), and one AYUSH practitioner, either by relocation or on contractual basis. All effort should be made, such as contractual appointment or walk-in interviews, making the District Cadre for Medical Officers and even appointment of retired MBBS doctors on contractual basis, and other incentives provided by the State government to see that all the PHCs have the Medical Officers.
- All the existing Primary Health Centres buildings as far as possible should be made environment-friendly, disabled-friendly, with a good source of water supply, electricity/solar power/other alternative energy sources and telephone. Rain water harvesting should also be promoted in the PHC building. This can be ensured with the help of Panchayat and related sectors such as water supply sanitation, horticulture, etc. All the proposed new buildings should have these components in their construction plan.
- Utilization of untied fund for strengthening the functioning of PHCs.
- Utilization of Annual Maintenance Grant for strengthening the infrastructure and basic necessities.
- Each PHC must have a Rogi Kalyan Samity and display of the Citizens' Charter.
- Once a specific PHC has achieved the 24×7/IPHS status, the district authority/state authority should declare the institution as 24×7/IPHS.

Community Health Centre (CHC)—First Referral Unit (FRU), Assured Services:

NRHM envisages a 30-bedded fully functional block level rural hospital. The greatest challenge of bringing these CHCs to FRU/IPHS is the non-availability of the specialists especially the critical ones like obstetric/gynecologist, anesthetist and pediatrician. The following steps may be taken up:

- Conduct an institution specific facility survey and identify the gaps.
- The bringing up the CHC to the level of the IPHS may be carried out in stages. First stage: It must be ensured that all the CHCs provides 24×7 services with appropriate referral transport service. The basic requirement for making it 24×7 service delivery, there should be four General Duty Medical Officers and seven Staff Nurses, one ANM and one LHV along with other support services and physical facilities. Each CHC must be certified by the State Government/District Authority that this is functioning as a 24×7 service delivery.

Second stage

All the CHCs, declared as 24×7 may be upgraded to First Referral Units (FRUs). The Minimum requirement of FRUs including manpower, i.e. gynecologist, anesthetist, pediatrician, and round the clock services of nurses and general duty officers should be ensured. Blood storage facility and other supportive services such as laboratory, X-ray, OT, labour room, laundry, diet, waste management system, referral transport, etc. must be ensured. Each CHC should be clearly demarcated as FRU. CHCs, as FRU, will provide the 24 Hours delivery services including normal and assisted deliveries, emergency obstetric care including surgical intervention like cesarean section and other medical intervention, newborn care, emergency care of sick children, full range of family planning services including laparoscopic services, safe abortion services, treatment of STI/RTI, availability of blood storage unit or effective linkage facilities with blood banks, and referral transport services.

Third stage (IPHS): Once the CHCs are qualified for FRU, next step would be to post adequate number of other specialists and support manpower as per the IPHS. Once these existing gaps in relation to manpower, equipments, drugs, supplies and other support services, are filled up, the CHCs can be declared to have achieved IPHS. The CHCs declared as IPHS, apart from above mentioned services by FRU, also must provide the following services:

- Care of routine and emergency cases in surgery.
- Care of routine and emergency cases in medicine.
- Services of a Public Health Manager.
- Delivery of all National Health Programmes including communicable and non-communicable diseases and RCH services.

Manpower

- Appointment of specialists may be made on contractual basis. All out efforts should be made, such as contractual appointment or walk-in interviews, making the specialist cadre in the State and even appointment of retired specialists on contractual basis, public private partnership, and other incentives provided by the State government. Short-term training course on anesthesiology and emergency obstetric care to the existing serving general duty doctors may also be undertaken, to see that all the CHCs have requisite manpower depending on the bed occupancy level.
- Appointment of Public Health Programme Manager on contractual basis.
- Appointment of Eye Surgeon (one for five CHCs) on contractual basis.
- Appointment of nine Nurses Midwives/Staff Nurses on contractual basis.
- All the existing Community Health Centres buildings as far as possible should be made environment-friendly, disabled-friendly, with a good source of water supply, electricity/solar power/

other alternative energy sources and telephone. Rain water harvesting should also be promoted in the CHC buildings. This can be ensured with the help of Panchayat and related sectors such as water supply sanitation, horticulture, etc. All the proposed new buildings should have these components in their construction plan.

- Dislocation of the existing centres for the sake of achieving the Standards may not be required, unless compulsory due to unavoidable circumstances. In that case, they could be resettled to an accessible place where the original client group could easily get the services.

As far as manpower is concerned, optimum strength should be taken into consideration.

Others

- Utilization of untied fund for strengthening the functioning of CHCs.
- Utilization of Annual Maintenance Grant for strengthening the infrastructure and basic necessities.
- Utilization of fund for up-gradation of CHCs to IPHS.

Implementation of achieving the Standards should keep into account the linkage of the referral system right from Sub-centre to Community Health Centres and to higher up institutions from CHCs.

Appendix 3

INVEST IN CHILDREN (DON'T BE DAZZLED BY THE GDP FIGURES)

by **A.J. Philip**, *The Tribune*, March 7, 2007 Chandigarh

The first five years are critically important in the life of a person. Studies have shown that 90 percent of the brain growth happens during this period. To put it differently, if children in the 1-5 age group are not given nutritious food, they will never be able to reach their full potential. A large number of our children are born so poor that they do not get good food and are, consequently, unable to attain the capabilities they would have otherwise attained. Though un-quantified, the national loss on this count is gigantic. The only national programme to address this gargantuan problem is the Integrated Child Development Services (ICDS) scheme, initiated as far back as in 1975.

In his Budget for 2007-08, Finance Minister P. Chidambaram has increased the allocation for ICDS from Rs. 4,087 crore to Rs. 4,761 crore—an increase of Rs. 674 crore, a sizeable sum in absolute terms, as most people would see it. To be fair, the allocation for ICDS has been increasing every year. It was just Rs. 1,600 crore in 2004-05. However, even this increased allocation is less than one-tenth of 1 percent of India's GDP. Compare it with the allocation for defence—Rs. 96,000 crore!

Allowance also has to be made for the fact that as of now, ICDS is provided to about 4 crore children through 7 lakh anganwadis. To make the programme universal, there is need to extend the services to a total of 16 crore children in 17 lakh settlements. Once this realisation sinks in, the meagerness of the increase in the allocation for ICDS will automatically dawn on.

But the question here is not exactly about how much money the Central government spends on children but how effective the programme is in addressing the problem of under-nourishment of children. A recent study found that out of every rupee the government spent, only 5 paise went to child-related programmes. This removes the fig leaf of the Central government's pretence to childcare.

What's the state of the Indian children 32 years after ICDS was started? Some statistics are quite revealing. A recent study of ICDS covering six states, including Himachal Pradesh, which was appropriately titled Focus On Children Under Six (FOCUS), found that though it is operational in almost every block, barely one-fourth of all children under six are covered under the very important supplementary nutrition component of the programme.

Variations among the states on the money spent on the nutrition of children in anganwadis are startling, to say the least. For instance, Tamil Nadu, which was the first to introduce a mid-day meal programme in schools in 1982, i.e., two decades before the Supreme Court mandated all the states to do so, the cost per meal per child was Rs. 1.20. In Bihar, the spending was 15 paise per meal per child. What kind of food can be given at 15 paise, when you have to factor in corruption also?

The FOCUS study also found that in some states the programme was run in a spasmodic manner. "There is no feeding of children in the first few months of the financial year due to procedural delays". In other words, the children must wait till the budgetary allocations trickle down to the anganwadis. Corruption is rampant. For instance, in Uttar Pradesh, a bland, monotonous, ready-to-eat mixture called panjiri is distributed. It has little nutritional value and is supplied by one state-level contractor. The anganwadis in the state spend more time in fudging of records than in serving the needs of children and lactating mothers.

The net result is that half of all Indian children are undernourished, more than half suffer from anaemia and a similar proportion escapes full immunisation. India loses 6 percent of its newborns before their first birthday, 50 percent of the toddlers to malnutrition and a whole generation to poor health, low skills and poverty. A Lancet study found that all over the world, 200 million children fail to reach their full potential. Out of them, the single largest group—65 million—belongs to India.

The Economic Survey presented in Parliament a day before the Budget contained some statistics, of course, sourced from the Human Development Report, 2006, which are quite revealing. India and China attained freedom almost around the same time. Yet, China has overtaken India on all the health parameters. For instance, the life expectancy at birth is 63 years in India, against 71 in China. Far more interesting is how poverty-stricken Bangladesh has stolen a march over India on all these indices.

In 1990, out of every 1,000 children born in India, 123 died before they could reach the age of 5. The corresponding figure for Bangladesh was 144 children. Just 14 years later, i.e., in 2004, Bangladesh had a much better figure of 77, against India's 85. The infant mortality rate and the maternal mortality ratio are now better in Bangladesh than in India. This is an impressive achievement given that in 2004 Bangladesh reported a per capita income of $406—58 percent lower than India's $640.

Perhaps, this has something to do with the fact that "public expenditure on health as a proportion of GDP is almost twice as high in Bangladesh (1.6 percent) as in India (0.9 percent). The reverse applies to military expenditure: 2.3 percent of GDP in India compared with 1.1 percent in Bangladesh". However, the nutrition situation is no better in Bangladesh than in India. In both countries half of all children are undernourished.

The UNDP report says India has the highest proportion of undernourished children in the world, along with Bangladesh, Ethiopia and Nepal. Surely, these figures are not complimentary to "Shining India".

Even within the country there are substantial pockets where children live in dreadful conditions as, say, among the Musahars of Bihar or the Sahariyas of Madhya Pradesh. And it is worth remembering that Musahars alone represent a population of about 2.5 million—more than the entire population of Bhutan or, for that matter, of 45 of the 177 countries listed in the Human Development Report.

The Economic Survey says the economy is projected to grow at 9.2 percent in 2006-07 building on the 9 percent growth in the previous year. There is a perception that once the desired economic growth is achieved, improvements in child nutrition and health will automatically follow. But this happens only at a very modest rate. Can the children be asked to wait till then, i.e., till the GDP growth rate reaches the double-digit level and infrastructure has developed to the desired extent?

A democracy will become meaningful to the citizens only when the state can ensure the safe delivery of a healthy child and the survival of both mother and child. Surely, the government cannot claim lack of resources with the foreign exchange reserves overflowing at $180 billion as Mr. Chidambaram says and uncollected tax revenue pegged at Rs. 80,000 crore. What is sorely lacking is the will to invest in children. It is time the government realised that healthy children were synonymous with healthy economy.

Child abuse guidelines for assessment

June 7, 2007—The American Academy of Pediatrics has issued guidelines providing a clinical approach to accurately evaluate and diagnose children who appear to have been physically abused in the past or present. The new recommendations are published in the June issue of *Pediatrics*.

"Physical abuse remains an underreported (and often undetected) problem for several reasons including individual and community variations in what is considered 'abuse,' inadequate knowledge and training among professionals in the recognition of abusive injuries, unwillingness to report suspected abuse, and professional bias," write Nancy D. Kellogg, MD, and colleagues from the Committee on Child Abuse and Neglect. "Misdiagnosed victims [are] more likely to be younger, white, have less severe symptoms, and live with both parents when compared with abused children who [are] not initially misdiagnosed. Such studies suggest a need for practitioners to be vigilant to the possibility of abuse when evaluating children who have atypical accidental injuries or obscure symptoms that are suggestive of traumatic etiologies but who do not have a history of trauma."

In the United States, 152,250 children and adolescents were confirmed victims of physical abuse in 2004, but the estimated number of victims is much higher. One retrospective cohort study of 8613 adults showed that 26.4% reported having had some form of physical abuse during childhood, and approximately 1.3% to 15% of childhood injuries leading to emergency department visits are thought to be abuse related.

The serious sequelae of child abuse may include death, severe incapacitation, and behavioural and functional problems including conduct disorders, physically aggressive behaviours, poor school performance, cognitive impairment, anxiety, depression, and problems with social adjustment and relationships.

Accurate and timely diagnosis of children who are suspected victims of abuse is essential to facilitate appropriate evaluation, investigation, and optimal outcomes for these children and their families. The current guidelines describe the evaluation of suspected physical abuse in children, including the medical evaluation encompassing the history, physical examination, and additional testing as appropriate. The clinician should evaluate the characteristics of the injury or injuries, the consistency of the explanation, and the child's developmental capabilities; report suspected abuse; and act as a liaison to other professionals to offer immediate and long-term treatment and follow-up for victims.

"Tests should be ordered judiciously and in consultation with the appropriate genetics, hematology, radiology, and child abuse specialists," the authors write. "Careful consideration of the patient's history, age, and clinical findings should guide selection of the appropriate tests."

Specific diagnostic tests that may be useful in the medical evaluation of suspected physical abuse and differential diagnoses are as follows:

- A skeletal survey for fractures is recommended for all children with fractures and children younger than 2 years with any suspicious injuries. This should include radiographs of the humeri, forearms, femurs, lower legs, hands, feet, skull, cervical spine, thorax (including oblique views), lumbar spine, and pelvis. For high-risk cases, the skeletal survey should be repeated in 2 weeks. Single whole-body x-ray films are not an acceptable substitute for the skeletal survey.

- For evaluation of bruises, tests for hematologic disorders are recommended when bleeding disorder is a concern because of the clinical presentation or family history. Testing should include complete blood count, platelets, prothrombin time, partial thromboplastin time, international normalized ratio, and bleeding time. After the initial screening tests, additional testing, such as factor levels, may be indicated. Platelet function activity, measured with the Platelet Function Analyzer-100, is better than bleeding time for establishing platelet function but is not widely available.
- For patients with intracranial injury, a disseminated intravascular coagulation screening should be performed, because intraparenchymal damage can affect coagulation.
- Liver enzyme tests, including those for aspartate aminotransferase and alanine aminotransferase, may be useful to diagnose occult hepatic injury.
- Pancreatic enzyme tests, such as those for amylase and lipase, may help diagnose pancreatic injury or pseudocyst.
- Urinalysis may assist in detection of urinary system or renal injury.
- For evaluation of intracranial and extracranial injury, magnetic resonance imaging of the head and neck may provide better dating of intracranial injuries than computed tomography (CT). To determine the extent of intracerebral edema, the diffusion-weighted scan may be better than CT. Other advantages of magnetic resonance imaging include greater sensitivity than CT for subtle

intracranial injuries in patients with normal CT results and abnormal neurologic examinations, and greater sensitivity than plain radiographs and CT for detecting cervical spine fractures and injury.

- However, CT scan used together with radiographs may enhance detection of skull fractures. Other tests that may be useful include urine testing for organic acids and screening for glutaric aciduria type 1.
- Abdominal CT scan is recommended for intra-abdominal injuries, using intravenous contrast, which is preferable to orally administered contrast.
- Levels of the cardiac enzymes troponin and creatine kinase with muscle and brain subunits can help detect cardiac injury.
- For acute rib fractures and subtle, non-displaced long-bone fractures, a skeletal radionuclide bone scan is preferable to plain x-ray films.
- If osteogenesis imperfecta is suspected, a skin biopsy for fibroblast culture and/or venous blood for DNA analysis are needed. Calcium, alkaline phosphatase, phosphorus, vitamin D, and parathyroid hormone levels are useful in the diagnosis of bone-mineralization disorders or rickets.

"The physician is responsible for reporting suspected abuse, documenting his or her opinions clearly, and providing the necessary information and expertise to investigative and legal personnel and parents, when appropriate," the authors conclude. "In addition, pediatricians are uniquely qualified to work with parents and caregivers to prevent abuse by providing anticipatory guidance on normal child behaviour and its management. Finally, physicians must advocate that children in foster care who have medical or mental health problems receive the appropriate services and medications and continuity of care through a medical home, and that a medical passport is maintained for these children."

Pediatrics. 2007;119:1232-1241.

Clinical context

According to the authors of the current study, in 2004 more than 150,000 adolescents and children were confirmed victims of child physical abuse in the United States, and this is believed to be an underestimate of the true incidence. Of the 4 types of child maltreatment—neglect, physical abuse, sexual abuse, and emotional abuse—approximately 18% of cases are physical abuse, which is second to neglect. An estimated 1.3% to 15% of childhood injuries resulting in emergency department visits are caused by abuse, according to the authors. Children with abusive head or abdominal injuries are more likely to die than those with accidental trauma, and they have higher incidence of subsequent behavioural and functional problems if they survive.

This is a review of risk factors associated with child physical abuse and recommendations for management by clinicians, summarized by the Committee on Child Abuse and Neglect of the American Academy of Pediatrics.

Study highlights

- Child physical abuse affects children of all ages, sexes, ethnicity, and socio-economic classes.
- Adolescents are more likely than younger children to receive physical assault injuries, but the risk for death from physical abuse is greater for children younger than 2 years.
- Risk factors for abuse include homes with incomes of less than $15,000 per year, maternal smoking, the presence of more than 2 siblings, low infant birth weight, and an unmarried mother.
- Homes with annual incomes of less than $15,000 have 3 times as many fatalities, 7 times as many serious injuries, and 5 times as many moderate injuries in children *vs.* homes with incomes of more than $15,000.
- Children living in households with unrelated adults are 50 times more likely to die of inflicted injuries than those residing with 2 biological parents.

- The rate of physical abuse is 2.1 times higher among children with disabilities than in those without.
- Child abuse is 4.9 times more likely in families with identified spousal abuse than in those without.
- Clinicians should educate parents about the normal range of behaviours in infants and children, provide anticipatory guidance, recognize parental stress, and provide resources when behaviours become unmanageable for parents.
- Clinicians can also be vigilant to identify spousal abuse, maternal depression or drug abuse, and other children at risk for abuse.
- Clinicians should be able to recognize suspicious injuries, perform a comprehensive examination and auxiliary tests, detect injuries, report child abuse, and document injuries for legal use.
- Clinicians in the 50 US states are mandated by law to report suspicion of child abuse, and mode of reporting (written, telephone, and online) differs among states.
- Some states include corporal punishment within the definition of child physical abuse.
- Many regions have child protective services and child abuse teams to whom clinicians may refer.
- Information on specific state laws are provided by the Children's Bureau at http://www.childwelfare.gov/systemwide/laws_policies/search/index.cfm.
- Many states have laws that allow clinicians, without parental consent, to evaluate and conduct tests and take photographs of children suspected of being abused or neglected.
- The American Academy of Pediatrics has recommended that hospitalization of children suspected of being abused or neglected be considered medically necessary.

- A history suggestive of child abuse includes no or vague explanation of injuries, changing details about the events, inconsistent explanation, and different eyewitness accounts.
- Complete physical examination should include a neurologic examination, growth charting for growth failure, and examination of extremities, neck, skin, face, and head.
- Fundoscopy for retinal hemorrhages for children suspected of having repetitive abusive acceleration-deceleration (shaking) injuries should be routine.
- Thoracoabdominal injuries may present late, and victims of such injuries tend to be younger.
- For abdominal injuries, CT scanning and other tests may be indicated because physical examination may be unreliable.
- Long-bone fractures that should be evaluated for non-accidental causes include metaphyseal and spiral-oblique fractures, especially in non-ambulatory infants.
- Documentation should include digital or other photography of observed injuries for peer review and court testimony.
- If a child has serious injury caused by suspected neglect or poor supervision, the clinician should report this to child protective services.
- The primary clinician should be notified to assure appropriate follow-up services.

Pearls for practice

- Risk factors for child physical abuse include annual household income less than $15,000, maternal smoking, spousal abuse, child with disabilities, household with more than 2 siblings, low infant birth weight, unrelated adults in household, and an unmarried mother.

- Child abuse reporting is mandated in all 50 US states, and specific guidelines for each state are available to clinicians. Generally, clinicians should be able to recognize suspicious injuries, perform a comprehensive examination and auxiliary tests, detect injuries, report child abuse, and document injuries for legal use, among other evaluation and management strategies.

Bibliography

Arora, V.K., Sarin, R., Lonnroth, K., Feasibility and effectiveness of a public-private mix project for improved TB control in Delhi, India. *Int J Tuberc Lung Dis,* 2003; 7:1131-38.

Bal, A.M., Private health sector in India: line between profit and profiteering is often thin. *BMJ* 2005; 331:1339.

Baru, R.V., Reproductive technologies and the private sector —implications for women's health. *Health Millions,* 1993; 1:6-8.

Bhat, R., Characteristics of private medical practice in India: a provider perspective.

Bhat, R., Regulation of the private health sector in India. *Int J Health Plann Manage* 1996; 11:253-74.

Bhatia, J,, Cleland, J., Healthcare of female outpatients in south-central India: comparing public and private sector provision. *Health Policy Plan* 2004;19:402-9.

Bhatia, J.C., Cleland, J., Health-care seeking and expenditure by young Indian mothers in the public and private sectors. *Health Policy Plan.* 2001; 16:55-61.

Brugha, R., Antiretroviral treatment in developing countries: the peril of neglecting private providers. *BMJ* 2003; 326:1382-84.

Buse, K., Waxman, A., Public-private health partnerships: a strategy for WHO. *Bull World Health Organ* 2001; 79:748-54.

Dandona, L., Enhancing the evidence base for HIV/AIDS control in India. *Natl Med J India* 2004; 17:160-166.

Dandona, R., Dandona, L., Mishra, A., Dhingra, S., Venkatagopalakrishna, K., Chauhan, L.S., Utilization of and barriers to public sector tuberculosis services in India, *Natl Med J India* 2004; 17:292-99.

Deshpande, K., Ravi Shankar, Diwan, V., Lonnroth, K., Mahadik, V.K., Chandorkar, R.K., Spatial pattern of private healthcare provision in Ujjain, India: a provider survey processed and analysed with a Geographical Information System. *Health Policy* 2004; 68:211-22.

Dewan, P.K., Lal, S.S., Lonnroth, K., Wares, F., Uplekar, M., Sahu, S., Granich, R., Chauhan, L.S., Improving tuberculosis control through public-private collaboration in India: literature review. *BMJ* 2006; 332:574-78.

Duggal, R., Healthcare utilisation in India. *Health Millions* 1994; 2:10-12.

George, R., Abraham, R., Private health in India. *Lancet* 2002; 359:1528.

Health Policy Plan, 1999; 14:26-37.

Hogg, R.S.., Heath, K.V., Yip, B., Craib, K.J., O'Shaughnessy M.V., Schechter M.T., Montaner J.S., Improved survival among HIV-infected individuals following initiation of antiretroviral therapy. *JAMA* 1998; 279:450-454.

International Labour Organization (ILO). Assessing the Socio-economic Impact of HIV/AIDS on People Living with HIV/AIDS (PLWHAs) and their families in India. New Delhi, India: ILO; 2004.

Kamat, V.R., Nichter, M., Pharmacies, self-medication and pharmaceutical marketing in Bombay, India. *Soc Sci Med,* 1998; 47:779-94.

Kamat, V.R., Nichter, M., Pharmacies, self-medication and pharmaceutical marketing in Bombay, India. *Soc Sci Med* 1998; 47:779-94.

Kamat, V.R., Private practitioners and their role in the resurgence of malaria in Mumbai (Bombay) and Navi Mumbai (New Bombay), India: serving the affected or aiding an epidemic? *Soc Sci Med,* 2001; 52:885-909.

Kielmann, K., Deshmukh, D., Deshpande, S., Datye, V., Porter, J., Rangan, S., Managing uncertainty around HIV/AIDS in an urban setting: private medical providers and their patients in Pune, India. *Soc Sci Med,* 2005; 61:1540-1550.

Kumarasamy, N., Generic antiretroviral drugs—will they be the answer to HIV in the developing world? *Lancet,* 2004; 364:3-4.

Mahal, A., Rao, B., HIV/AIDS epidemic in India: An economic perspective. *Indian Journal of Medical Research,* 2005; 121:582-600.

Mahal, A., Yazbeck, A.S., Peters, D.H., and Ramana, G.N.V. The Poor and Health Service Use in India. August, 2001. World Bank Report. Washington DC. 2001.

Mertens, T.E., Smith GD, Kantharaj K, Mugrditchian D, Radhakrishnan KM. Observations of sexually transmitted disease consultations in India. *Public Health,* 1998; 112:123-28.

Mudur, G., Inadequate regulations undermine India's healthcare. *BMJ,* 2004; 328:124.

Murthy, K.J., Frieden TR, Yazdani A, Hreshikesh P. Public-private partnership in tuberculosis control: experience in Hyderabad, India. *Int J Tuberc Lung Dis,* 2001; 5:354-59.

Nagelkerke, N.J., Jha, P., de Vlas, S.J., Korenromp, E.L., Moses, S., Blanchard, J.F., Plummer, F.A., Modelling HIV/AIDS epidemics in Botswana and India: impact of interventions to prevent transmission. *Bull World Health Organ,* 2002; 80:89-96.

National, AIDS Control Organization, Ministry of Health and Family Welfare, and Government of India. HIV/AIDS epidemiological Surveillance and estimation report for the year 2005.

National AIDS Control Organization. Annual Report, 2002-2004, 2005, New Delhi.

National AIDS Control Organization. HIV Annual Report 2002-2004. New Delhi, 2005.

National Commission of Macroeconomics and HealthMinistry of Health and Family Welfare and Government of India. Financing and Delivery of Healthcare Services in India. 2005.

National Commission on Macroeconomics and Health, Ministry of Health and Family Welfare, Government of India, and New Delhi. Burden of Disease in India. 2005.

Ogden, J., Rangan, S., Uplekar, M., Porter, J., Brugha, R., Zwi A., Nyheim, D., Shifting the paradigm in tuberculosis control: illustrations from India. *Int J Tuberc Lung Dis* 1999; 3:855-61.

Over, M., Heywood, P., Gold, J, Gupta, I, Hira, S, and Marseille, E., HIV/AIDS Treatment and Prevention in India. World Bank Report. Washington DC, 2004.

Palella, F.J., Jr., Delaney, K.M., Moorman, A.C., Loveless, M.O., Fuhrer, J., Satten, G.A., Aschman, D.J., Holmberg, S.D., Declining morbidity and mortality among patients with advanced human immunodeficiency virus infection. HIV Outpatient Study Investigators. *N Engl J Med* 1998; 338:853-60.

Peters, D.H., The role of oversight in the health sector: the example of sexual and reproductive health services in India. *Reprod Health Matters* 2002;10:82-94.

Peters, D.H., Yazbeck, A.S., Sharma, R.R., Ramana, G.N.V., Pritchett, L.H., and Wagstaff, A. Better Health Systems for India's Poor: Findings, Analysis, and Options. The World Bank. Washington D.C. 2002.

Population Division of the Department of Economic and Social Affairs of the United Nations Secretariat (2003) 'World population Prospects: the 2002 revision', Highlights, New York, February, p. 78-90. 2002.

Ramachandani, S., Mehta, S., Saple, D.G., Vaidya, S., Pandey, V., Vadrevu, R., Rajasekaran, R., Bhatia, V., Chowdhary, A., Bollinger, R.C., and Gupta, A., Knowledge, attitudes, and practices of antiretroviral therapy among HIV-infected persons attending public and private clinics in India. AIDS Patient Care and STDs . 2006.*In press.*

Rangan, S.G., Juvekar, S.K., Rasalpurkar, S.B., Morankar, S.N., Joshi, A.N., Porter, J.D., Tuberculosis control in rural India: lessons from public-private collaboration. *Int J Tuberc Lung Dis* 2004; 8:552-59.

Rao, S., Section II Delivery of health services in the private sector in Financing and Delivery of Health Services in India. National Commission on Macroeconomics and Health 2005. pg. 89-124, New Delhi, 2005.

Sengupta, A., Nundy, S., The private health sector in India. *BMJ* 2005; 331:1157-58.

Shah, B., Walshe, L., Saple, D.G., Mehta, S., Kharkar, J.P., Ramnani, J.P., Bollinger, R.C., and Gupta, A., Adherence to Antiretroviral Therapy Among Indian

HIV Infected Persons Seeking Care in the Private Sector in Mumbai, India.*Submitted for publication.*

Sheikh, K., Porter, J., Kielmann, K., Rangan, S., Public-private partnerships for equity of access to care for tuberculosis and HIV/AIDS: lessons from Pune, India. *Trans R Soc Trop Med Hyg* 2006; 100:312-20.

Sheikh, K., Rangan, S., Deshmukh, D., Dholakia, Y., Porter, J., Urban private practitioners: potential partners in the care of patients with HIV/AIDS. *Natl Med J India* 2005;18:32-36.

Sheikh, K., Rangan, S., Kielmann, K., Deshpande, S., Datye, V., Porter, J., Private providers and HIV testing in Pune, India: challenges and opportunities. *AIDS Care* 2005;17:757-66.

Shepard, D.S., Public-private collaborations in healthcare: lessons from India. *Int J Qual Healthcare* 2001; 13:277-78.

Subbanna, J., Public-private mix in the National Leprosy Elimination Programme. *Indian J Lepr* 2004;76:179-80.

Sudha, G., Nirupa, C., Rajasakthivel, M., Sivasusbramanian, S., Sundaram, V., Bhatt, S., Subramaniam, K., Thiruvalluvan, E., Mathew, R., Renu, G., Santha, T., Factors influencing the care-seeking behaviour of chest symptomatics: a community-based study involving rural and urban population in Tamil Nadu, South India. *Trop Med Int Health* 2003;8:336-41.

Uplekar, M., Juvekar, S., Morankar, S., Rangan, S., Nunn, P., Tuberculosis patients and practitioners in private clinics in India. *Int J Tuberc Lung Dis* 1998; 2:324-29.

Uplekar, M., Pathania, V., Raviglione, M., Private practitioners and public health: weak links in tuberculosis control. *Lancet* 2001;358:912-16.

Uplekar, M.W., Cash, R.A., The private GP and leprosy: a study. *Lepr Rev* 1991; 62:410-419.

World Bank 'South Asia Region (SAR)—India', Regional Updates, www.worldbank.org/ungass/India.htm accessed 22/4/06.

Index